THE
LAUNCH
PATH

Getting from a startup idea to a
launch-ready venture.

Bret Waters

Paperback—ISBN: 979-8-9890904-0-2
Hardbound—ISBN: 979-8-9890904-1-9
Ebook—ISBN: 979-8-9890904-2-6

Sundquist Press
Redwood City, CA 94061
Contact: ping@4thly.com

Revised edition: March, 2024.
Papaya 2550

For Britt–Marie.

TABLE OF CONTENTS

PREFACE

Late one evening last year, I was enjoying a glass of wine with my friend David at his home in the hills above Silicon Valley. We've both been involved in the startup world for most of our careers—David became a venture capitalist while I stayed on the entrepreneur path, but we each spent much of our careers hunting unicorns (startups with billion-dollar valuations). Yet here we were, sipping a delicious Rafanelli Zinfandel and talking about *Mittelstand*, the German term describing decidedly non-unicorn companies that form the rock-solid foundation of the economy.

Mittelstand companies are small-to-medium in size and privately owned. They have strong local linkages, grow prudently, and use conservative long-term financing—so pretty much the exact opposite of the "burnout or bust in the pursuit of billions" ethos that many people associate with Silicon Valley today.

The conversation that night is part of the genesis of this book. In recent years Silicon Valley has sometimes felt as if it's become a cult of fundraising and unicorn-chasing. I feel we need to return to the cult of just building a great business.

So my first goal for this book is to provide a path for just building a great business—whether you intend to create a billion-dollar unicorn, a solid member of the Mittelstand, or a social venture focused on saving the world through sustainable impact.

My other goal with this book is to help make entrepreneurship more accessible. I believe in the democratizing of entrepreneurship, and with this book, I hope to help demystify the process of getting from a startup idea to a successful, thriving operation. You don't need an

MBA, Ivy League connections or a rich uncle. All you need is passion, intention, and a good dose of tenacity.

Steve Jobs once said that everything in the world was "made by people who were no smarter than you. And you can change it, you can influence it, you can build things that other people can use."

Over the years, through my work at Stanford and Miller Center, I've worked with hundreds of startup founders. I've seen some succeed wildly and some fail miserably. From watching those patterns, I've developed a framework I call the **Launch Path**. It's a process designed to help entrepreneurs everywhere get efficiently and effectively from an early startup idea to a successfully launched venture.

That's the book you're now holding in your hands.

INTRODUCTION TO THE LAUNCH PATH

When I teach entrepreneurship at Stanford, in our first classroom session I ask how many students signed up for the course because they were hoping to get a business plan template of some sort. Typically, around a third of them raise a hand. I encourage those students to drop the course immediately.

Startup success is not about writing business plans. It's mostly about mindset, honestly. It's also about identifying problems worth solving, learning about customers, and following an iterative process for testing your assumptions (most of which will turn out to be wrong).

Investors know this, of course. Paul Graham, one of the world's most famous seed-stage startup investors, says, "I have never read a business plan or a balance sheet." Never.

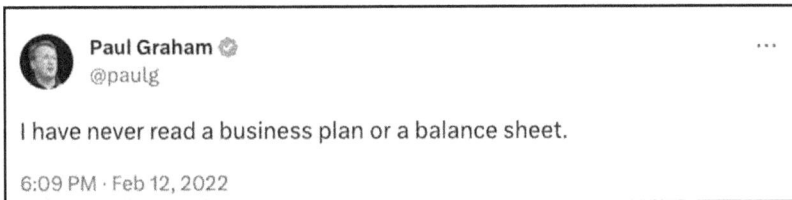

Paul Graham @paulg · · ·

I have never read a business plan or a balance sheet.

6:09 PM · Feb 12, 2022

Paul Graham is a famous startup investor and co-founder of Y Combinator.

So, this book is not about writing business plans, nor will it provide a business plan template. Feel free to ask for a refund.

Instead, this book is about a process—a process I call the **Launch Path**—that anyone can use to get effectively from a startup idea to a launch-ready, funding-ready venture. It's based on my experience as a Silicon

Valley entrepreneur as well as my experience working with hundreds of entrepreneurs through my work at Stanford and Miller Center. By following my process in this book, you will not end up with a 300-page business plan that no one wants to read (and will be obsolete about ten minutes after you finish it). Instead, you will end up with a clear path to a launch-ready, funding-ready venture with assumptions validated, risk mitigated, and economics articulated. I guarantee you that will be **way more valuable** than a silly business plan template.

The structure of this book and the tools provided

Each chapter in this book describes one step on **The Launch Path**. I present the concept around each step, tell a few relevant stories from my career, and mix in various examples from startup history. Each chapter also contains a case study with key takeaways. If you are working on your own startup venture, I've included the following for you:

- **An assignment for each step.** The last page of each chapter is called "For your startup" and has an assignment to complete for your own venture. As you complete them, you will document them on your **Launch Path Canvas** (see below).
- **Fitaco—my awesome fictional venture!** For each step on the Launch Path, I provide an example for a fictional venture named Fitaco. It's a new startup that will provide on-demand delivery of healthy tacos that keep you fit! (I have a bit of a taco obsession. When you visit, I'll take you to Sancho's Taqueria, home of the best fish tacos on the planet). I've provided these example deliverables for each step with the hope that they will be helpful to you as you develop your own.
- **The book's companion website:** On **thelaunchpath.com,** you will find additional resources referred to in this book. For example, in Chapter 5, we discuss creating an economic model for your startup venture, and if you go to **thelaunchpath.com,**

you will find an example spreadsheet you can copy and use. You'll find many other tools and resources on the companion website, and I keep it updated for you.

- **The Launch Path Canvas:**[1] I've designed a special canvas for you to use as you work your way through this book. The individual boxes on the Launch Path Canvas have descriptions in them and are explained in greater detail in Chapter 4 of this book. You can download a PDF of my canvas from **thelaunchpath.com** and then fill it out in whatever way is best for you. The **Launch Path Canvas**, once completed, represents all the elements of your business model. It's a visualization of all the moving parts and how they will interact together to drive your venture's success and growth.

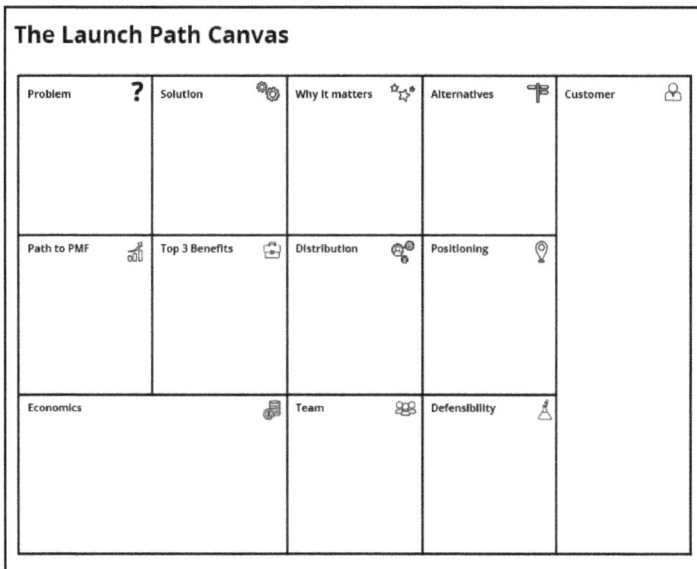

The Launch Path Canvas

Problem ?	Solution	Why it matters	Alternatives	Customer
Path to PMF	Top 3 Benefits	Distribution	Positioning	
Economics	Team	Defensibility		

Download a blank PDF at theaunchpath.com

1: My Launch Path Canvas is an expanded version of the seminal Business Model Canvas, originally developed by Alexander Osterwalder and updated/modified by many others. I recommend his book, Business Model Generation, ISBN 978-0470876411

The Launch Path Canvas
Lorem ipsum

Name of Startup Venture: Fitaco, Inc
Prepared by: Bret Waters
Date: November 8, 2023
Iteration: 8

Problem	Solution	Why it matters	Alternatives	Customer
One clear sentence that articulates the problem your startup solves. Consumers in the US spend $331 billion/year on fast food, and most of it is really unhealthy. The paradox is that consumers today want to eat healthy, but also have a busy life that often drives them to resort to the convenience of fast food.	How does your venture solve the problem you have articulated? Keep this short and concise! Fast food doesn't need to be unhealthy. Our startup is developing a new brand of health-conscious fast food (healthy tacos!), delivered directly to your home or office.	Why is this a problem worth solving? The National Institutes for Health say that today a fast food diet may kill more people prematurely every year than cigarette smoking.	When a customer looks at alternative ways to solve the problem we solve, what will they see? This is a list of competitors and alternatives. Link to a graphic representation of the landscape. There are many many food delivery services, from Uber Eats to Doordash to Grubhub. See visualization at this link.	It's all about understanding customers. Write a one-sentence description of key customer personas and the problem we solve for each. Circle the one that is most influential. **Adventurous Alex:** A thrill-seeking foodie always on the hunt for unique and spicy taco creations to satisfy their daring palate. **Health-Conscious Haley:** A fitness enthusiast looking for wholesome and fresh ingredient options that align with their nutritious lifestyle at the taqueria. **Busy Ben:** An on-the-go professional seeking quick, flavorful, and portable taco choices to enjoy during a busy workday. **Vegetarian Victoria:** A plant-based eater in search of flavorful and creative vegetarian and vegan taco selections that cater to their dietary preferences. **Traditional Tony:** A lover of classic flavors, Tony enjoys indulging in authentic and time-honored taco recipes that remind him of his cultural heritage. **Family-Oriented Felix:** A parent looking for a family-friendly meal delivery with a variety of options to cater to the taste preferences of both kids and adults. **Budget-Conscious Bella:** A student or frugal diner in pursuit of affordable yet flavorful taco choices that won't break the bank at the taqueria.
Path to PMF What is our path to Product-Market Fit? Customer Development, MVP's, etc. 1. Farmers' markets where we can get input on our menu items. 2. One truck in the Palo Alto area for a pilot project. 3. Scale slowly to additional markets, based on our learnings.	**Top 3 Benefits** What are the top 3 benefits that your product or services provides to customers? 1. Convenience. Use our mobile app to place a custom order and it's delivered directly to you. 2. Healthy food, designed by a nutritionist. 3. Tacos. Everybody loves tacos.	**Distribution** What are our distribution channels? Direct to consumer, via resellers, or? We intend to sell direct-to-consumer, via our mobile app and website, with delivery via our own vans. In the future, we may be open to distribution partnerships.	**Positioning** Within this landscape of competitors and alternatives, how is your venture positioned? Our positioning can be summed-up in two words: healthy, and delicious. There are many food delivery apps that can deliver something that is delicious but not very healthy. Or you could eat a kale salad. We serve delicious tacos designed by a nutritionist. That's our unique positioning.	
Economics What are the Unit Economics for this venture, and how we expect the CAC<LTV to look like, and what are out capital needs? (Link to full spreadsheet.) One unit = one taco: Sell price $5, on which our gross profit is 4.74. Early tests indicate CAC of $11, and we expect an initial LTV of three orders per customer ($25.50), which will grow with time. Our initial capital needs are $22.0K, which will get us through the pilot launch. We will propose to investors structuring this as a SAFE. See full spreadsheet at this link.	**Team** What are the characteristics of the right team to make this venture a success? The right team aligns with our target demographic - people who want to eat healthy and also enjoy the convenience of a quick taco meal. The economics of our venture are such that we'll need drivers and cooks who are affordable, so we will work hard to make it an attractive part-time job for students, and a great evening second job for anybody.	**Defensibility** What is your secret sauce that is difficult for competitors to copy? The fact that we own the customer and customer data is a big part of our defensibility. A restaurant selling through a 3rd-party like Doordash owns neither the customer nor the data.		

A completed Launch Path Canvas for my fictional venture, Fitaco. See a larger version at **thelaunchpath.com**

On the shoulders of giants

Much of my **Launch Path** framework stands on the shoulders of giants. It incorporates aspects of design thinking (developed by David Kelley and others), Customer Development (from the mind of Steve Blank), Lean Startup and MVP (popularized by Eric Ries), and the Business Model Canvas (created by Alex Osterwalder). Collectively, these authors created a toolset that Silicon Valley startups have successfully used for many years.

But this toolset has some holes, notably financial modeling and competitive landscape. Also it's twenty years old at this point and has become slightly dated. So, the **Launch Path** is my attempt to create an updated framework that builds upon the well-established Silicon

Valley canon while expanding it a bit, bringing it up to date, and incorporating some new ideas into the mix.

Case Studies

I've included brief case studies as part of each chapter in this book. Some are directly relevant to that particular chapter, some are more general with key takeaways that span several of this book's chapters. Some are from companies founded long ago (Trader Joe's and NExT), some are more recent (Venmo). These aren't the sort of in-depth case studies that you'd find in an MBA course, but I hope you find them interesting stories that highlight some of the key factors that tend to drive startup success and failure.

Move fast and ~~break~~ _build_ things

Silicon Valley startup culture has sometimes been criticized as being too much "move fast and break things," a phrase suggesting a chaotic, destructive process.

This characterization isn't exactly right, so let me reframe it. In the 1990s, the legendary Carol Bartz was CEO of Autodesk, a San Francisco software company. She developed what she called the "Fail Fast Forward" (FFF) methodology that transformed her company into one of the most innovative and successful in Silicon Valley.

With the **Launch Path,** I am channeling Carol by encouraging you to fail fast (find out early which of your assumptions are wrong) in a way that pushes you forward down the path to success—no chaotic breaking of things required.

So, here we go, down the Launch Path. Let's build a startup together. Let's dream in Technicolor but execute in black and white—because that's how great ventures are created.

"*You can't wait for inspiration. You have to go at it with a club.*

JACK LONDON

CHAPTER 1

LISTEN TO THE WAVES

How do great startups begin?

From my house in the heart of Silicon Valley, I can hop in my car and be on the coast in about a half-hour. I typically do this several times a week and take my dog for a long walk on the beach. The beaches here in Northern California are often foggy and moody, and I do some of my best thinking while walking the coast, throwing a tennis ball for the dog, and watching the steady parade of waves crashing up on the shore.

But where do great startup ideas come from? Do they suddenly spring into your head during a long walk on the beach?

We'll get to that, but first, let's start with a definition of entrepreneurship. The one I like to use comes from Harvard Business School professor Howard Stevenson:

> *"Entrepreneurship is the pursuit of opportunity without regard to resources currently controlled."*

What I love about this definition is that it captures the notion that when a great entrepreneur sees opportunity, he doesn't worry about whether he currently has the necessary resources to go after that opportunity. He may currently have no money, no team, no customers, no distributors, and no technology. But that doesn't deter him because he believes he can assemble whatever resources he needs. That's what great entrepreneurs do.

That may be why you bought this book. Perhaps you see an opportunity, and you're ready to put together the right resources in order to pursue it. Over the following few chapters, that's exactly what we'll do. But let's start by dispelling some common startup myths.

It all starts with thinking up an idea— (no, it doesn't)

The mythology is that startup success begins with some brilliant idea that suddenly comes to you like a bolt of lightning that ignites your brain (and then you're a billionaire by Tuesday). If you look at startup history, however, it's actually very difficult to find examples where it was the <u>idea</u> that made a startup a success.

Most original startup ideas fail. The Twitter team's original idea was a podcasting app called Odeo. Instagram's original idea was a mobile check-in app called Burbn. YouTube thought their primary use case would be video dating. Slack's original idea was a video game studio.

In all of those examples, the original ideas failed, but the teams still turned the companies into billion-dollar successes. My goal with this book is to make you like one of those teams.

Also, note that Mark Zuckerberg didn't come up with the idea of social networking, Steve Jobs didn't come up with the idea of a personal computer or a smartphone, and Elon Musk didn't come up with the idea of electric cars. So it ain't about the idea—it's about the execution.

Your idea is worth millions – (no, it's not)

I hate to burst your bubble already since you probably bought this book because you have a startup idea, but honestly, your startup idea is probably worthless. All startup ideas are. Want proof? There are online marketplaces where you can buy and sell pretty much anything, yet there are no marketplaces for startup ideas. Nobody wants to buy ideas, so, by definition, they are worthless. As I tell my Stanford students, **ideas are cheap; execution is hard.**

So, if success isn't actually about thinking up an awesome startup idea, then where do great startups begin?

Paul Graham, co-founder of the startup accelerator Y Combinator, wrote a great essay[1] saying, "The verb you want to be using with respect to startup ideas is not 'think up' but 'notice.' The way to get startup ideas is **not to try to think of startup ideas. It's to look for problems.**"

From my experience, this is precisely where most successful startups begin—with **an entrepreneur who notices a problem worth solving.**

Uber was born when a group of friends spent eight hundred dollars to hire a private driver and then listened to the driver talk about how much downtime he had every week, waiting for business. Airbnb was born when roommates in San Francisco needed to rent out a spare bedroom with an air mattress to pay the rent. Cisco was born when two computer administrators at Stanford were frustrated by slow network speeds. In all of these examples, the founders not only noticed a problem worth solving, but they also fell passionately in love with solving that problem.

Max Levchin is one of the original founders of PayPal. He's now Founder & CEO of Affirm, which offers a consumer-friendly alternative to credit card financing. I had a chance to chat with him one afternoon about where the idea for Affirm came from.

1: You can find all of his great essays on startups at paulgraham.com. His website looks like it's stuck in 1994, but his essays are updated and always excellent.

"I was already kinda in love with solving financial services problems," he said (he had co-founded PayPal, after all), "and then I spent some time doing research on the credit card business, trying to figure out what opportunities might be there. The more I learned about the predatory practices of the credit card industry, the more enraged I became."

He went on to talk about how the traditional credit card business works: high-interest rates, late fees, and "the flip," which means if you miss a single payment, some credit cards actually hike your interest rate retroactively. Many credit card companies make most of their profits from practices like these. Learning about these predatory practices enraged Max. "So, I guess that's how I founded Affirm," Max said. "**It was love plus rage.**

Today, Affirm has a market capitalization of five billion dollars and so many happy customers they've earned an NPS score of 83 —all because Max was a startup founder driven by "love plus rage."

You need a completely unique startup idea— (no, you don't)

When I ask my students to write a sentence describing the problem their startup ideas solves, there's always at least one who submits some version of: "The problem our startup solves is that there is no product like ours on the market today!"

To me, this is like saying: "We're going to make frog-flavored cookies because there are no frog-flavored cookies available today!" Maybe there's a good reason why there are no frog-flavored cookies on the market.

If you really are planning to enter a market that has no existing products like yours, you'll need to spend a lot of money creating demand where there isn't any. You may still fail. Saying you are launching something that doesn't currently exist is a big red flag for investors, and it should be for you too.

To put it another way, if you want to go into the cookie business, we already know that people spend millions of dollars on chocolate chip cookies, so selling chocolate chip cookies that are different in some way is much more likely to succeed than launching the first-ever frog-flavored cookies.

Gray markets can sometimes point you toward a problem worth solving. One of the most famous examples is digital music. In the early 2000s, college kids were busy sharing illegal music downloads, and the record labels were busy suing college kids and forcing Napster into bankruptcy. Steve Jobs saw this as an opportunity, created iTunes, and successfully convinced all the major record labels to sign to the idea of legally selling songs for one dollar per download, turning an underground market into a billion-dollar above-the-table business. iTunes begat Pandora, which begat Spotify, and now here we are.

Gray markets flourish where consumer demand gets ahead of the law. Lots of people rented out bedrooms against local laws; Airbnb came along and turned it into a four-billion-dollar business. Lots of private car companies flouted the oppressive taxi regulations; Uber came along and normalized it to the tune of twelve billion dollars. Throughout Latin America, there existed a large, informal market of people who would run errands for you. Three guys from Colombia founded Rappi to formalize this market, and they are now one of the fastest-growing companies in all of Latin America.

In my work with Miller Center for Social Entrepreneurship, we've graduated several successful microfinance startups, replacing predatory loan sharks in the developing world with normalized financial services.

Again, the existing gray market of lenders proved market demand, and that provided opportunity for new startups to provide more structured, legal solutions.

So, as you look for entrepreneurial opportunities, think about gray markets. The flourishing ones often indicate where consumer demand is ahead of the regulators and incumbents. There's likely to be an opportunity there.

You'll need to write a business plan— (no, you don't)

As I previously mentioned, there may have been a time when startup founders wrote business plans and investors read them, but that rarely happens anymore.

Steve Blank is the godfather of Silicon Valley startup methodology— I'll quote him frequently in this book. He famously wrote that "No business plan ever survived first contact with customers," and I've experienced this myself. I once spent six months writing a very detailed business plan, raised money with it, built a team around it, built a product around it, and then went out and met with prospective customers. Within about two weeks it was apparent that everything in my business plan was wrong.

Paul Graham writes, "The reason I don't care about business plans is that I can learn more from five minutes of interrogating the founders than from ten pages of fluff they've written. The reason I don't care about balance sheets is the same reason I don't care who's leading one hundred yards into a marathon."

You may still want to write a business plan for your own benefit (I definitely find that by writing about something I get better clarity for myself), but don't fool yourself into thinking that investors will care. Plus, I already told you that your original idea will likely fail, so why would you write two hundred pages about it?

Someone is going to steal your idea— (no, they're not)

Some first-time entrepreneurs are hesitant to talk to anyone about their startup idea because they are afraid someone will steal it.

For the most part, I think this fear is unfounded. Most people aren't interested in stealing your idea. Also, any great entrepreneur has the ability to tell the story without giving away any secrets, so great really good at that.

Business is all about weighing the risks versus the benefits. In this case, you have to weigh the risk that someone is going to steal your idea against the benefit of talking to people, getting their input, asking for referrals, etc. In ninety-five percent of cases, I believe the benefits from sharing your idea far exceeds the risk that someone is going to steal it.

So, make a list of ten people you're going to take out for coffee (or just have a call). People whose opinions you trust, people who are subject matter experts, people who are prospective customers, random people you find on LinkedIn who you think might be helpful. You'll be amazed at how willing people are to help, and you'll be amazed at the value of the input and referrals you will get. Nobody is going to steal your idea.

Passion is what matters (yes, always)

When a startup founder is pitching, I want to see their passion shining through. I want to see that they've fallen in love with a problem worth solving and are passionate about solving it. The reason that matters to me is simple, really: running a startup is hard. It's like running a marathon, except you don't know where the water stations are or what the weather will be like. Also, there is no actual finish line. To be successful, you will need to be driven by something deep inside you.

If I'm an investor looking at a startup, all I really care about is whether you have the grit and resilience to see it through to success. Yes, all the other things we talk about in this book matter too—you need to have found a problem worth solving, you need to understand the landscape of competitors and alternatives, and you need to have a solid economic model. But ultimately, resilience wins the day—and underlying passion is the best predictor of that.

But walks are awesome (just ask my dog)

So go for a walk on the beach if that's where you do your best thinking. Personally, I recommend the Wavecrest Open Space trail in Half Moon Bay, and then you can stop at Tres Amigos Taqueria afterward. Get the fish tacos. Tell them I sent you.

As you're on your walk, staring out at the waves, think about what matters to you and what problems you have seen. Great startups begin with an entrepreneur who notices **a problem worth solving and develops a passion for solving it.**

And that's where our Launch Path begins.

TESTING YOUR STARTUP IDEA

In my own career, I learned the hard way that building an unvalidated idea can be a very expensive mistake. The underlying philosophy of the **Launch Path** is that your chances of success will dramatically improve if you test and validate your assumptions at every stage.

But how do you do some quick testing at this very early stage? Or maybe you have a couple different startup ideas; how do you decide which one to go all-in on?

Fortunately, there are incredibly powerful tools and processes available so you can do some quick validation right now, before you even start down the rest of the Launch Path.

Start with Dr. Google and Ms. ChatGPT.
You will learn a lot by Googling around for a couple of hours. You'll probably discover competitors you don't know about (don't worry, this is a good sign!), and maybe you'll find discussion threads on Reddit or a Facebook group around something related to your idea. Read product reviews. As you're Googling around, you may also discover previous failed companies with a similar idea. Again, this isn't necessarily discouraging, but we'd like to try to understand why they failed. Is the website for a failed company now gone? No problem. You can probably time travel using the Wayback Machine at archive.org—they have snapshots of 833 billion websites of the past!

Now, make sure demand exists.
The leading cause of startup death is lack of market demand. Fortunately, Google search traffic is often a pretty good proxy for market demand, and that data is readily available. Use free tools such as Google Keyword Planner, Moz, Semrush, Ubersuggest, or Ahrefs to see what search traffic exists for people who may be looking to solve the problem

your startup idea addresses. Google Trends is also a great source of free information on consumer search trends. Again, we're looking for evidence that customers are looking to solve the problem your startup idea solves (see the Zapier case study in Chapter 6).

Your friends are great, but don't ask them.

All of us tend to socialize ideas with our friends, but for this process, you won't really get meaningful data that way. It's too small a sample size, and your friends are biased. I had a student once who told me he had "thoroughly tested" his startup idea by texting the idea to 10 friends, and 9 of them thought it was awesome. Friends are a great source of personal affirmation but not a very good source of objective data on your startup idea. Same with your mom.

For a B2B idea, LinkedIn can be your friend.

Will your target customers be Vice Presidents of Marketing for mid-size industrial companies in the Northeast region? By using LinkedIn Sales Navigator, you can find people who fit this exact profile! Reach out to ten of them and ask if you can have a short call to get their insights (make sure you're clear that you're not selling anything). Have a relaxed conversation in which you try to understand their world and the problems they face. Do not bias the conversation by telling them all about your specific startup idea! You're looking for the sort of insights that come from an organic discussion. Now, talk to some more people who fit your prospective customer profile. You want to hear at least twenty percent of them say they have the problem you've articulated.

Landing pages are easy and powerful.

With a tool like Unbounce or Squarespace, you can build a "Coming Soon" landing page for your startup idea in about ten minutes and slap an email signup box front and center. Then spend fifty dollars on Facebook/Instagram ads that click through to your landing page. From this modest investment, you'll be able to begin to learn what your cost-per-click will be for online ads and see the demographics of who clicks on your ads. You'll be able to reach out to people who signed up to learn about why they are interested. To get all that for fifty dollars is pretty remarkable, so why wouldn't you do it?

To reiterate, the bottom line is simply that most startups fail due to lack of market demand. Investors know this, and they tend to avoid investing in startups with unproven demand. Every passionate entrepreneur is <u>sure</u> their idea will be an awesome success, but the really great entrepreneurs combine passion with data by spending the time to test and validate their startup ideas.

As legendary Silicon Valley venture capitalist Marc Andreessen says, "If you come in with a theory, a plan, and no data, you're just one in a thousand."

Startups don't usually fail because of competition, but they do fail because founders don't spend enough time gathering data, validating their ideas, and learning about customers. Fortunately, there are many tools to help you start gathering data long before you actually start building a company.

Competition can be addressed, but a lack of demand is hard to fix. Spend some time understanding current demand for products like yours <u>before</u> you start building your startup.

B2B VERSUS B2C

In the startup world, you'll often hear about companies having either a business-to-business model (B2B, where your business sells to other businesses) or a business-to-consumer model (B2C, where your business sells directly to consumers).

You may say to yourself, "My startup will do both!" but for the most part, you'll need to pick one or the other. B2B and B2C models are very different, and there are not many examples of companies that have succeeded at both.

The process of getting a customer in the consumer world is typically different from the process of gaining a business customer. With consumer products, advertising and marketing are expensive, but the sales cycle tends to be short. In the enterprise (B2B) world, purchasing is more relationship-driven, and it tends to be a multi-step process that leads to longer sales cycles. A company the size of Microsoft can put consumer products in a different division (Xbox) that uses a completely different customer acquisition process than selling enterprise software. Amazon's most profitable business today, of course, is Amazon Web Services (AWS), which is strictly focused on B2B and runs much differently than their consumer business.

My general advice for startups is to focus on one or the other. As the old proverb says, "If you try to chase two rabbits, they'll both get away."

The Value Propositions for B2C and B2B

The term Value Proposition essentially answers the question, "Why should a customer buy our product or service?"

Consumers can be a bit fickle, but for B2C I like to use the "Theory of Jobs to Be Done," which was developed by Harvard Business School's Clayton Christensen. He writes: "When we buy a product, we essentially 'hire' something to get a job done. If it does the job well, when we are confronted with the same job, we hire that same product again. And if the product does a crummy job, we 'fire' it and look around for something else we might hire to solve the problem."

This applies pretty well to consumer products across many different categories and dimensions.

B2B is a little different in that for the most part, businesses make purchase decisions strictly based on ROI (return on investment). You have to have a very solid proposition that if a business customer spends $X to buy your product, that will get more than $X in cost savings and/ or revenue growth.

I spent most of my career running enterprise (B2B) software companies. Over time, I realized that there is a sort of value proposition hierarchy, and your ability to sell and price your product is almost entirely determined by your ability to position your product as far up that ladder as you possibly can.

Here's a breakdown of the hierarchy as I see it:

- If your product is perceived as able **to improve an existing process,** that's nice (everyone wants their sock drawer to be more organized!), but it's not something a company would pay a lot of money for. Maybe you'll get two points in the customer's mind.
- However, if your product is going to **save the company real money,** now you get five points in the customer's mind, because the CFO will be happy.

- If your product will **help the company drive revenue**, everybody wants that, including the CEO! So, now you are worthy of eight points in the customer's mind. What if your product will **drive the company's share price** and valuation/market capitalization? The CEO herself will jump at the opportunity to approve that purchase. You've earned ten points and two tacos in the customer's mind!

This hierarchy explains how customer relationship management (CRM) became the most successful enterprise software category ever. A CRM vendor is selling a value proposition that says their product will help you **improve a process, reduce costs, drive sales, and (by extension) drive shareholder value**. That right there is the home run. Salesforce (whose stock ticker symbol is "CRM," by the way) has built this into a $260 billion business.

If you're launching a B2B business, think about positioning your offering as far up this ladder as possible. If you're still down at the "improve a process" level, that's fine, but consider how you can create a product roadmap that will move you up the ladder over time. Your sales process will improve, your sales cycles will shorten, and you will be able to charge more for your product.

Throughout this book, we'll discuss customers and customer growth strategies that apply to both B2C and B2B startup ventures.

Case Study:
TRADER JOE'S

I'm a regular shopper at Trader Joe's. If I'm making a big taco spread for a hungry group of family and friends at home, TJ's will have everything I need (the pickled jalepeño peppers are especially delicious, so always make sure you get two jars of those).

The origin story of Trader Joe's is an interesting one, so let's take a look at it and discuss the lessons that entrepreneurs everywhere can learn.

The founder was Joe Coulombe. After graduating from Stanford in 1958, he went to work for Rexall, the largest retail pharmacy chain at the time. Rexall gave him the task of developing a new line of convenience stores in Southern California.

He successfully got six Pronto Markets up and running, and then suddenly, the Rexall corporate bigwigs back at headquarters changed their minds and told him to shut the stores down. But he didn't want to, so instead, he borrowed money, bought them himself, and transformed his career from a corporate lackey into being a determined entrepreneur.

Coulombe grew his Pronto Markets to eighteen locations around the Los Angeles area and was doing great until 7-Eleven, the Dallas-based convenience store giant, announced they were entering the Los Angeles market.

"They were so huge, I decided I'd better get the hell out of convenience-store retailing," he recalled later. Rather than try to compete head-to-head with 7-Eleven, he came up with a new name, revamped his stores, and (in an era of unironic Tiki culture) gave them a South Seas motif with an eclectic set of products.

Boeing was about to launch the 747 jetliner, and suddenly international travel would be available to millions of Americans. Coulombe predicted this would **increase consumers' interest** in exotic foods and what today we would call "ethnic cuisine." Instead of carrying the same boring American food found in most grocery stores, he focused his stores on a mix of interesting tastes from around the world. Nailing that particular consumer trend would turn out to be a key component of his success.

"What you want is a coherent group of customers," Coulombe told Investor's Business Daily in 1998, "and you shape yourself around it." In 1960s America, more people than ever were college-educated, and Coulombe was based in Southern California, where many of them landed to vie for jobs in the entertainment industry. He said he envisioned his new stores as havens "for overeducated and underpaid people, for all the screenwriters, classical musicians, museum curators, and journalists."

Bingo—he identified and described a target market he could build a product offering around.

Most chains have identical retail spaces, no matter the location. The interior of a 7-Eleven in Chicago is identical to the interior of a 7-Eleven in Atlanta, for example. Coulombe knew that he needed the scale economies of a chain, but he wanted consumers to feel as if their neighborhood stores were **connected to their communities.** Trader Joe's hired in-house artists who matched each store's decor to the neighborhood it served. To this day, they create signature wall murals (the Manhattan store has a rainbow Statue of Liberty, while the Santa Cruz store has surfers, for example), and the same in-house artists create all the signs and labels in each unique store. Customers like the benefits of a big chain, but they also like supporting businesses that feel integrated into their communities.

Over time, Coulombe added more organic and healthy items because that's what his "overeducated and underpaid" consumers were asking for. In 2007, Trader Joe's phased out food imported from China due to customer concerns. They discontinued sales of six species of fish deemed unsustainable by Greenpeace, and today they only carry dairy products without added hormones. Their shelves are stocked with items containing no artificial colors, flavors, preservatives, or genetically modified ingredients. In recent years, they've been criticized for their use of plastic packaging, which they are now phasing out. From the beginning, Coulombe had managers dressed in tropical shirts standing behind the front desk, **asking customers what they liked**, what they didn't like, and what they wanted to see more of. Coulombe consistently listened and responded accordingly.

No discussion of Trader Joe's would be complete without mentioning the wine section (my favorite part!). When Coulombe founded Trader Joe's, a typical grocery store might have one percent of their shelf space dedicated to wine; Trader Joe's **devotes nearly fifteen percent of their retail space to that one product category.** Coulombe was a wine lover himself, and he once said he had read that "educated people tended to drink more wine," so that fit his vision of the customers he was targeting. In the 1960s, most consumers thought of fine wine as expensive and imported from France, but the California wine industry was just getting going, so he decided he'd focus on value wines, mainly from California. Soon after came the famous Two-Buck Chuck, a private-label California wine exclusive to Trader Joe's that sold for its eponymous price. Consumers were being introduced to Trader Joe's variety of goods via their wine selection—they would come in for the wine and discover that the store sold food, too!

Today, Trader Joe's is owned by a guy in Germany, but it is still run on the principles established by its founder, Joe Coulombe, many years ago.

The story of Trader Joe's is a great parable of entrepreneurial success. A guy quits his corporate job, creates a new startup, dodges well-financed competition, listens to customers, gains millions of loyal followers, drinks a lot of good wine, and becomes a cultural icon. Sounds like a life well-lived to me. Here's to Joe Coulombe and to "overeducated and underpaid" people everywhere.

KEY TAKEAWAYS:

Trader Joe's is a decidedly old-fashioned, non-tech business founded long ago, but I think there are some timeless lessons in the story that entrepreneurs today can learn from:

◊ Coulombe identified a "coherent group of customers" and built a product offering around them. In Chapter 2, we will discuss how successful product development begins by talking to customers, and in Chapter 7, we will discuss the idea of creating Customer Personas and referring to them constantly. You can't build a product "for everyone"—you have to have a very specific set of personas you are building a product offering about, and Joe Coulombe did that.

◊ Competition didn't scare Coulombe off, but it did make him realize that positioning within the landscape mattered. So he built an offering that was clearly positioned as something that was different than convenience stores and traditional grocery stores.

◊ Never stop iterating. By continuing to talk to customers (and have his managers do the same) he was able to stay on top of consumer trends as they shifted and he made sure that the product offerings in his stores shifted as well.

◊ The hockey player Wayne Gretsky once said, "I skate to where the puck is going, not where it has been." A big part of Joe Coulombe's success is that he saw patterns that helped him correctly predict changes to customer preferences that traditional grocery stores didn't see.

Problem ?

One clear sentence that articulates the problem your startup solves.

Consumers in the US spend $331 billion/year on fast food, and most of it is really unhealthy.

The paradox is that consumers today <u>want</u> to eat healthy, but also have a busy life that often drives them to resort to the convenience of fast food.

Solution

How does your venture solve the problem you have articulated? Keep this short and consise!

Fast food doesn't need to be unhealthy. Our startup is developing a new brand of health-conscious fast food (healthy tacos!), delivered directly to your home or office.

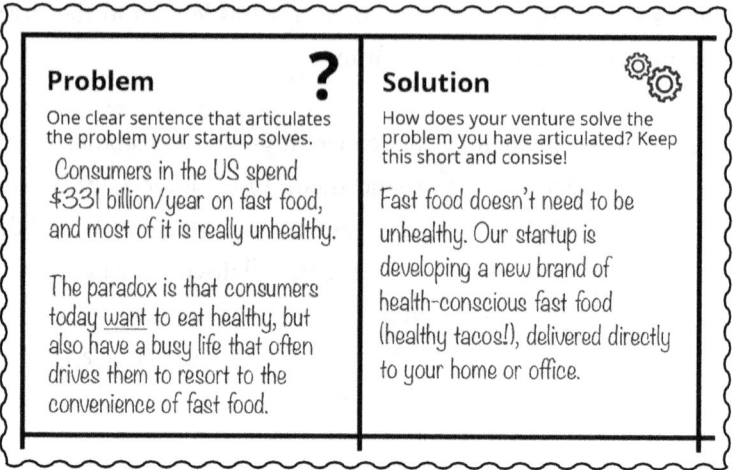

The Launch Path Canvas
Lorem ipsum

Name of Startup Venture: Fitaco, Inc

Prepared by: Bret Waters

Date: November 8, 2023

Iteration: 8

Problem ?
One clear sentence that articulates the problem your startup solves.

Consumers in the US spend $331 billion/year on fast food, and most of it is really unhealthy.

The paradox is that consumers today <u>want</u> to eat healthy, but also have a busy life that often drives them to resort to the convenience of fast food.

Solution
How does your venture solve the problem you have articulated? Keep this short and consise!

Fast food doesn't need to be unhealthy. Our startup is developing a new brand of health-conscious fast food (healthy tacos!), delivered directly to your home or office.

Why it matters
Why is this a problem worth solving?

The National Institutes for Health say that today a fast food diet may kill more people prematurely every year than cigarette smoking.

Alternatives
When a customer looks at alternative ways to solve the problem we solve, what will they see? This is a list of competitors and alternatives. Link to a graphic representation of the landscape.

There are many, many food delivery services, from Uber Eats to Doordash to Grubhub.

See visualization at this link.

Customer
It's all about understanding customers. Write a one-sentence description of key customer personas and the problem we solve for each. Circle the one that is most influential.

Adventurous Alex: A thrill-seeking foodie always on the hunt for unique and spicy taco creations to satisfy their daring palate.

Health-Conscious Haley: A fitness enthusiast looking for wholesome and fresh ingredient options that align with their nutritious lifestyle at the taqueria.

Busy Ben: An on-the-go professional seeking quick, flavorful, and portable taco choices to enjoy during a busy workday.

Vegetarian Victoria: A plant-based eater in search of flavorful and creative vegetarian and vegan taco selections that cater to their dietary preferences.

Traditional Tony: A lover of classic flavors, Tony enjoys indulging in authentic and time-honored taco recipes that remind him of his cultural heritage.

Family-Oriented Felix: A parent looking for a family-friendly meal featuring a variety of options to cater to the taste preferences of both kids and adults.

Budget-Conscious Bella: A student or frugal diner in pursuit of affordable yet flavorful taco choices that won't break the bank at the taqueria.

Path to PMF
What is our path to Product-Market Fit? Customer Development, MVP's, etc.

1. Farmers' markets where we can get input on our menu items.
2. One truck in the Palo Alto area for a pilot project.
3. Scale slowly to additional markets, based on our learnings.

Top 3 Benefits
What are the top 3 benefits that your product or services provides to customers?

1. Convenience. Use our mobile app to place a custom order and it's delivered directly to you.
2. Healthy food, designed by a nutritionist.
3. Tacos. Everybody loves tacos.

Distribution
What are our distibution channels? Direct to consumer, via resellers, or?

We intend to sell direct-to-consumer, via our mobile app and website, with delivery via our own vans.

In the future, we may be open to distribution partnerships.

Positioning
Within this landscape of competitors and alternatives, how is your venture positioned? Our positioning can basically be summed-up in two words: healthy and delicious.

There are many food delivery apps that can deliver something that is delicious but not very healthy. Or you could eat a kale salad.

We serve delicious tacos designed by a nutritionist. That's our unique positioning.

Economics
What are the Unit Economics for this venture, what do we expect the CAC<LTV to look like, and what are out capital needs? (Link to full spreadsheet).

One unit = one taco: Sell price $5, on which our gross profit is 4.74

Early tests indicate CAC of $11, and we expect an initial LTV of three orders per customer ($25.50), which will grow with time.

Our initial capital needs are $220K, which will get us through the pilot launch. We will propose to investors structuring this as a SAFE.

See full spreadsheet at this link.

Team
What are the characteristics of the right team to make this venture a success?

The right team aligns with our target demographic - people who want to eat healthy and also enjoy the convenience of a quick taco meal.

The economics of our venture are such that we'll need drivers and cooks who are affordable, so we will work hard to make it an attractive part-time job for students, and a great evening second job for anybody.

Defensibility
What is your secret sauce that is difficult for competitors to copy?

The fact that we own the customer and customer data is a big part of our defensibility.

A restaurant selling through a 3rd-party like Doordash owns neither the customer nor the data.

See full example at **thelaunchpath.com**

STEP 1, FOR YOUR STARTUP

Most great startups begin with a founder who notices a problem worth solving. So, what problem does your startup solve? Can you articulate it clearly, along with your proposed solution?

▶ *For your Launch Path Canvas:*

Write a simple, clear **problem statement** for your startup venture, and then write an equally simple and clear, **solution statement**. You're not writing marketing copy, so stay away from fluff—you're just writing a simple and clear articulation of the problem and your proposed solution. Remember, these are just drafts for now. As we work our way through **The Launch Path**, we'll validate and refine everything.

Download a blank copy of **The Launch Path Canvas** from thelaunchpath.com and begin filling it out as shown below. Throughout the book I will give you examples based on my awesome (fictional) startup, Fitaco—tacos that keep you fit!

"The only way to win is to learn faster than anyone else.

ERIC RIES

CHAPTER 2

LEARN WHAT CUSTOMERS WANT

If you don't do this, nothing else matters

Back in 1999, I had an awesome idea for a new startup. I was so excited I could barely contain myself. It was the height of the dot-com boom in Silicon Valley, and all my friends were getting filthy rich.

I spent late nights producing a pitch deck for my startup. Surely, this set of slides would convince investors that my idea was brilliant and worthy. After many long hours, my pitch deck was finally perfect, and I asked for a meeting with a friend who had recently joined a venture capital firm. I walked into his conference room early on a chilly November morning, feeling confident and prepared.

By the end of the meeting, we were high-fiving about how awesome my idea was. His firm led a $5 million initial round of financing, and I was off to the races.

With funding secured, I quickly recruited an all-star team of twenty software engineers to build my awesome idea. We labored for two years, fully convinced that our idea would be a big hit with customers. All the ingredients were in place—we had a great startup idea, we were obviously a brilliant team, and we were backed by incredibly smart venture capital investors—what could go wrong?

Well, after spending two years and $5 million building a product we thought was fantastic, we released it, only to find out that no customer wanted it. Customers didn't care about all the work we put into building the product because it didn't solve problems they cared about. My awesome idea was a complete failure.[1]

This has been a recurring issue since the dawn of entrepreneurship: how does one reliably create new products that succeed?

We've all seen examples of companies large and small that put enormous effort into developing a new product they are sure will be a success, only to find out that customers don't want it.

The research firm CB Insights conducts an annual post-mortem survey of failed startups, and year after year, they find that **"no market need"** remains a leading cause of startup death. How the hell do you build and fund an entire company without first determining whether there's a market need? It seems ridiculous, yet it happens over and over again. I've done it myself.

The worst new product failure in history:

While my own experience was painful, others have had it much worse. The greatest new product failure in American history was probably the Ford Edsel. It's still legendary for how spectacularly it failed, and the name has become synonymous with disastrous product development.

The Ford Motor Company had an initial public offering (IPO)in 1956. Led by Goldman Sachs, the offering raised $650 million (more than $7 billion in 2023 dollars). It was the most successful IPO in American history at the time, and Ford decided to spend a chunk of that shiny new cash developing the most sophisticated automobile

---

1: I have modified the story slightly for dramatic effect. We actually got a few customers, but we never had anywhere near the success we anticipated. We eventually sold the company in a disappointing deal that lost money for the investors.

line on Earth. They hired the world's top automotive engineers, who then spent three years and $250 million developing the new car they called the Edsel, named for Henry Ford's grandson. The engineers had developed exciting new features like push-button transmission shifting, self-adjusting brakes, triple-thermostat cooling, and a state-of-the-art 410-cubic-inch engine.

Ford executives were so sure of success that they launched the Edsel with not just one but <u>eighteen</u> new models spread across four lines and a $12 million advertising campaign developed by the famous Madison Avenue ad agency Foote, Cone & Belding. The Edsel's tagline, glamorizing it as "the newest expression in fine engineering from the Ford Motor Company," drove home the idea that it was indeed the most advanced automobile ever produced.

THE EDSEL RANGER FOUR-DOOR HARDTOP

Ford launched the new Edsel in 18 models spread across 4 lines.

But despite the huge engineering and advertising investment, the Edsel failed to sell. Out of the projected sales of one million units, only sixty thousand were sold the first year, followed by fifty-six thousand the second year, and then Ford shut down the entire production in the third year. The Edsel line lost $350 million (over $3 billion in today's dollars) and went down in history as the most spectacular new product failure ever.

Successful product innovation occurs at the intersection of what is technically feasible, has positive economics, and aligns with what customers want. The Edsel had one of those: the engineering was feasible. But it didn't align with what customers wanted, and the manufacturing economics were upside down.

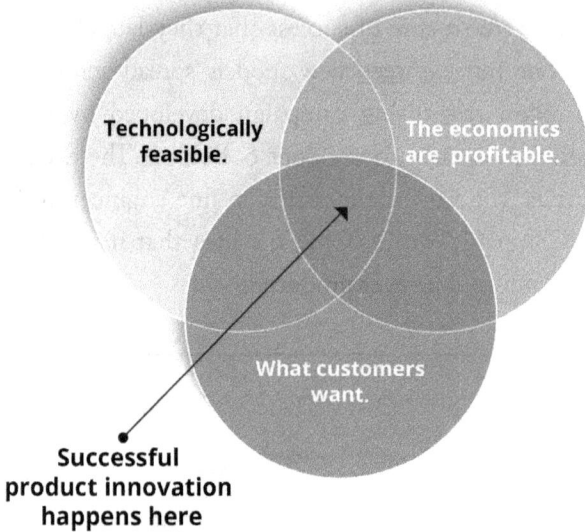

Ford launched the new Edsel in 18 models spread across 4 lines.

Entire books have been written about the Edsel's failure, and as a case study, it has been taught in MBA classrooms for many years. Yet we continue to see companies spend a lot of money developing products they are sure will be a success, only to find out customers don't want them.

PRODUCT-MARKET FIT

A few years ago, in an attempt to put a framework around developing products that actually succeed, Silicon Valley venture capitalist Andy Rachleff developed the concept of **Product-Market Fit**, suggesting that the entire goal of a startup is to achieve a fit between what your product does and what the market wants. I didn't achieve Product-Market Fit with my startup in 1999, and Ford didn't achieve it with the Edsel in 1958 (nor did several thousand companies since then). The notion of Product-Market Fit is a critical one that every startup founder needs to understand.

Marc Andreessen expanded on the Product-Market Fit concept in an article he wrote for the Stanford School of Engineering[2]:

"Product/market fit means being in a good market with a product that can satisfy that market", emphasizing that the concept only works if you've found a good market for your product.

"You can always feel when Product-Market Fit isn't happening. The customers aren't quite getting value out of the product, word of mouth isn't spreading, usage isn't growing that fast, press reviews are kind of 'blah,' the sales cycle takes too long, and lots of deals never close."

"And you can always feel when Product-Market Fit <u>is</u> happening. The customers are buying the product just as fast as you can make it— or usage is growing just as fast as you can add more servers. You're hiring sales and customer support staff as fast as you can. Reporters

---

2: https://web.stanford.edu/class/ee204/ProductMarketFit.html

are calling because they've heard about your hot new thing and they want to talk to you about it. You could eat free for a year at Buck's[3]."

Marc Andreessen succinctly summarizes the whole concept by stating that, with startups, "the <u>only</u> thing that matters is getting to Product-Market Fit."

If this is indeed "the only thing that matters" for startups, then there is only one question: how do we achieve Product-Market Fit most effectively? There are three concepts I wish I had understood when I founded that software business back in 1999: **Customer Development**, **Lean Startups/MVP**, and **Design Thinking**.

Customer Development

Steve Blank coined the term Customer Development. Steve is a crusty startup veteran often called the godfather of Silicon Valley startup methodology. He and I had lunch together at a Thai restaurant a few years ago, and he told me a story about an experience he once had when he was a startup CEO.

"We had a new product under development," Steve said. "It wasn't quite ready, but my top salesperson and I decided to go out and meet with some customers so we could tell them about our exciting new product that would be available next quarter."

They built a slide deck about the product and all its amazing features, then hit the road to meet customers. "After the first customer meeting, we realized the product was all wrong, so while my sales guy drove us to the next customer meeting, I sat in the passenger seat and edited the

---

3: Buck's is a restaurant up the street from my house, famous for meetings with venture capitalists. Funding for PayPal, Netscape, Hotmail, and Tesla were all secured over breakfast at Buck's. I recommend the huevos rancheros. Tell them I sent you.

slide deck based on the feedback we had received." The day continued, repeating the same process. After each meeting, they would update the slide deck about the product based on the input they received. Steve finished his story to me with "By the end of the day, the product in our slide deck was perfect, but unfortunately, it wasn't the product our engineering team had been building".

From that experience (and others), he realized that we were all doing it backward. We needed to be doing what he called Customer Development <u>before</u> we did product development.

Steve founded eight companies in his career. Four had successful IPOs, while four failed so spectacularly that they left (in his words) "giant craters in the ground." He then semi-retired and wrote a book called *The Four Steps to the Epiphany: Successful Strategies for Products that Win.*[4]

In his book, Steve writes about how startups tend to conduct product development, then after the product is developed, they go out and try to find customers (I did that and ended up losing a lot of money). A process with a much higher likelihood of success, Steve writes, would be first to spend a whole lot of time talking to customers and <u>then</u> build a product based on what you've learned from their real-life experiences.

He breaks Customer Development down into four steps:

- **Customer discovery** first captures the founders' vision and turns it into a series of business-model hypotheses. Then it develops a plan to test customer reactions to those hypotheses and turn them into facts.

4: Available on Amazon (ISBN 978-1119690351); for a distilled version, find his 2013 article in Harvard Business Review.

- **Customer validation** tests whether the resulting business model is repeatable and scalable. If not, founders should return to customer discovery.
- **Customer creation** is the start of execution. It builds end-user demand and drives it into the sales channel to scale the business.
- **Company building** transitions the organization from a startup to a company focused on executing a validated model.

For the purposes of the **Launch Path**, we will focus on the first two steps, as they are the most applicable to early-stage startup ventures.

In a nutshell, early-stage Customer Development is about validating your assumptions by talking to actual customers and making sure your product development roadmap is informed by these validated assumptions. Like everything else in our Launch Path methodology, it's an ongoing process—you don't just do one set of Customer Development interviews and declare that you're done. Instead, you want to have the mindset of <u>always</u> making sure that what you're building has been tested and validated by interactions with real customers.

As startup founders, we have a set of untested hypotheses about who the customer is, what features they want, what channels to use, etc. But you don't want to build a product based on untested hypotheses, you want to build a product based on <u>actual validated facts</u>. That's the heart of the Customer Development concept.

Lean Startup/MVP

The term "Lean Startup" was popularized by Eric Ries in his 2009 book of the same name[5], based on the previous work of Steve Blank. It's a

---

5: The Lean Startup: How Today's Entrepreneurs Use Continuous Innovation to Create Radically Successful Businesses ISBN 978-0307887894

methodology for developing businesses and products by **shortening development cycles via experimentation and validated learning.**

Contrary to popular belief, the "lean" in the title doesn't mean cheap. You could use the Lean Startup methodology with a $100 million budget. The name "Lean Startup" comes from the auto industry and the fact that Toyota revolutionized that sector with their Lean Manufacturing methodology, which advocated shorter production cycles and a more iterative approach to building products.

Ries preaches that startups can successfully use the principles of Lean Manufacturing combined with the scientific method. Your assumptions are just hypotheses, so find ways to test them empirically!

Central to the lean startup methodology is the concept of a Minimum Viable Product (MVP). The idea is simple: a startup should test their product idea by first building a bare-bones prototype with a minimum set of features, then put it into the market to learn from. Based on those early learnings from your MVP, you can develop a product roadmap informed by real users.

The key thing many people miss is that the purpose of building an MVP is **learning, not showing** (more on this in the next section).

Think of how Facebook launched with just a bare minimum set of features, but today it has a zillion features, all informed by watching the interactions of real users. That is the lean startup concept in action.

Design Thinking

David Kelley, who designed many of the early Apple products, went on to found the design consultancy IDEO (and then the d.school at

Stanford) and popularized a product-engineering framework known as Design Thinking. Its five steps are to:

- **Empathize** (develop a deep understanding of the user).
- **Define** (develop a point of view around a problem)
- **Ideate** (brainstorm about how you can solve that problem)
- **Prototype** (build an early set of MVP's)
- **Test** (get input on your prototype from actual customers)

By iterating through the Design Thinking process, you will end up with an innovative product that aligns with the needs of your customers. Over the years, several related frameworks have been developed, including User Centered Design, Value Centered Design, Product Thinking, and others. They all have proponents and adherents, but to me, they are all variations of the same theme: don't just build a product <u>you</u> think is awesome; use a process that helps you build a product <u>customers</u> think is awesome.

Design Thinking: A 5-Stage Process

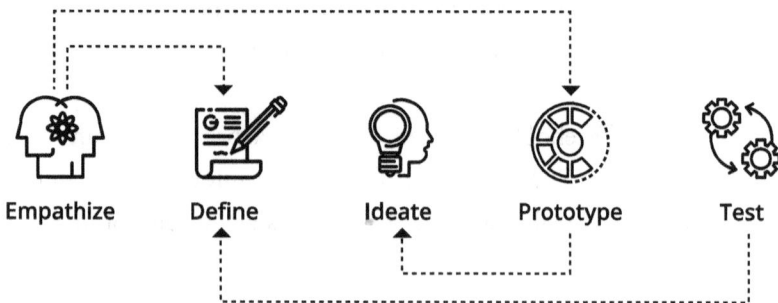

Empathize   Define   Ideate   Prototype   Test

(Despite the name, Design Thinking isn't inherently about design at all. It's an approach to solving problems by putting structure around brainstorming. It's been used across many disciplines. Maybe someday someone will come up with a better name for it).

But it's just common sense, really

All of these terms, "Product-Market Fit," "MVP," "Lean Startup," and "Design Thinking," get tossed around as if they were magic elixirs. Honestly, it's really just the common-sense way that successful businesses have always been built.

Let's say we wanted to open a neighborhood bakery. Our goal is to bake bread that our neighborhood actually wants to eat (**Product-Market Fit**). We might begin by asking our neighbors about their taste in bread so we can understand what they care about (**Customer Development**). Based on this, we'll brainstorm some recipes (**Design Thinking**). Then we'll make some small batches for them to taste and give us feedback on (**prototyping**).

Now we'll do a neighborhood pop-up some one weekend (an **MVP).** Then maybe we should set up a booth at some farmers' markets to learn a little more about the economics of selling bread (another **MVP!**).

If we take these steps <u>before</u> we lease an expensive building and build out an expensive bakery kitchen, we will have a much greater chance of success (**Launch Path**, baby!).

The fancy management consulting companies will be happy to sell you some magic elixir advice filled with buzzwords if you'd like.

But fundamentally, it's just the common-sense way that successful businesses have always been built.

WHO DA CUSTOMER?

All of the concepts discussed in this chapter are about making sure you are building something **that customers will buy.** And so, you must be careful to distinguish between random feedback and actual <u>customer</u> input. If you put a digital MVP out in the marketplace and then just start creating new features for every troll who gives you input, you'll be spinning your wheels. On the other hand, if ten people say they would buy your product now if you had one particular feature, that might be worth working on (see the Zapier case study later in this book). My colleague Edwin Oh teaches an entire course on Product-Market Fit, and as he puts it, "The only real validation is a monetary commitment in either the form of cash, a credit card number, a binding letter of intent, or dedication of resources to a beta test. Everything else is a pat on the back or unqualified opinion." So beware of making changes to your product based on an "unqualified opinion." Unqualified opinions don't pay the bills.

Remember also that there are many businesses where the user differs from the customer. Social media companies, for example, have users (you and me), and then they have customers (advertisers).

Two-sided marketplaces (discussed further in Chapter 4) need two sets of Product-Market Fit. Airbnb needed Product-Market Fit with people looking for a room to rent and also with people looking to get some income from the extra room in their house. With medical device startups, your user is the patient, but the customer actually making the purchase decision is often a physician (working within a purchase environment shaped by insurance companies). So, as you are working on getting to Product-Market Fit, ensure you are fitting the right thing(s)!

THE MVP: A WIDELY MISUNDERSTOOD CONCEPT

"Minimum Viable Product" (MVP) has become one of the most overused terms in Silicon Valley. If you walk into any of Palo Alto's many coffee shops, you'll hear the term being used by wannabe entrepreneurs at nearly every table.

But what is an MVP, exactly? Some people seem to think it's a pretty slide deck of their startup idea; some think it's a nice design mockup of the product; some people seem to actually be writing software code.

As Eric Ries explained in his book, *The Lean Startup*, "The minimum viable product (MVP) is that version of a new product a team uses to collect the maximum amount of validated **learning about customers** with the least effort." Learning about customers is the important part of that sentence. That's the purpose of an MVP.

History is littered with the dead bodies of startups that built a product no actual customers wanted. Some spent millions of their investors' money proving there was zero market demand for their product (hey, I did that!). The value of an MVP is to avoid that sort of startup death by creating a bare-bones product first, getting it in front of real customers to see how they react, and then building out and refining the product in a way that is informed by actual customers.

Tesla launched by buying car bodies and chassis from Lotus, putting Tesla's EV motors in them, and selling them branded as the Tesla Roadster. They made and sold five hundred of those, and from the learnings gained, they developed the Model S, the first car that was actually entirely their own design.

Peloton launched by creating a picture of a prototype and making the product available for pre-sale on Kickstarter. Two hundred ninety-seven people paid $1,000 each to get one of the first models, and based on the feedback from that first production run, they built a company now worth over $3 billion.

The concept of an MVP is straightforward: get an **early, imperfect version of the product out into the market so you can learn from actual customers** as you refine the product offering. Yet there still seems to be confusion about what an MVP is, so here are my own thoughts. First, let me tell you (from my personal experience) what an MVP is not:

1. **An MVP is not something you build to show;** it's something you build to learn from. Many people working on their MVPs think they are building a demo to impress someone. That's nice, but the purpose is to learn actionable insights from real customers.
2. **It's not going to get you funded.** No doubt you've heard someone say, "As soon as our MVP is complete, we'll show it to venture capitalists and raise lots of money!" In truth, this is backward thinking because it implies that the purpose of an MVP is to show something. Showing that you can create a clickable prototype isn't going to impress investors—any fifth-grader can do that. But proving to them that you have discovered **key insights into the wants and needs of real-world customers** by having an initial product out in the actual marketplace? In investors' minds, that's golden (see the Dollar Shave Club case study in Chapter 4).
3. **It's not even a thing; it's a process.** If you embrace the MVP concept, you are embracing an iterative process of idea generation, data collection, analysis, and learning. You're embracing the concept of optimizing your path to Product-Market Fit by getting early product releases into the hands of customers so you can learn from them. Marc Andreessen has written that,

if you do this right, **"the market actually pulls the successful product out of the startup**." That's what you want from your MVP. Twitter thought they were developing a group SMS platform when they released their MVP at the 2007 SXSW festival, but the market pulled out a real-time media platform that has been a billion-dollar success (until Elon touched it).

Now I'll tell you (again, from my own personal experience) what a good MVP is:

1. **It's Simple.** When DoorDash launched, it was a simple landing page with PDF menus and a phone number that the founders answered themselves. It probably cost less than one hundred dollars to build, but the learnings they got from it allowed them to build a company with a market capitalization of $35 billion.

2. **It tests the right things.** When Pandora first launched, the playlists were manually managed by humans. The question they needed to test was: Will people pay for a streaming music service? (Note that the test question was not: Can we write a software algorithm that chooses good music?) Once they successfully proved market demand with their MVP, they made the investment to write the complex software required to algorithmically choose music.

3. **It's built for rapid iteration.** The whole idea of an MVP is to rapidly try out new features and see how the market responds. Rapid iteration accelerates the process of **getting from your guess as to what the market wants to something that the market has proven it wants**.

Want one more example? Here's one you can eat

My favorite kind of MVP is food trucks. For a relatively small investment, an aspiring restaurateur can take her menu on the road, get feedback from real customers, create daily menu iterations based on that feedback, and then—after having proven market demand—can make the investment in leasing restaurant space and building a kitchen and full dining room. That's how a good MVP should work.

I've already mentioned my favorite Steve Blank quote: "No business plan survives first contact with actual customers." The entire purpose of an MVP is to avoid this by getting early learnings from actual customers before you start executing a plan.

PUT SOME TURK IN YOUR MVP

In the eighteenth century, a guy named Wolfgang von Kempelen created a machine that seemingly could play chess. It was a large wooden box with a chessboard and a Turkish-looking mechanical man sitting at it, ready to place chess with anyone. As a person made moves on the chessboard, the Turk would reach out its mechanical hand and make its counter-move. This amazing device was demonstrated in all European royal courts and became known as the Mechanical Turk. People were astonished and entertained by the magic of a mechanical figure that could play chess and make smart moves.

Eventually, of course, it was discovered that there was actually a human hidden inside the box who was controlling the Mechanical Turk. It wasn't magic after all, but everyone still loved it.[6]

6: I highly recommend Tom Standage's book, The Turk: The Life and Times of the Famous Eighteenth-Century Chess-Playing Machine. ISBN 978-0802713919.

There are several examples of startups using the Mechanical Turk approach to build an MVP that looks like magic is going on, but the magic is actually being done manually. I mentioned previously how, when the streaming music pioneer Pandora launched, humans manually created the playlists, even though users thought the software was personalizing playlists on the fly.

When Wealthfront launched their automated investing platform, the "automation" was just plain old humans sitting at desks. In both cases, they were able to get learnings from their Mechanical Turk MVPs that then informed the building of the actual automated product.

Zappos began as a website called ShoeSite.com. Founder Nick Swinmum would take pictures of shoes at stores around town and post them to the website. When orders came in, he would literally drive to the store, buy the shoes, and manually ship them to the customer. Customers thought it was a slick digital process, but it was actually just Nick doing everything manually and learning as much as possible about customers. Based on the learnings, he met Tony Hsieh, changed the name to Zappos, raised the necessary capital, and built out the digital process and inventory that is Zappos today.

Sometimes this is called a Wizard of Oz MVP since it appears to be "great and powerful," but it's just an average dude behind the curtain.

Whether you want to call it Wizard of Oz or Mechanical Turk, many great startups have used this approach to create an MVP for a new product or service.

CUSTOMER DEVELOPMENT INTERVIEWS

I once had a student tell me, "I've done market testing for my startup, and ninety percent of people say they will buy my product when it's available!" I was impressed, so I asked him about his methodology. He said he had texted ten friends about his startup idea, nine of whom thought it was awesome. Then I was much less impressed.

As this student demonstrated, most new entrepreneurs do customer interviews wrong because they are more interested in affirmation than insights. We all want to be told our startup idea is awesome (and that we're handsome, too!). Humans crave affirmation, but if you approach customer development interviews as a search for affirmation, your new venture is likely doomed from the start.

Steve Blank, who first articulated the Customer Development concept, suggests that early-stage startups mostly have a bunch of untested hypotheses about their business models (who the customers are, what features they want, how much they'll pay, etc.), and it's a mistake to build a product around untested hypotheses. So, **get out there and talk to a bunch of customers** before you start developing the product!

It's a simple enough concept, but as the student I mentioned proves, many entrepreneurs go through the customer development motions without uncovering meaningful customer insights. Worse yet, they get false positives and build the wrong thing.

Common Mistakes:

Here are some of the common mistakes in conducting customer development interviews:

Thinking you're pitching.

Entrepreneurs work hard on their startup pitches, and then they want to use them everywhere, including on customer development calls. But remember, the point of these calls is to learn about customers and discover hidden insights. Once you go into pitch mode, you're not learning anything; you're just telling them what the solution is before you even understand what their problems are.

Digging for compliments.

Deep down, we're all insecure people who crave compliments. But, as Rob Fitzpatrick's terrific book, *The Mom Test,* puts it: "Compliments are the fool's gold of this process: shiny, distracting, and worthless."[7] Digging for compliments isn't going to give you any market insights; it will just give you false positives.

Not asking why.

When your interviewee states their biggest problem, always ask them why. When they tell you, ask why again. Keep peeling back the onion until you find the customer's real underlying problems. In the consulting business, it's axiomatic that the problem a client hires you to solve is always different from the problem the client actually has. The same is true with customer development.

Staying inside your echo chamber.

Most of us surround ourselves with friends who think like we do. We all love our friends, but they are the wrong people to interview in a customer development process because you won't learn much from people who think like you do. Get out of your echo chamber

---

7: I highly recommend this book. The Mom Test: How to Talk to Customers & Learn If Your Business Is a Good Idea When Everyone Is Lying to You, ISBN 978-1492180746 It's an easy read, and it's worth every penny as you prepare for your startup's customer development interviews.

for your customer development—it's less comfortable but much more insightful.

Not asking about purchase authority.

I once had a software startup that thought production managers at advertising agencies would be our core customers. We talked to production managers nationwide until we were one hundred percent confident that we were building a product they would love. When we launched, we discovered that they did love it—but they didn't have the spending authority to buy it. There are many kinds of businesses where it's important to understand how the money flows. Don't hesitate to ask.

Talking more than listening.

The more you're talking, the worse you're doing. It's certainly true for dating, and it's just as true for customer development interviews.

Sending out a survey.

Many people put together a survey and send it out for their customer development process rather than have one-on-one calls. I am not a fan of this. Real insights happen during actual conversations between humans. To me, sending out a survey is lazy, pre-defines the answer set, and is very unlikely to uncover hidden insights.

Not focusing on learning.

Again, I can't tell you how often I've seen entrepreneurs think this process is about pitching and hearing people say, "Wow, cool idea!" They finish the call quite pleased with the affirmation, but they've learned absolutely nothing. These calls are about uncovering insights and learning about customers. Before the call, list what you'd like to understand about this customer so you can steer the conversation in ways that uncover those things.

Not ending with an ask.

Many entrepreneurs end a customer development call with something like, "Well, thanks. I'd love to stay in touch!" This is really pretty meaningless and contains no commitment on the other person's part. True commitment comes with time, reputation, or money. My favorite way to end a customer discovery call is to say, "Thank you so much! Is there anyone else you think I should talk to?" You'll get some great referrals, and someone making an introduction means they are investing their reputation in helping you. That's a powerful signal.

Here's the thing—I did customer development interviews wrong for a long time, and I lost a lot of investor money before I finally figured it out. Be better than me. Ask good, open-ended questions that may provide unexpected insights. Don't pitch your solution; instead, aim to understand their problems.

And don't dig for compliments and affirmation. You can get those from your mom.

PMCF > PMF

One day, I had a conversation with veteran venture capitalist Tim Connors in which he said, "Everyone talks about Product-Market Fit, but what actually matters is Product-Market-<u>Channel</u> Fit."

Tim's point is that, ultimately, you'll need a great product, <u>and</u> you'll need to find the right channels through which to sell it. Many startups have died because they had the right product but the wrong distribution channels. Without the right distribution channels, your product will never succeed.

If you're selling home improvement tools, you'll probably need distribution through Home Depot or a similar big retailer. It's hard to sell books these days without being on Amazon. For mobile apps, garnering good reviews in the app stores is the only way your distribution will succeed.

Clothing brands have historically needed distribution through large retailers (or maybe a focus on selling through small boutiques). Today, clothing brands can choose to go direct-to-consumer instead, but a DTC distribution approach can be difficult and expensive.

So, as you're doing your Customer Development interviews, ask people where they currently buy products and services like yours. Understand the distribution channels available in your sector and the patterns of purchase behavior. You may even be able to test distribution channels at this early stage and see which ones appear to be most effective for your particular product.

Ultimately, you'll need a great product <u>and</u> effective distribution channels. So Tim is right—the sooner you start thinking about Product-Market-Channel fit, the better.

CHAPTER 2 SUMMARY

Successful startups are built upon a series of small experiments. As entrepreneurs, we go into the startup process with many assumptions about what we <u>think</u> customers will buy. But building a new product or service entirely based on what you think the world needs has a very low likelihood of success (I've tried it and lost a lot of money).

So always be thinking about small experiments you can do to validate your assumptions with real customers.

Ultimately, what matters is achieving Product-Market fit, a fit between what your product does and what the market wants. Therefore, your focus should be on whatever will help you get there efficiently and effectively.

1. Spend a lot of time **talking to prospective customers** up-front (do Customer Development before you do product development).
2. Embrace the fact that most of your assumptions will be wrong, and success depends on **testing your assumptions** before the market tells you just how wrong you are.
3. Always be thinking, "What's the smallest experiment I could do right now that would provide the **greatest possible learning**?"
4. Embrace the concept of your Minimum Viable Product (MVP) as a great way to learn from the marketplace. Don't think of an MVP as a one-time deal; instead, using multiple MVPs is part of the process by which you are getting **validated knowledge of the market** as you continue to iterate upon and improve your march toward Product-Market Fit and beyond.

Remember that everything in this chapter is best thought of as an **ongoing process.** I once had a student ask me, "So when can I stop iterating on my product?" and the answer, of course, is never!

Successful companies are continually iterating on product offerings based on input from real customers. Product-Market Fit is an ever-shifting target as customers change, markets change, and competitive landscapes change.

Journey sang, "Don't stop believing," and I'll add to that, "Also, don't stop iterating."

That's how great ventures (and great rock n roll) are built.

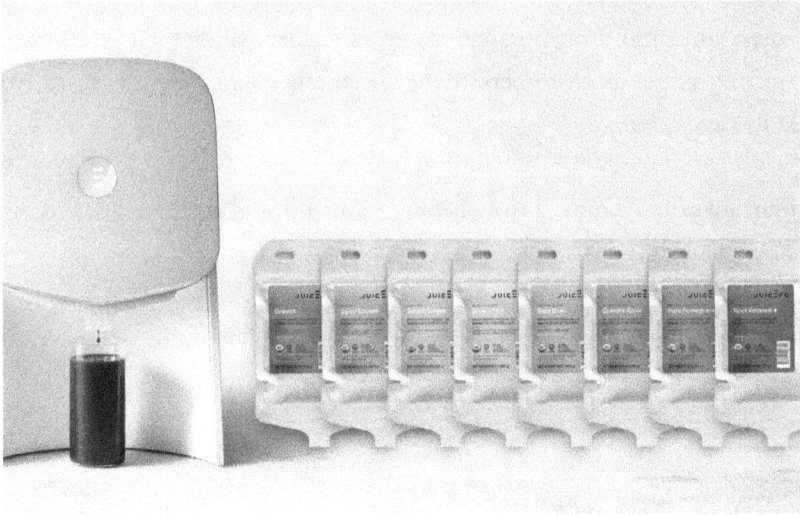

Case Study:

JUICERO

One of Silicon Valley's most infamous failures was Juicero. In 2016 the startup received $120 million in venture capital from leading investors, including Kleiner Perkins and Google Ventures, and then proceeded to go bankrupt within three years.

The Juicero press was a wifi-connected device that sat on your kitchen counter and made delicious fruit and vegetable juice on demand. It used proprietary single-serving packets of pre-juiced fruits and vegetables, which were sold exclusively by the company on a subscription basis.

The founder compared himself to Steve Jobs and hired expensive industrial designers to create a beautiful machine (beware of any founder who compares himself to Steve Jobs).

People love fresh fruit and vegetable smoothies, and the startup was sure that people would love the convenience of a beautiful machine like this in their own homes.

The machine initially sold for $699 (eventually dropping in price), while the juice packets sold for around $5 each and were only available on a subscription basis. Each juice packet had a printed QR code to be scanned while the machine connected to the internet to validate the packet and check the expiration date.

Investors loved the very profitable business model since the high-margin packets were required to use the machine and could only be bought from the company.

But, as you've probably already guessed, it failed miserably. The machine was too expensive, too unreliable, and couldn't be used for anything else (there was no way to press your own fruits and vegetables, for example).

The death knell came when Bloomberg ran an article pointing out that the machine itself was completely unnecessary—you could just buy the juice packets and squeeze them by hand, yielding exactly the same result. The company shut down in 2017, just seventeen months after launching (and after $120 million in investor capital had been flushed down the toilet).

In retrospect, the business model was fatally flawed from the beginning. Juicero had an expensive solution to a problem no one really had, and the profit margin was based on the consumer lock-in of a proprietary machine and consumables that could only be bought from the company.

What consumers really want (and continue to buy) is juicers that you can toss your own fruits and vegetables into—no internet connection required. Remember, in the previous chapter, we talked about how your product exists in a landscape of competitors and alternatives. Juicero may not have been competing with other wifi-connected, stupidly expensive juicing machines, but it was certainly competing with all sorts of alternative ways of juicing!

It's hard to understand how venture capitalists sank $120 million into this project, but on the other hand, VCs do all sorts of inexplicable things. I suppose the investors fell in love with the economic model, the subscription lock-in, and the whole health/nutrition trend. But when something fails as immediately as Juicero did, it's clear that the market didn't like the product nearly as much as the founders and investors did.

KEY TAKEAWAYS:

The schadenfreude runs deep on this one. It's easy to laugh at the whole Juicero thing and feel as if the investors got what they deserved. But let's look at the story through our Launch Path lens:

◊ Most great startups begin with a founder who notices a problem worth solving. The fundamental flaw in the Juicero journey is that juicing wasn't really a problem that customers were willing to pay $699 to solve.

◊ Consumers have lots of ways to make fresh juice. So Juicero's competitive landscape included not only head-to-head competitors but also all the alternative ways to make juice (including buying it from a juice bar). Within that broader landscape, consumers just didn't find the expensive Juicero machine all that compelling (something the company clearly should have tested earlier)

◊ Engineers develop features, but customers buy benefits. The Juicero engineers might have thought it was cool that the device used a wifi connection and QR codes on each juice packet, but customers were just annoyed by features that provided no particular benefit to them.

Path to PMF

What is our path to Product-Market Fit? Customer Development, MVP's, etc.

1. Farmers' markets where we can get input on our menu items.
2. One truck in the Palo Alto area for a pilot project.
3. Scale slowly to additional markets, based on our learnings.

The Launch Path Canvas

Lorem ipsum

Name of Startup Venture: Fitaco, Inc

Date: November 8, 2023

Prepared by: Bret Waters

Iteration: 8

Problem ?
One clear sentence that articulates the problem your startup solves.

Consumers in the US spend $331 billion/year on fast food, and most of it is really unhealthy.

The paradox is that consumers today want to eat healthy, but also have a busy life that often drives them to resort to the convenience of fast food.

Solution
How does your venture solve the problem you have articulated? Keep this short and consise!

Fast food doesn't need to be unhealthy. Our startup is developing a new brand of health-conscious fast food (healthy tacos!), delivered directly to your home or office.

Why it matters
Why is this a problem worth solving?

The National Institutes for Health say that today a fast food diet may kill more people prematurely every year than cigarette smoking.

Alternatives
When a customer looks at alternative ways to solve the problem we solve, what will they see? This is a list of competitors and alternatives. Link to a graphic representation of the landscape.

There are many many food delivery services, from Uber Eats to Doordash to Grubhub.

See visualization at this link.

Customer
It's all about understanding customers. Write a one-sentence description of key customer personas and the problem we solve for each. Circle the one that is most influential.

Adventurous Alex: A thrill-seeking foodie always on the hunt for unique and spicy taco creations to satisfy their daring palate.

Health-Conscious Haley: A fitness enthusiast looking for wholesome and fresh ingredient options that align with their nutritious lifestyle at the taqueria.

Busy Ben: An on-the-go professional seeking quick, flavorful, and portable taco choices to enjoy during a busy workday.

Vegetarian Victoria: A plant-based eater in search of flavorful and creative vegetarian and vegan taco selections that cater to their dietary preferences.

Traditional Tony: A lover of classic flavors, Tony enjoys indulging in authentic and time-honored taco recipes that remind him of his cultural heritage.

Family-Oriented Felix: A parent looking for a family-friendly meal delivery with a variety of options to cater to the taste preferences of both kids and adults.

Budget-Conscious Bella: A student or frugal diner in pursuit of affordable yet flavorful taco choices that won't break the bank at the taqueria.

Path to PMF
What is our path to Product-Market Fit? Customer Development, MVP's, etc.

1. Farmers' markets where we can get input on our menu items.
2. One truck in the Palo Alto area for a pilot project.
3. Scale slowly to additional markets, based on our learnings.

Top 3 Benefits
What are the top 3 benefits that your product or services provides to customers?

1. Convenience. Use our mobile app to place a custom order and it's delivered directly to you.
2. Healthy food, designed by a nutritionist.
3. Tacos. Everybody loves tacos.

Distribution
What are our distribution channels? Direct to consumer, via resellers, or?

We intend to sell direct-to-consumer, via our mobile app and website, with delivery via our own vans.

In the future, we may be open to distribution partnerships.

Positioning
Within this landscape of competitors and alternatives, how is your venture positioned?

Our positioning can basically be summed-up in two words: healthy, and delicious.

There are many food delivery apps that can deliver something that is delicious but not very healthy. Or you could eat a kale salad.

We serve delicious tacos designed by a nutritionist. That's our unique positioning.

Economics
What are the Unit Economics for this venture, what do we expect the CAC<LTV to look like, and what are out capital needs? (Link to full spreadsheet).

One unit = one taco: Sell price $5, on which our gross profit is $.74

Early tests indicate CAC of $11, and we expect an initial LTV of three orders per customer ($25.50), which will grow with time.

Our initial capital needs are $220K, which will get us through the pilot launch. We will propose to investors structuring this as a SAFE.

See full spreadsheet at this link.

Team
What are the characteristics of the right team to make this venture a success?

The right team aligns with our target demographic - people who want to eat healthy and also enjoy the convenience of a quick taco meal.

The economics of our venture are such that we'll need drivers and cooks who are affordable, so we will work hard to make it an attractive part-time job for students, and a great evening second job for anybody.

Defensibility
What is your secret sauce that is difficult for competitors to copy?

The fact that we own the customer and customer data is a big part of our defensibility.

A restaurant selling through a 3rd-party like Doordash owns neither the customer nor the data.

See full example at **thelaunchpath.com**

STEP 2, FOR YOUR STARTUP

For your startup to succeed, your product or service will need to achieve Product-Market Fit—a fit between what your product does and that the market wants. Typically the most effective way to get there is through a series of experiments—small at first, then growing in complexity.

▶ *For your Launch Path Canvas:*

Write a paragraph describing how you will use the concepts described in this chapter in order to effectively get your startup's product or service to Product-Market Fit.

For example, our Fitaco venture looks awesome on paper: delicious, healthy tacos, delivered directly to your home or office! But now we have to test whether the market wants it and how we can adjust our product to align it better with what people want. We will get to Product-Market Fit through a series of small experiments.

"I looked at my competitors, and I thought, if they could do it, I could do it. And if they are popular and doing well, I could compete with them.

TOMMY HILFIGER

CHAPTER 3

DRAW THE LANDSCAPE

Every venture operates within a landscape of competitors and alternatives

I had dinner with my friend Richard Draeger one evening before a jazz show in Menlo Park. His Draeger's Markets—big, beautiful food emporiums brimming with all things delicious—operate several locations around the Bay Area. The business dates back to Richard's grandfather, who quickly obtained the very first liquor license in San Francisco County when US prohibition laws were repealed in 1933. That's my kind of entrepreneur.

Richard and I were enjoying our Chinese meal when I asked how business was going for him. For many years, Draeger's Markets were the upscale grocery stores in the area, but then Whole Foods moved in, Trader Joe's started to proliferate, and now even the big supermarket chains have embraced the sort of artisan, premium, fresh foods that Draeger's is known for. Yet somehow, even in the face of all that new competition, Draeger's Markets seem to continue to grow and thrive.

Richard is clearly doing something right, so I asked him what brilliant strategy he was using to battle all the new competition. "I don't know," Richard shrugged as he reached for another serving of yummy Szechuan string beans. "I just focus on making my business better."

I think Richard's response is excellent advice for startup founders everywhere. Rather than obsess about competitors, just **focus on making your business better.**

Some founders become too obsessed with competition; the fact is that startups rarely fail because of competition. Startups fail because their product doesn't meet market needs; they fail from bad financial management; they fail because the unit economics are upside down. In short, ninety percent of them fail because the team doesn't properly execute. The data is clear on this. Someone else with the same idea ain't what kills startups.

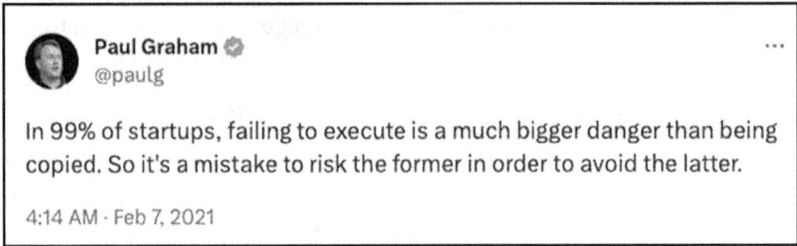

> **Paul Graham** ✔
> @paulg   ⋯
>
> In 99% of startups, failing to execute is a much bigger danger than being copied. So it's a mistake to risk the former in order to avoid the latter.
>
> 4:14 AM · Feb 7, 2021

Paul Graham is the co-founder of Y Combinator

But how you are positioned within your competitive landscape <u>does</u> matter. If you want to be a successful entrepreneur, you'll need to hold two truths in your mind at the same time:

> Obsessing about competition is a waste of time because that's not what matters, but it's still important to research and understand the landscape of competitors and alternatives you are operating within.

One former student has been working on his startup for two years. He's in "stealth mode" because he doesn't want anyone to steal his idea. Every time I check in on him, he tells me all about what the competitors are doing. He's spent two years obsessing about competitors instead of talking to actual prospective customers and building a company. At this point, I'd estimate that he has an approximately 100% chance of failure. As Jeff Bezos (founder of Amazon) has said, "If you're competitor-focused, you have to wait until there is a competitor doing something. Being customer-focused allows you to be more pioneering."

Don't pretend you have no competition

One of the worst statements an entrepreneur can make in an investor pitch is, "Best of all, we have no competition!" There is competition for everything. If you claim you have no competition, then that either means there is zero demand for what your startup does or you don't know how to use Google search. Either way, you look like a fool.

In fact, competition is usually good. If other companies are successfully selling something like what you're selling, that means there is established demand for what you offer. Now you just have to be better/different in some way. That's much easier than needing to create demand for a product where there isn't any.

No competitors is a red light, not a green one

During the dot-com boom, there was a notion known as the "the first-mover advantage." It suggested that if you were the first to launch an e-commerce website dedicated to selling toasters, for example, you would end up owning the toaster market. The notion turned out to be almost completely false—there are very few examples of companies that now own a category because they were the first in.

In fact, for the most part, history indicates that it's the other way around. Webvan was the first online grocery delivery company, and they failed miserably, blowing through $800 million in capital and paving the way for "second movers" to develop many subsequent successful online grocery delivery services.

Palm, General Magic, and Blackberry were early smartphone pioneers who failed, paving the way for Apple and Android to make it a billion-dollar business. There are many other examples. As Willie Nelson said, "The early bird may get the worm, but the second mouse gets the cheese."

So, don't obsess too much about competition, and especially don't think that it's an advantage to find a startup idea where there is no competition. A hole in the market usually doesn't represent a green light—it's usually a giant red flag.

But do conduct solid research

Create a spreadsheet that lists all your competitors and their salient information: how big they are, their focus within the space, etc. You also may know of some companies in the space that failed. You'll want to have a list of those too, especially if their failures can provide important insights. The Wayback Machine at archive.org comes in handy here.

Remember that ultimately we want to have a list of competitors **and alternatives**. With many startups, you are competing less with direct competitors than with alternative ways of solving the problem your startup addresses. In the Juicero case study (Chapter 2), they failed because there were plenty of other ways to juice fruits and vegetables without the hassle of a subscription.

Clayton Christensen, the late, great Harvard Business School professor, wrote that when consumers buy your product, they are actually "hiring it to do a job," so when a consumer looks at a landscape of products, it's because they have a job to be done. As we saw with Juicero, when a consumer is looking to "hire" the right product to make juice, there are many options—some direct Juicero competitors and some not.

Later in this chapter, you'll find lots of tools for competitive research. So, do your homework, then make a comprehensive list of your competitors and alternatives. Keep the list in a spreadsheet you can regularly update and share with your team.

Competition

	Our App	Brand X	Brand Y
User Friendly	✓	✗	✗
Encryption	✓	✗	✓
Keywords	✓	✓	✗
AI-Powered	✓	✓	✗
Cloud Bookmarks	✓	✗	✗
Social	✓	✗	✓
API's	✓	✗	✓

Do not create a "feature checklist"

I often see newbie entrepreneurs create a "feature checklist" slide and think that's their competitive landscape. The slide always shows their features compared to their competitors' features (and of course, it always shows that the new startup has more). It's an entirely useless slide because it assumes that the product with the most features will win (which is seldom true). A feature checklist tells us nothing about the landscape of competitors and alternatives. And it assumes the wrong thing, so why the hell would you do this?

Engineers develop features, but customers buy benefits. Don't put a boring feature checklist slide in your pitch deck. It may appeal to engineers, but it's meaningless to customers and investors. Instead, figure out a way to draw a visualization of the landscape of your competitors and alternatives and how you fit in. Remember, competition is good, so don't be afraid to add a lot of competitors. In the retail world, for example, there's room for Target, Nordstrom, and Costco, but they occupy very different spots within the landscape.

This is not meaningful. Don't be this guy.

Think about whether you can create a nice, two-dimensional representation of the landscape showing how you and the other players fit in. One axis could represent price, and the other one could represent a focus on durability. Or one axis could be consumer-focus versus enterprise-focus, and the other could be bandwidth consumption, maybe.

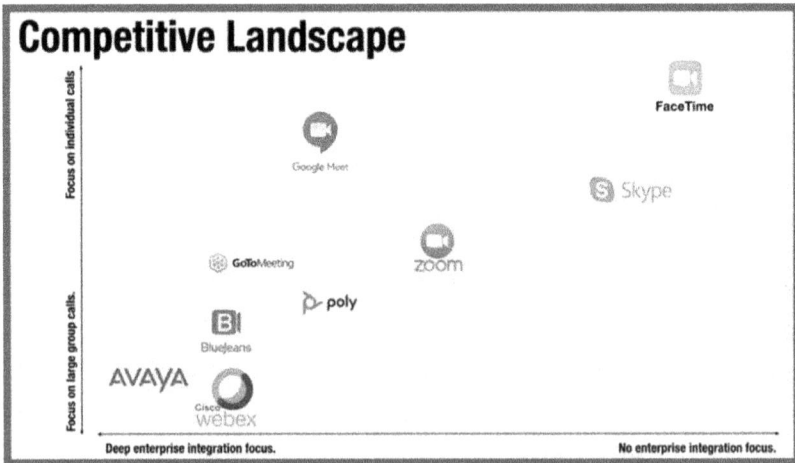

When Zoom launched, there were many many competitors.
They just focused on solid positioning,
and building a product that met customer needs.

Competitive Landscape
Fitaco is uniquely positioned as freshly-prepared and healthy.

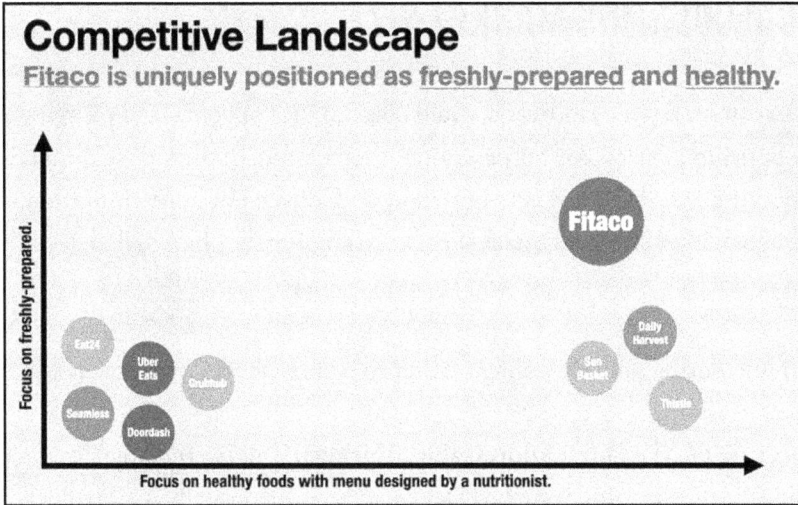

There are many ways to create a visualization of a landscape of competitors and alternatives, so choose a method that you think represents your landscape well. If your startup is a marketplace (see further discussion of this in Chapter 4), then you'll probably want to create two landscapes, one for each side of your marketplace.

But don't pretend you have no competition, and don't think that a feature checklist means anything because it doesn't. Nobody wants to buy your frog watch.

Come up with a visualization that shows you understand the landscape and have intention with regard to positioning.

Every venture operates within a landscape of competitors and alternatives, and every great startup CEO knows that positioning matters. Do your research on all the competitors and alternatives—that's important—but then stop worrying about that and obsess about execution, not competitors.

CALCULATING MARKET SIZE

As you survey the landscape, you'll need an idea of your startup's market opportunity size. Don't obsess about this too much; startups seldom fail because the market wasn't big enough. Conversely, don't think that a huge market size guarantees success. Many startups have failed despite a pitch deck touting the "$500 billion available market!"

In measuring and expressing market size, three terms are typically used:

- **TAM (Total Addressable Market):** This is the total market demand for your product or service. It's usually a ridiculously large number that sounds very impressive but is relatively meaningless because your applesauce startup will never get one hundred percent of the worldwide applesauce market.
- **SAM (Serviceable Addressable Market):** This is the amount of the TAM you could potentially reach, given your geography and business model. Maybe our applesauce startup is targeting just the direct-to-consumer applesauce market in the United States. That's our SAM.
- **SOM (Serviceable Obtainable Market):** Unless you're a monopoly, you'll never get one hundred percent of the SAM. Given the benefits your applesauce offers customers, what percentage of the total available customers could potentially become yours, and how much would they buy?

When it comes to finding market size data for your startup, Dr. Google is your friend. A few minutes of searching usually turns up some data from reputable sources. Industry associations typically have market size data available, as do research firms such as Gartner and CB Insights. Find some data, and then cite your sources.

Your startup will operate within a landscape where customers spend a certain amount of money, in the aggregate, to solve the problem your startup solves. Be realistic about this fact. Don't claim that you have no competition, and don't suggest that you can get one hundred percent of the market. Instead, do some research on the size of the market you could potentially reach, think about how your startup will be positioned within that landscape, and do a realistic assessment of how much of the market your startup might reach.

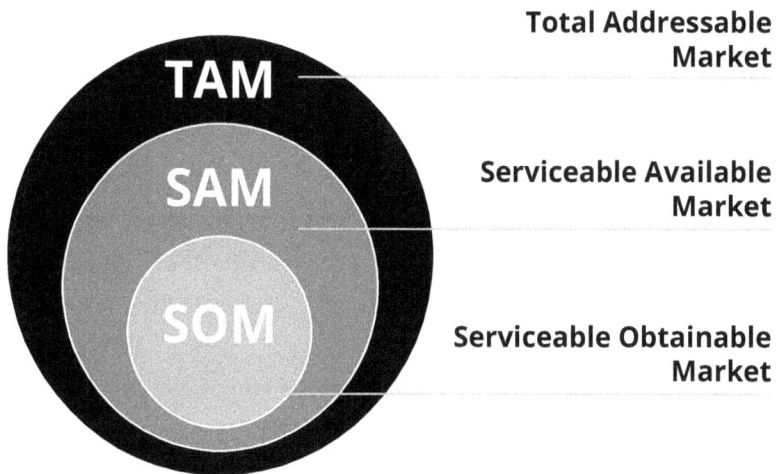

TAM — **Total Addressable Market**

SAM — **Serviceable Available Market**

SOM — **Serviceable Obtainable Market**

The standardized way of representing market size.

COMPETITIVE RESEARCH TOOLS

A generation ago, doing comprehensive competitive research would have meant hiring an expensive market research firm. Today, there are incredibly powerful tools available, many of them free. Here's my quick list of some resources you should be aware of:

- **Old-Fashioned Customer Interviews**
  Your best insights are always going to come from talking to prospective customers. Remember, you're trying to understand the alternative ways customers address the problem your startup will solve. If you're making a shopping list app, your competition isn't just other shopping list apps, it's spreadsheets, notes on scraps of paper, and all the other ways people create shopping lists. When you do customer development interviews, make sure you ask how they are currently solving the problem that your startup proposes to solve.

- **Google, Google Trends, Google News**
  Google searches are an obvious tool for competitive research, but do you know about Google Trends? It shows search volume trends that can be very helpful for your research. Finally, of course, Google News may help you find press releases and articles about competitors. Remember to set Google alerts for your competitors so that Google will automatically notify you whenever they make announcements.

- **The Wayback Machine**
  Did one of your competitors change their pricing two years ago? Would it be helpful to know how their pricing changed? You can use the Internet Archive's Wayback Machine to see exactly what their pricing page looked like in the past! It's a cool tool for many facets of competitor research.

- **Crunchbase and PitchBook Data**

  Figuring out the financial strength of your competitors may be important. If one of them recently raised one hundred million dollars in new funding, that would be good to know! Crunchbase and PitchBook will give you this data (the free versions will provide some data, but you may have to pay for deeper insights).

- **Customer Reviews**

  If your startup is building enterprise software for digital asset management, you'll want to check out G2 and Capterra and read customer reviews of current digital asset management platforms. I guarantee you'll learn a lot. For consumer products, there are many review sites ranging from Yelp to Amazon.

- **Web Traffic Data**

  If web traffic will be important to your startup, you may want to see what sort of traffic your competitors are currently getting. Platforms such as Semrush and Similarweb will give you insights into competitors' web traffic, search engine optimization (SEO), pay-per-click (PPC), and sales and service management (SSM).

- **LinkedIn**

  LinkedIn is an underutilized research tool. Find out how many employees work for each of your competitors. See what the employees are currently posting about. Discover whether they brag about funding milestones or operating metrics. Upgrade to LinkedIn Sales Navigator for deeper tools.

On this book's companion website, **thelaunchpath.com**, I have provided links to all these resources and many more.

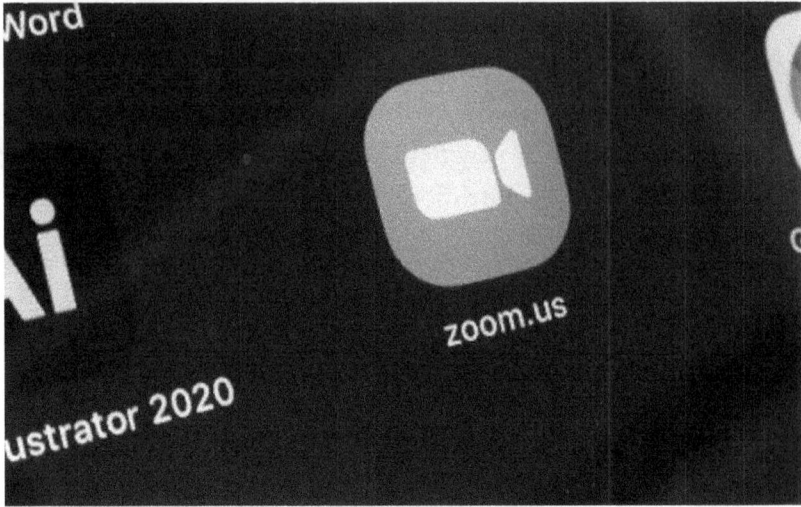

Case Study:
ZOOM

I was first introduced to Zoom in mid-2013. I was running a company in San Francisco, and for video calls, we used Skype, GoTo Meeting, Webex, etc. We hated them all.

One day, Dariusz, the head of our engineering team in Europe, sent me a Zoom link and said, "Hey, let's try this." I loved it and bought a subscription the next day. The domain was zoom.us, and since I'd been introduced to it by Dariusz, we called our new video platform "Zoomiusz." And Zoomiusz was awesome.

Today, Zoom is a household name (a verb, even!). Let's look at the company's history and the success patterns that other entrepreneurs can learn from.

Zoom was founded by Eric Yuan, who several years earlier had experienced the frustration of attending college thousands of miles away from his girlfriend. He missed her.

Eric finished his studies, came to the US, and landed a job with Webex, which was then acquired by Cisco. He did well there and ended up running the engineering group. Webex was the leading video conference platform at the time, and many large companies standardized on its use. Most individual users, however, hated WebEx—people used it because they had to, not because they wanted to.

Eric Yuan says, "Before I left Cisco, I spent a lot of time talking with Webex customers, and every time … after the meeting was over, I felt very, very embarrassed because I did not see a single happy customer, and I tried to understand, why is that?" By then, Webex was a mature product, doing very well in the marketplace, and Cisco wasn't interested in plowing money into re-inventing an existing product. So Yuan decided to leave and try to build something better.

The video call sector was extremely crowded. Webex was the leader in the enterprise market, and Skype had the largest share of consumers. GoTo Meeting was very popular amongst small and medium-sized businesses, Apple had just released FaceTime, and Google was putting a lot of effort into the product that became Google Meet. BlueJeans had raised a lot of venture capital in order to own the high-end enterprise market, while private equity-backed Avaya was working hard to make their video conference platform part of the communications infrastructure at every company in the world.

In other words, absolutely no one looked at the video call market and thought there was an opportunity for yet another company in the crowded space—no one, apparently, except for Eric Yuan.

They launched the product, but Yuan didn't want to spend a lot of money on customer acquisition. He knew that, in a crowded sector with a product that hadn't yet proven Product-Market Fit, you can waste a lot of money on marketing and advertising. Zoom had no dedicated marketing team at that point. They relied on word of mouth, and when a customer canceled their account, Yuan would email them personally, asking to interview them to find out why the product didn't meet their needs.

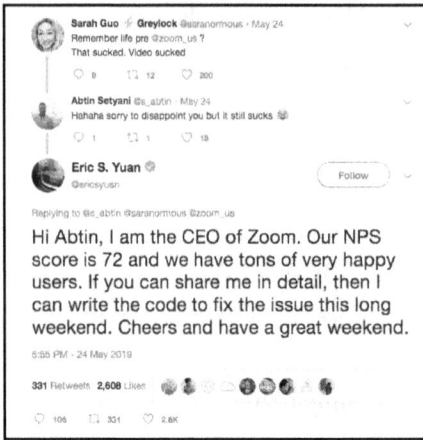

He monitored Twitter, and if he saw anyone complain about a problem with Zoom, he'd contact them personally, even offering to write new code over a weekend to fix bugs customers had found.

Higher Education was a market that WebEx and the other players didn't pay much attention to, so Eric decided that might be their beachhead market. The company entered into agreements with a range of higher-education institutions and got great traction. Graduating students then went out, got jobs, and introduced their new bosses to the Zoom experience. Today, ninety percent of US universities use Zoom.

By mid-2013, more than 1.2 million participants had joined over four hundred thousand meetings in 2,500 cities across the globe. As Zoom continued to grow their customer base, Eric Yuan made sure to stay close to customers, understand their needs, and add features based on customer conversations. Over the next couple of years, Zoom added breakout rooms, virtual backgrounds, automated meeting transcripts, support for different languages and webinars, and more.

Large companies were struggling with the trend toward "bring your own device" policies, as employees wanted to use their personal devices instead of being required to carry company-issued ones, so Zoom made sure they could provide a seamless and secure experience across a wide range of computers and phones. Meanwhile, the large legacy incumbent players were struggling to update their products amid the rapidly changing needs of enterprise companies.

As the Zoom team developed the product further, they did more customer interviews than ever, constantly looking for unexpected pain points they could address by adding certain features. Eric Yuan said, "We always prioritize the features requested by our existing customers.... We truly believe if you do not make the existing customer happy, even if you get more new customer prospects, it may not be sustainable."

By 2015, Zoom was really gathering steam. The company raised $30 million in a round led by Emergence Capital after Yuan insisted that the pitch meetings be conducted over Zoom so that investors could experience the product themselves. The new "breakout rooms" feature was a hit in academia, and Zoom was gaining good traction in enterprise settings, especially in Silicon Valley.

Meanwhile, Slack was changing the way many large companies operate as "enterprise chat" became a fast-growing sector. In response, Zoom developed deep Slack integration. Zoom calls could now be scheduled and launched right within Slack. You could see confirmed Zoom attendees from within Slack, as well as launch ad-hoc calls. Since Outlook was the preferred scheduling system of many large companies, Zoom developed integrations for that as well. Many people at large companies were learning about Zoom because it appeared on their Outlook calendars and Slack channels.

Zoom continued to grow and succeed. In April 2019, they had their IPO and exceeded analysts' projections by 72%. I bought some stock and am still a happy shareholder today.

	As of January 31,	
	2018	2019
	(in thousands)	
Consolidated Balance Sheet Data:		
Cash and cash equivalents	$ 36,146	$ 63,624
Marketable securities	103,056	112,777
Working capital	114,633	124,378
Total assets	215,019	354,565
Deferred revenue, current and non-current	54,262	125,773
Convertible promissory notes, net(1)	—	14,858
Convertible preferred stock	159,552	159,552
Accumulated deficit	(32,737)	(25,153)
Total stockholders' deficit	(26,671)	(7,439)

(1)   Included in other liabilities, non-current on our consolidated balance

At the time of Zoom's IPO, most of the venturre capital
they had raised was still in the bank.

Here's an extraordinary fact: Zoom raised $146 million from investors but if you look at their balance sheet when they had their IPO they still had most of that sitting in cash accounts! Zoom effectively built a public company on less than $20 million of outside capital. That's pretty remarkable.

A year later, the COVID-19 pandemic hit, and Zoom got an unexpected boost that drove usage into the stratosphere. But that never would have happened without the eight years of hard work Eric Yuan and his team spent building a product customers loved.

Yuan says that money was never his driver for founding Zoom—he was just obsessed with trying to build a better product. When he quit Webex, he never dreamed of making something bigger; he just wanted to make something better. When people referred to his startup as a potential "unicorn," he said, "I don't use that word at all. It doesn't matter. Even if you're a unicorn for many years, if customers don't like your product, very soon you become nothing."

KEY TAKEAWAYS:

There are many great lessons for entrepreneurs everywhere in the Zoom story:

◊ Eric Yuan entered a very crowded sector with lots of competition. But Yuan knew that all that competition meant there was solid market demand, now, he just needed to build something that was positioned well and focused on what what customers wanted.

◊ He remained relentlessly focused on engaging with customers and understanding their needs. Because a startup is inherently more nimble than large incumbents, they were able to react more quickly to things like the "bring your own device" trend in the enterprise world.

◊ He identified a good beachhead market—education—and after succeeding there, that market helped him spread to others.

◊ He successfully rode the coattails of other products with a larger footprint—Slack and Outlook—to gain new customers, using the "land and expand" approach of getting into large organizations.

◊ He operated with solid capital efficiency, not spending big money on marketing until Product-Market Fit had been achieved.

◊ Like most great entrepreneurs, he wasn't motivated by riches, per se, but he had fallen passionately in love with building a better way to solve a problem customers have.

Alternatives

When a customer looks at alternative ways to solve the problem we solve, what will they see? This is a list of competitors and alternatives. Link to a graphic representation of the landscape.

There are many, many food delivery services, from Uber Eats to Doordash to Grubhub.

See visualization at this link.

Positioning

Within this landscape of competitors and alternatives, how is your venture positioned?

Our positioning can basically be summed-up in two words: healthy, and delicious.

There are many food delivery apps that can deliver something that is delicious but not very healthy. Or you could eat a kale salad.

We serve delicious tacos designed by a nutritionist. That's our unique positioning.

Defensibility

What is your secret sauce that is difficult for competitors to copy?

The fact that we own the customer and customer data is a big part of our defensibility.

A restaurant selling through a 3rd-party like Doordash owns neither the customer nor the data.

Name of Startup Venture: Fitaco, Inc **Date:** November 8, 2023

Prepared by: Bret Waters **Iteration:** 8

Canvas

Why it matters

Why is this a problem worth solving?

The National Institutes for Health say that today a fast food diet may kill more people prematurely every year than cigarette smoking.

Alternatives

When a customer looks at alternative ways to solve the problem we solve, what will they see? This is a list of competitors and alternatives. Link to a graphic representation of the landscape.

There are many, many food delivery services, from Uber Eats to Doordash to Grubhub.

See visualization at this link.

Customer

It's all about understanding customers. Write a one-sentence description of key customer personas and the problem we solve for each. Circle the one that is most influential.

Adventurous Alex: A thrill-seeking foodie always on the hunt for unique and spicy taco creations to satisfy their daring palate.

Health-Conscious Haley: A fitness enthusiast looking for wholesome and fresh ingredient options that align with their nutritious lifestyle at the taqueria.

Busy Ben: An on-the-go professional seeking quick, flavorful, and portable taco choices to enjoy during a busy workday.

Vegetarian Victoria: A plant-based eater in search of flavorful and creative vegetarian and vegan taco selections that cater to their dietary preferences.

Traditional Tony: A lover of classic flavors, Tony enjoys indulging in authentic and time-honored taco recipes that remind him of his cultural heritage.

Family-Oriented Felix: A parent looking for a family-friendly meal delivery with a variety of options to cater to the taste preferences of both kids and adults.

Budget-Conscious Bella: A student or frugal diner in pursuit of affordable yet flavorful taco choices that won't break the bank at the taqueria.

Path to PMF

What is our path to Product-Market fit? Customer Development, MVP's, etc.

1. Farmers' markets where we can get input on our menu items.
2. One truck in the Palo Alto area for a pilot project.
3. Scale slowly to additional markets, based on our learnings.

Top 3 Benefits

What are the top 3 benefits that your product or services provides to customers?

1. Convenience. Use our mobile app to place a custom order and it's delivered directly to you.
2. Healthy food, designed by a nutritionist.
3. Tacos. Everybody loves tacos.

Distribution

What are our distribution channels? Direct to consumer, via resellers, or?

We intend to sell direct-to-consumer, via our mobile app and website, with delivery via our own vans.

In the future, we may be open to distribution partnerships.

Positioning

Within this landscape of competitors and alternatives, how is your venture positioned?

Our positioning can basically be summed-up in two words: healthy, and delicious.

There are many food delivery apps that can deliver something that is delicious but not very healthy. Or you could eat a kale salad.

We serve delicious tacos designed by a nutritionist. That's our unique positioning.

Economics

What are the Unit Economics for this venture, what do we expect the CAC+LTV to look like, and what are out capital needs? (Link to full spreadsheet).

One unit = one taco: Sell price #5, on which our gross profit is 4.74

Early tests indicate CAC of 4¢, and we expect an initial LTV of three orders per customer (#25.50) which will grow with time.

Our initial capital needs are #22.0K, which will get us through the pilot launch. We will propose to investors structuring this as a SAFE.

See full spreadsheet at this link.

Team

What are the characteristics of the right team to make this venture a success?

The right team aligns with our target demographic - people who want to eat healthy and also enjoy the convenience of a quick, taco meal.

The economics of our venture are such that we'll need drivers and cooks who are affordable, so we will work hard to make it an attractive part-time job for students, and a great evening second job for anybody.

Defensibility

What is your secret sauce that is difficult for competitors to copy?

The fact that we own the customer and customer data is a big part of our defensibility.

A restaurant selling through a 3rd-party like Doordash owns neither the customer nor the data.

STEP 3, FOR YOUR STARTUP

Make a comprehensive list of competitors and alternatives (remember that you're making a list of actual competitors plus alternative ways of solving the problem your startup solves).

Now think about how your startup will be positioned within that landscape of competitors and alternatives, and see if you can create a visualization that shows what the landscape looks like and how you fit in. Remember, you're not trying to prove that you're the best, you're just trying to realistially think about how you fit into that landsape.

▶ *For your Launch Path Canvas:*

After you have done comprehensive research on the landscape of competitors and alternatives for your startup, write sentences for your Launch Path Canvas that distill down these three important points:

- **Alternatives:** How would you describe the landscape of competitors and alternatives? Add a link to a visualization (see pages 74-75 for examples).
- **Positioning:** Can you write 1-2 succinct sentences describing your positoining within the landscape?
- **Defensibility:** What is it that you have that would be diffi-cult for competitors to copy? (Eventually this will be things like patents, copyrights, and exclusive distribution agreements. You probably don't have those things yet—for an early stage compa-ny it may just be your amazing passtionate team).

"Luck is not a business model.

ANTHONY BOURDAIN

CHAPTER 4

DESIGN AN ENGINE OF GROWTH

You're gonna need a great business model

What is a business model, exactly? If you ask five people, you'll probably get six or seven different answers, but the definition I like to use is very straightforward:

> *A business model describes the rationale by which an organization creates, delivers, and captures value.*

We **create value** by solving a problem customers have, we **deliver** that value to customers in some way, and we **capture** the value in the form of economic profit.

Some business models are simple. A baker knows that people value fresh bread, so she delivers that value to them via a convenient shop location, and she captures the value by selling a loaf of bread for more than it costs her to make it. Easy peasy.

Some business models are more complex. Social media companies need to provide value to both users and to advertisers, banks have an elaborate set of products and risk factors, and medical devices have to deal with unique complications, including the fact that the customer and the payer are different. Fundamentally, however, every venture has to **create, deliver, and capture value** to succeed.

Your business model is your venture's engine of growth, one that, once it gets going, attracts customers and delivers value to them over and over again. Miraculously, it's also an engine that eventually creates its own fuel (money) to keep itself running. Many moving parts have to work together for the whole operation to work. If you remove one part, the whole engine can stop running, even though all the other parts are working fine.

Business model innovation—new ways of creating and delivering value—has transformed many sectors in recent years. Amazon's AWS has been wildly successful by offering a completely different way to "buy" servers and infrastructure. Stitch Fix offers consumers a completely different way to buy clothing, as does Rent the Runway. Rolls Royce Engines has applied the pay-for-use model to jet engines; instead of buying them, airlines can now just pay by the hour—thrust as a service, if you will.

All of these are examples of innovation that is not product innovation, per se; it's business model innovation. A new way to sell established products. An innovative new way of creating, delivering, and capturing value for customers.

Back in 2005, a PhD student by the name of Alexander Osterwalder developed the Business Model Canvas as a way of expressing the business model of any business.[1] Since then, it's been used by many in the startup community, and a few variations exist, including the Lean Canvas, developed by Ash Maurya, which maps Eric Reis's book, *The Lean Startup*, a little more closely.

A lot has changed since Osterwalder's original work was published, so I've developed **the Launch Path Canvas** to go with this book. It

---

1: He also wrote a great book called **Business Model Generation:** *A Handbook for Visionaries, Game Changers, and Challengers,* which I highly recommend. ISBN 978-0470876411 includes several aspects of the original Business Model Canvas, plus some updates, and I've designed it to align with the **Launch Path** process presented in this book.

Once you fill it out, you will have a representation of all your particular business model's elements and how they fit together. I find this visual representation helpful in several ways:

- Filling it out helps ensure you consider all the different elements of your business model. Sometimes entrepreneurs can be so deep in the weeds about one aspect of their venture that they forget about some of the other components they will need in order for the engine to work properly.
- Every entrepreneur begins with a set of assumptions, most of which turn out to be wrong. As you fill out your **Launch Path Canvas**, think of everything you write as being a hypothesis, and then think of ways in which you can test, validate, and refine those hypotheses.
- Different startups have risk in different places. For some startups, the risk is on the market side (Will people buy this?); for others, the risk is on the product side (Can we successfully make this?); for still others, the risk is in the economics (Can we really operate more efficiently than anyone else?). This is how an investor will look at your startup—Where is the risk?—so that's precisely how you should look at it as well. The **Launch Path Canvas** is a good way to visualize all the different aspects of your venture that will need to work together so that you can think about where the risk is.
- For startup success, you will need everyone on the team—founders and employees alike—to have a clear understanding of what makes your engine run. The Launch Path Canvas can be a great collaboration tool for working with your team to achieve clarity and consensus.

Every venture has a business model, and each is a little different. You almost certainly will end up with a slightly different model than you started out with, but ultimately to be successful, you need to create, deliver, and capture value for customers. Using the **Launch Path Canvas** in an iterative way will help you get to a sustainable and scalable engine of growth for your venture.

The Launch Path Canvas

The Launch Path Canvas by Bret Waters is marked with Creative Commons 1.0 Universal License, meaning that you are free to use it and/or modify it for any use. The creator is giving up their copyright and allowing anyone to distribute, remix, adapt, and build upon the material in any medium or format, even for commercial purposes. No attribution required.

Name of Startup Venture:

Date:

Prepared by:

Iteration:

Problem	Solution	Why it matters	Alternatives	Customer
One clear sentence that articulates the problem your startup solves.	How does your venture solve the problem you have articulated? Keep this short and consise!	Why is this a problem worth solving?	When a customer looks at alternative ways to solve the problem we solve, what will they see? This is a list of competitors and alternatives. Link to a graphic representation of the landscape.	It's all about understanding customers. Write a one-sentence description of key customer personas and the problem we solve for each. Circle the one that is most influential.

Path to PMF	Top 3 Benefits	Distribution	Positioning	
What is our path to Product-Market Fit? Customer Development, MVPs, etc.	What are the top 3 benefits that your product or services provides to customers?	What are our distribution channels? Direct to consumer, via resellers, or?	Within this landscape of competitors and alternatives, how is your venture positioned?	

Economics	Team	Defensibility		
What are the Unit Economics for this venture, what do we expect the CAC<LTV to look like, and what are out capital needs? (Link to full spreadsheet).	What are the characteristics of the right team to make this venture a success?	What is your secret sauce that is difficult for competitors to copy?		

Download your blank canvas from **thelaunchpath.com**

BOXES ON THE LAUNCH PATH CANVAS

Each box on the **Launch Path Canvas** represents an aspect of your venture's business model. They are cogs in the wheel that creates, delivers, and captures value, and once that wheel gets spinning it's a beautiful thing. Here is a description of each and how they map to chapters in this book:

Problem (see Chapter 1).
As Charles Kettering said, "A problem well-stated is a problem half-solved." Write down, **in one concise sentence**, what problem your startup will solve.

Solution (see Chapter 1).
How does your product or service solve this problem? Be specific, without hyperbole (you aren't writing marketing copy!).

Why it matters (see Chapters 1 and 11).
Startups fail when the problem they solve isn't really a problem that anyone cares much about. Avoid that by making sure you can articulate why your startup is working on **a problem worth solving**.

Alternatives (See Chapter 3).
This is your competitive landscape. As customers look at alternative ways they could solve the problem your startup addresses, what will they see? Link to a document that provides more detail on your landscape of competitors and alternatives.

Positioning (see Chapter 3).
As customers look at the landscape of your competitors and alternatives, how do you fit in? What is your startup's unique value proposition?

Defensibility (see Chapter 3).

Once your startup is successful, others will try to copy what you are doing. What do you have that's defensible? Patents? Trademarks? Exclusive distribution agreements?

Customer (see Chapter 7).

Startup success is all about understanding customers. What are your various customer segments? Sometimes it's demographic groups, e.g., teenagers, adults, or seniors. Sometimes it's usage, e.g., professionals or hobbyists. Sometimes the economic buyer for a product differs from the consumer. For example, kids' cereal is consumed by the kid (brightly colored packaging!), but it is purchased by the parent (healthy and wholesome!). If this is the case for your venture, then write both down.

Now circle which customer segment you expect to be early adopters. Within your customer segments, which one do you think will be the easiest to sell to? Let's sell to them first, especially if they will be influential in some way.

Distribution (see Chapter 2).

Products and services can be delivered through different distribution channels. A venture can, for example, sell to its customers directly (through their own website or their own stores), through partner retailers, or through a combination of both. A software company might sell via a direct salesforce or through resellers. Which channels will you use to sell your product or service?

Path to Product-Market Fit (see Chapter 2).

What is your path to Product-Market Fit? What will your MVPs look like, and how will you learn from them? Link to a document that goes deeper into your proposed path to Product-Market Fit.

Top three benefits (see Chapter 7).

Engineers develop features, but customers buy benefits. What are the top three benefits your product/service provides to customers? (The ones they will pay for!)

Economics (see Chapters 5 and 6).

Ultimately, the economics of your venture will need to work out. List the three key elements: (1) Initial capital needs; (2) Estimated time to profitability; and (3) Your best guess on CAC:LTV. Then link to your full economic model.

Team (see Chapter 10).

In the land of startups, nothing matters more than the team. Write some thoughts on the sort of team you think this venture will need to grow and succeed.

Remember that your first pass at filling out the **Launch Path Canvas** will mostly be writing down guesses since you won't know any of these things for sure yet. Think of them as hypotheses that can be tested, validated, and refined as you go along. You'll be revisiting your **Launch Path Canvas** regularly, so fill it out in a way that makes it easy to update and revise over and over again.

That's how great ventures are built: they begin as a set of assumptions that then, through an iterative hypothesis-testing process, will be refined into a fully functioning business model that creates, delivers, and captures value as a sustainable and profitable engine.

MARKETPLACE MODELS

Some of the most successful internet businesses have been digital marketplaces—platforms for matching buyers and sellers. eBay, which created a global marketplace for buying and selling pretty much anything, pioneered the space. On the enterprise side, Ariba (now owned by SAP) built Ariba Network, a digital marketplace for connecting companies with vendors of all types. Airbnb, of course, is a marketplace connecting property owners with short-term renters, and even Uber can be seen as a digital marketplace that connects people who need a ride with a driver who wants to give them one. In developing and producing this book, I used Upwork, a marketplace for connecting freelancers to people looking for freelancers, to find a skilled illustrator, a talented cover designer, and the world's best copy editor. Even Amazon, which started as an e-retailer, is now also a digital marketplace; many items are placed on the platform by independent sellers who fulfill orders directly.

If you're building a digital marketplace startup venture, how will the **Launch Path** process described in this book be different?

- **Two sides means two sets of customers.**
  Because you have two groups of customers (one on the buy-side of the marketplace and one on the sell-side), you will need to achieve two sets of Product-Market Fit. For example, Airbnb has to meet the needs of people looking for a place to rent, and it also has to meet the needs of people looking for a short-term renter.

- **Trust drives transactions.**
  With marketplaces, trust becomes a crucial component because you are asking strangers to do business together. Digital marketplaces often deploy a range of strategies to increase the

level of trust between buyers and sellers, such as supporting buyer and seller reviews as a way to foster community trust. Shortly after Airbnb launched, they were involved in a highly publicized incident where someone's house suffered extreme damage from an Airbnb renter. Airbnb quickly negotiated with an insurance company to bundle a million dollars' worth of insurance into every booking, in order to further build trust.[2]

- **You're the Governor.**
  The policies and governance structure, essentially the "rules of the road" for using the marketplace, are critically important for marketplace businesses: who can join the marketplace? Are there qualification requirements? What is considered good behavior? What happens if I don't comply with the marketplace's policies? As a marketplace operator, you will need to develop a policy and governance system that, on the one hand, creates a healthy, vibrant environment for its users but on the other hand, does not stifle demand by being too stringent. For example, during Covid 19, Airbnb unilaterally relaxed their cancellation policies for guests, which in many cases exceeded levels that had already been set by their hosts, causing a small revolt among affected hosts who lost thousands of dollars in booking revenue.

- **Threat of disintermediation**
  In Chapter 5, I've included a case study on Tutorspree, a marketplace for connecting tutors with people looking for a tutor. The platform took a fifty-percent share of each tutoring session booked. One of the reasons they failed was that, in the

---

2: Interesting backstory: Jeff Jordan of the VC firm Andreessen Horowitz had recently led a $60M investment in Airbnb because their marketplace model reminded him of the early days of eBay where he had been an executive for five years. When Airbnb suffered a PR disaster with the well-publicized incident in which an Airbnb host's home was trashed, Jeff quickly jumped in and helped create the new insurance program called Airbnb Guarantee, modeled after a similar program at eBay. If you want to successfully run a digital marketplace, trust is absolutely essential.

first tutoring session, tutors said to students, "Hey, next time, just contact me directly, and we'll save some money." Successful marketplaces like Airbnb limit the threat of disintermediation by providing solid reasons why you should continue to conduct transactions on their platform (and pricing model that does not drive customers away), not outside it.

- **You need mass on both sides.**

  A digital marketplace with all sellers and no buyers will have no transactions. Same with one that has all buyers and no sellers. This ends up being one of the most challenging aspects of building a digital marketplace—you need two sets of customer acquisition efforts going on at the same time because, without a critical mass of users on both sides of the marketplace (who also have a mutual interest in each other), it will be difficult to drive transactions. Early in Airbnb's history, they were getting lots of people posting rooms for rent, but not enough people looking for a room to rent. The founders quickly wrote a script that automatically posted every new Airbnb listing to the Craigslist Rooms for Rent section, which gave them a way to build traffic on the buy-side.

- **Use two canvases.**

  With a two-sided marketplace, I recommend producing two **Launch Path Canvases.** Think about Uber: their model depends on not only recruiting enough riders but also recruiting enough drivers. The essential value proposition for a rider is different from the essential value proposition for drivers. So with a two-sided marketplace, it may be helpful for you to create two Launch Path Canvases as you develop and refine your startup, one for each side of the marketplace.

Case Study:
DOLLAR SHAVE CLUB

In 2010, Michael Dubin graduated from college and was learning comedy improv while working various marketing and advertising gigs, trying to decide what to do with his life.

One night, he met a friend's father at a party, and they started talking about the ridiculous cost and hassle of men's razors. The two chatted about how irritating it was to go to the store to buy overpriced razor blades every couple of weeks. To make it even more annoying, many stores keep razors in locked displays to prevent theft, so you need to find a clerk to unlock your razor blades before you can overpay for them. Dubin went home obsessed with the idea that this was a problem worth solving, and within a week, he had registered the **dollarshaveclub.com** domain.

His idea was brain-dead simple: buy razors and blades from an existing manufacturer in Korea and resell them in the US on a subscription basis. Consumers would sign up and enter their credit card numbers, then every month, a new box of reasonably priced razor blades would arrive in the mail.

Nothing about this business idea would impress most venture capitalists—no product innovation, no intellectual property, no defensibility, no differentiating technology—and the US razor market was 70% controlled by giants Gillette and Schick. Oh, and the founder had no business experience. Who would invest in that?

As an improv comedy enthusiast, Dubin knew the power of storytelling. He self-produced a ninety-second video about his new startup, named it "Our Blades are F***ing Great," and uploaded it to YouTube on March 6, 2012 (you can still find it on YouTube).

The video garnered millions of views and shares, and within two days of its release, the company received 12,000 orders. Dubin got his friends to help him fulfill the avalanche of orders, and Dollar Shave Club was off to the races.

The VCs were suddenly interested, and he ended up raising capital from Kleiner Perkins, Andreessen Horowitz, Shasta Ventures, and others to continue to scale the company.

In July of 2016, just five years after its founding, Dollar Shave Club had 3.2 million subscribers, and Dubin sold the company to Unilever for one billion dollars in cash. That's right, a billion dollars in cash. It's one of the most remarkable stories in the history of entrepreneurship.

KEY TAKEAWAYS:

There are a bunch of interesting insights and learnings from the Dollar Shave Club story, including:

◊ Many entrepreneurs would have been afraid to enter a space crowded with competition from such well-entrenched incumbents. The reality is that it's always easier to get a piece of an existing category than to create a brand-new one. People already spent a zillion dollars a year on razors; Dubin just needed to differentiate his business model enough to get a piece of that giant existing market. **He wasn't afraid of competition.**

◊ Although there was no product innovation, Dollar Shave Club offered **business model innovation**. It was a completely different way to buy razors, and customers loved the convenience of home delivery. Plus, the economics of a subscription business are powerful—automatic repeat purchases.

◊ **Storytelling matters.** Dubin's self-produced video went viral, and the products that arrived in the mail continued the story with messaging and packaging showcasing an attitude that fit Dollar Shave Club's brand voice.

◊ Every entrepreneur believes their startup idea will be a success, but venture capitalists want to see **actual proof of customer demand.** Dubin's proof was evident within forty-eight hours as thousands of people subscribed with their credit cards before ever actually seeing or using the product. No investor can ignore empirical proof of market demand on that level.

◊ With any startup venture, the **only element that really matters is CAC< LTV**. The unexpected success of the viral video gave Dollar Shave Club a low customer acquisition cost (at least for the first batch of customers), while a monthly subscription model (direct to consumer, with no retailer margin sharing) yields a very high lifetime value for each customer. Unilever paid a billion bucks to buy 3.2 million subscription customers, which equals $312 per customer. To Unilever, that was a reasonable CAC against what they believed they could make from the product.

◊ **It all starts with a problem worth solving**. People need to shave, but they hate having to go to the store and pay for overpriced razor blades. That's a very simple and clear problem Michael Dubin solved—all the way to the bank.

Problem ?

One clear sentence that articulates the problem your startup solves.

Consumers in the US spend $331 billion/year on fast food, and most of it is really unhealthy.

The paradox is that consumers today want to eat healthy, but also have a busy life that often drives them to resort to the convenience of fast food.

Solution

How does your venture solve the problem you have articulated? Keep this short and concise!

Fast food doesn't need to be unhealthy. Our startup is developing a new brand of health-conscious fast food (healthy tacos!), delivered directly to your home or office.

Why it matters ☆☆

Why is this a problem worth solving?

The National Institutes for Health say that today a fast food diet may kill more people prematurely every year than cigarette smoking.

Alternatives

When a customer looks at alternative ways to solve the problem we solve, what will they see? This is a list of competitors and alternatives. Link to a graphic representation of the landscape.

There are many, many food delivery services, from Uber Eats to Doordash to Grubhub.

See visualization at this link.

Customer

It's all about understanding customers. Write a one-sentence description of key customer personas and the problem we solve for each. Circle the one that is most influential.

Adventurous Alex: A thrill-seeking foodie always on the hunt for unique and spicy taco creations to satisfy their daring palate.

Health-Conscious Haley: A fitness enthusiast looking for wholesome and fresh ingredient options that align with their nutritious lifestyle at the taqueria.

Busy Ben: An on-the-go professional seeking quick, flavorful, and portable taco choices to enjoy during a busy workday.

Vegetarian Victoria: A plant-based eater in search of flavorful and creative vegetarian and vegan taco selections that cater to their dietary preferences.

Traditional Tony: A lover of classic flavors, Tony enjoys indulging in authentic and time-honored taco recipes that remind him of his cultural heritage.

Family-Oriented Felix: A parent looking for a family-friendly meal delivery with a variety of options to cater to the taste preferences of both kids and adults.

Budget-Conscious Bella: A student or frugal diner in pursuit of affordable yet flavorful taco choices that won't break the bank at the taqueria.

Path to PMF 📏

What is our path to Product-Market Fit? Customer Development, MVP's, etc.

1. Farmers' markets where we can get input on our menu items.
2. One truck in the Palo Alto area for a pilot project.
3. Scale slowly to additional markets, based on our learnings.

See full spreadsheet at this link.

Top 3 Benefits 🗂

What are the top 3 benefits that your product or services provides to customers?

1. Convenience. Use our mobile app to place a custom order and it's delivered directly to you.
2. Healthy food, designed by a nutritionist.
3. Tacos. Everybody loves tacos.

Distribution

What are our distribution channels? Direct to consumer, via resellers, or?

We intend to sell direct-to-consumer, via our mobile app and website, with delivery via our own vans.

In the future, we may be open to distribution partnerships.

Positioning

Within this landscape of competitors and alternatives, how is your venture positioned?

Our positioning can basically be summed-up in two words: healthy, and delicious.

There are many food delivery apps that can deliver something that is delicious but not very healthy. Or you could eat a kale salad.

We serve delicious tacos designed by a nutritionist. That's our unique positioning.

Economics

What are the Unit Economics for this venture, what do we expect the CAC<LTV to look like, and what are out capital needs? (Link to full spreadsheet.)

One unit = one taco: Sell price $5, on which our gross profit is $.74

Early tests indicate CAC of $11, and we expect an initial LTV of three orders per customer ($2.50!), which will grow with time.

Our initial capital needs are $220K, which will get us through the pilot launch. We will propose to investors structuring this as a SAFE.

See full spreadsheet at this link.

Team 🎖

What are the characteristics of the right team to make this venture a success?

The right team aligns with our target demographic - people who want to eat healthy and also enjoy the convenience of a quick taco meal.

The economics of our venture are such that we'll need drivers and cooks who make it affordable, so we will work hard to make it an attractive part-time job for students, and a great evening second job for anybody.

Defensibility

What is your secret sauce that is difficult for competitors to copy?

The fact that we own the customer and customer data is a big part of our defensibility.

A restaurant selling through a 3rd-party like Doordash owns neither the customer nor the data.

View and download a larger version at **thelaunchpath.com**

STEP 4, FOR YOUR STARTUP

A business model is the rationale by which your new venture will create, deliver, and capture value. We create value by solving a problem customers have, we have to deliver that value to them through distribution channels, and we capture that value in the form of profits. Every venture has a variety of components to its particular business model and they will all need to operate in harmony for the venture to succeed and scale. The Launch Path Canvas provides a way to make sure you are thinking-through all the different elements of your particular model.

▶ *For your Launch Path Canvas:*

If you haven't already, download a PDF of the Launch Path Canvas from thelaunchpath.com and fill out all the boxes. If you've already completed the deliverables from Chapters 1-3, then simply place those onto the Canvas in the appropriate spot. Some of the others are deliverables from Chapters 5-10, so just put your best guesses on there now.

Don't worry about getting it absolutely right; the idea at this point is to write down your best guesses, and then think about how you can test, validate, and refine those guesses as you go along.

"For every one of our failures, we had spreadsheets that looked awesome.

CHAPTER 5

ENGINEER AN ECONOMIC MODEL

Spreadsheets are fun. Really!

Startup success isn't about making pretty spreadsheets, but your venture will probably sink or swim depending on whether the numbers work, so we better start the process of creating an economic model for your venture long before operations actually begin.

In this chapter, I will walk you through the process of creating an economic model for your startup. Note that I said economic model, not financial statements. Financial statements are backward-looking documents detailing what happened last year for reporting and tax purposes. Right now, we are creating a **forward-looking model of how your venture's economics might look.** We don't care about GAAP accounting rules, depreciation tables, or accrual methods at this stage, so don't worry your pretty little head about any of that right now.

I also tend to avoid saying "financial projections" because, for a startup at this stage, revenue in year three is really just a wild-ass guess, so calling it a "projection" is a bit laughable. In fact, none of the numbers you come up with here will be right (especially for year three!), but you need a sense of the underlying economics of your proposed venture.

I had a student once who refused to do any spreadsheets for his startup idea. He claimed that early-stage investors don't care about financials anymore, just as they don't care about formal business plans these days. Good luck with that. Every investor I know wants to understand how a venture's numbers might work out. Most importantly, they want to invest in an entrepreneur who has actually spent some time thinking through the basic economics of their business model.

Yes, you need to build this yourself

Some inexperienced entrepreneurs may try to find a freelancer who can build spreadsheets for them, while others find a spreadsheet template somewhere. But my opinion is that a successful startup founder needs to really **understand and internalize their venture's basic economics**. If you're going to manage the organization successfully and make good decisions, you have to understand the underlying economics of the operation deep in your bones. That's just not going to happen unless you build the spreadsheets yourself.

Nothing is a brighter red flag for investors than asking a founder about a particular number on the spreadsheet and getting a response of: "I'm not sure; this is just a template I downloaded somewhere" or, worse yet, "I don't know; I found a freelancer on Fiverr to build that spreadsheet." Don't be that guy.

Let your Launch Path Canvas be your guide

In the last chapter, we talked about how a business model is the rationale by which an organization **creates**, **delivers**, and **captures** value. It's a beautiful engine that, once it's up and running, creates its own fuel in the form of profits. The Launch Path Canvas that you created is a visualization of all the various elements that will have to work together for your engine to run smoothly. In building your economic model, you're putting some numbers around this conceptual engine.

Most importantly (as we'll look at in the CAC<LTV section of this chapter), what are we likely to spend on customer acquisition activities,

and how will that compare to the money we can make from customers once we have them? Every business of every kind needs to have a way of getting a customer at a lower cost than they can make from them. It's a simple concept but a common reason startups fail. By beginning the process of putting down some numbers now, we can make sure we improve our chances of success.

You don't need a master's degree in accounting

Some first-time founders get nervous about building an economic model because they think it requires the specialized wisdom of a finance expert. It does not. **Don't overcomplicate this process**, and don't put off this task because you think you don't have good enough accounting knowledge. Like everything else on the **Launch Path**, just enter your best guesses first, and then you can refine, test, expand, and iterate as you go along.

Eventually, you can have a financial expert review it for you, but for now, just get it going yourself. You are good enough, you are smart enough, and doggone it, people like you![1]

1: From an SNL skit that may be from before you were born.

THE PURPOSE OF A GOOD ECONOMIC MODEL

The reason you're going to want to start creating this now, early in the venture-building process, is that there are a variety of important things that will emerge from the process.

- **Understanding the levers.** For any venture, there are often two or three key levers that really make a difference in the economics of the operations. For a manufacturing business, it might be the materials cost; for a consulting business, it might be the ratio of billable to non-billable hours; for a restaurant, it might be the table churn rate. Once you build a solid economic model, you'll be able to easily conduct sensitivity analysis that will help you understand where the meaningful levers are for your particular venture. I worked with a startup once that was desperately trying to get their materials costs down by a couple of percentage points in order to improve their profit margin. I looked at their numbers and saw that they were paying almost 4% of every sale for credit card processing. I suggested they shop around and see if they could find a better deal. They found a payment processor charging 1.5%, and that one switch added more to their bottom line than all of their efforts to reduce materials cost. Once you have a good financial model built, it's straightforward to do "what if" scenarios that help you see which levers really matter.

- **Informing the capital strategy.** Once you've built an economic model, you'll have a clearer picture of your capital needs at each stage. You'll also have a better idea of the type of capital that makes sense. For example, if you have a solid cash flow after year one, then debt financing may make much more sense than equity financing. We'll talk a lot more about capital strategies in the next chapter and how a good economic model will help you choose the best way to finance your startup.

Yes, I know this is impossible to read, but you can see
my whole economic model at **thelaunchpath.com**

- **Uncovering insights.** In your head, you probably have already
  made some assumptions about your venture's economics and
  your capital needs. But the process of actually building the
  economic model may yield insights that differ from your initial
  assumptions. Again, a fundamental part of the **Launch Path**
  process is always to be looking for ways to test and validate your
  assumptions.

- **Understanding scaling dynamics.** Scaling one sort of company
  is different from scaling another sort of company. Building
  the economic model for your particular venture will help you
  understand the particular scaling dynamics you will encounter.
  For a consulting firm, for example, headcount typically goes up
  with a linear relationship to revenue. Consulting firms bill by
  the hour, and so to double the revenue, you need to double the
  number of consultants. With a software company, doubling the
  revenue may not require doubling the people, but it may require
  additional investment in server infrastructure. Again, the point

is that you need to immerse yourself in what the economic dynamics of your particular venture will look and feel like.

- **Communicating with investors.** As Guy Kawasaki[2] has written, "The point of an economic model is to tell a story with numbers—a story about opportunity, resource requirements, market forces, growth, milestone achievements, and profits." Having a well-thought-through economic model is an essential part of being able to talk to investors about your startup. You're telling a story with numbers.

OK, Fire-Up Your Spreadsheet!

Are you ready to do this thing? I'll walk you through the process of creating the initial economic model for your brand-new startup concept—no accounting skills required! On thelaunchpath.com, you'll find an example economic model for our awesome fictional venture, Fitaco. You can make a copy of that spreadsheet, if that helps you to follow along with with my narrative here as you build one for your venture.

What you're building is a model of the economic rationale by which you expect to create, deliver, and capture value for your customers (which you'll remember as my definition of a business model).

I like to do the other parts of the **Launch Path Canvas** first so that I've got a reasonably good picture in my head of the elements of this particular venture, and then I use that to inform the creation of a spreadsheet representing the economic model. For the first year of your new startup, you'll want a spreadsheet with everything listed by month. For years two and beyond, you may want to use quarters instead of

---

2: Guy Kawasaki is an author, venture capitalist, and early Apple employee. He also likes tacos.

months, but for a new startup, it will likely be more helpful to look at months.

When you look at my example on **thelaunchpath.com**, you'll notice that I like to put everything on separate spreadsheet tabs. I do this for ease in making adjustments as I continue to refine a startup's economic model. Here are the various tabs on my spreadsheet and a description of each:

- **Assumptions**

  Put all your assumptions on one tab so you can change them in one place and see how they flow through the entire model. An example might be "credit card fees." If you're assuming you'll pay a credit card fee of three percent, then later you get a good deal and can get that down to 1.85 percent, you can just change it in one place on the Assumptions tab, and it will automatically flow everywhere else.

- **Setup Costs**

  There are always some one-time costs to get your venture going. For example, the cost of forming the corporation is a one-time cost, not a recurring cost. I like to put these one-time startup costs on a separate tab, as they are not part of ongoing operating expenses.

- **Sales, General, and Administrative (SG&A)**

  This is what most people would just call "overhead"—rent, insurance, utilities, stuff like that. Sometimes these are called "fixed costs" because they don't vary month to month depending on how many widgets we make and sell. Put all of your estimated overhead costs on this tab. Again, don't worry about all the numbers being right, just add in rows for all the different operating expenses you think your venture will likely incur.

- **People**

  People are the largest expense for most ventures, so put them on a separate tab. Group them by function because, eventually, salespeople will go into a different expense category than engineers, for example. Maybe you'll have some freelancers and contractors at first, and then you will hire full-time staff. Keep contractors and payroll employees separate because employees will cost you more than their salaries once you add payroll taxes and benefits. This added amount is called a load factor. For example, if we pay someone a salary of $100,000, they'll cost us more like $130,000 when we include payroll taxes and benefits, so the load factor is 30%. I like to put that load factor on the Assumptions tab, and then you can easily refine it later. Your venture will probably end up with a payroll load factor somewhere between 20-40%, depending on the labor law where you're operating and the extent of your benefits package. Just put 30% on the Assumptions tab for now.

- **Revenue**

  You won't yet really have any idea of your new venture's revenue, but you need to have it represented correctly in your model. Do you think you'll start earning revenue in the first month, or is yours the sort of venture where there will be no revenue until month seven? If you have a subscription business, then your revenue is the number of subscribers each month, times your monthly subscription fee. Of course, with a subscription business, there's always churn—the number of monthly people who cancel their subscriptions. All of that should be modeled in some way on the Revenue tab. Again, having the numbers right isn't as important right now as creating a logical model that produces clear and easy-to-understand results. You can refine the actual numbers as you go along.

- **Cost of Goods Sold (COGS)**

  Your cost of goods sold (COGS) is the traditional way of representing what the products you sold cost you to make. If you sold one hundred loaves of bread for one thousand dollars total, the COGS includes the flour, water, yeast, salt, and labor costs in making those one hundred loaves. The COGS is not the overhead costs of running the organization; it's just the costs related to making the products you sold. You, as CEO, are overhead, whereas the baker mixing bread dough all day is part of the COGS required to make each loaf of bread you sell. Sometimes you will hear this called "variable cost" or "direct labor" (meaning that, if you double the number of products you are shipping, you'll need to hire another shipping guy, so the cost is variable depending on how many products you ship each month). This gets a little squishy with some business models. For example, with a software-as-a-service (SaaS) business, there is no manufacturing cost, but you probably want to record the cost of running the servers (and support personnel) upon which your SaaS platform is delivered to customers.

- **Summary Tab**

  All of your data should roll up onto a single Summary tab that gives an overview of the story. Startups typically run at a loss at first and then eventually turn profitable, so I like to have a cumulative "running cash balance" across the bottom, as that will help inform how much capital you'll need to start and scale the business.

Once you fill out your spreadsheet, you can refine the numbers and test some assumptions, and after iterating on it a few times, you'll begin to have a functioning economic model for your venture. Remember, like everything else in the Launch Path process, you're putting down your best guesses first, then finding ways you can validate your guesses and refine them toward a final form.

Capital Expenses vs. Operating Expenses

You'll likely hear accountants and financial people talk about Capital Expenses and Operating Expenses. From an accounting perspective, CapEx and OpEx are different animals, represented on financial statements in a completely different way. Right now, for your early-stage venture, all you need to care about is cash. If you buy a one-hundred-thousand-dollar piece of equipment, it's cash out the door, just like paying one hundred thousand dollars for a marketing campaign. So, don't worry about CapEx and depreciation tables; let your CPA worry about that later.

Eventually, you will have financial statements

For now, we are creating a forward-looking economic model for our venture, which is different from the formal (backward-looking) financial statements you will eventually have, prepared by your bookkeeper and CPA. Eventually, every venture keeps a set of financial statements that typically have three components:

- **Balance Sheet**
  This is simply a list of the company's assets and liabilities at a particular snapshot in time. If we have one thousand dollars in the bank (assets), and we owe three hundred dollars in debt (liabilities), then the net of that (our equity) is seven hundred dollars. Equity plus liabilities equals assets (they balance). That's all there is to that. The first questions an investor asks about a balance sheet will be: How much cash do you have, and when does it run out? How healthy are your accounts receivable? Are you behind on your payables?

- **Income Statement (Profit & Loss Statement)**
  This shows a particular time period (maybe a year, divided up by month), along with your revenue and expenses during that same

time period. Revenue minus expenses equals income (profit). If you ended the year with five hundred dollars in net income (profit), then you'd expect that the assets on your balance sheet also increased by five hundred dollars.

- **Cash Flow Statements**
  If one month's expenses totaled two hundred dollars, and you billed your customers one thousand dollars, then you made eight hundred dollars, and you're happy, right? Except that maybe your customers aren't going to pay their bills until next month. For reasons like these, the income statement may not exactly represent how the cash flows and that's what cash flow statements are for.

But as I said, don't worry about these financial statements right now. You're simply going to build an economic model, a numbers-based story about how your venture will **create, deliver, and capture value for customers.**

You'll find example economic models, spreadsheets, and other resources on **thelaunchpath.com.**

Every startup venture needs to eventually have a profitable economic engine. Once you get the flywheel going, that engine will (hopefully) create more dollars than it consumes each year.

UNIT ECONOMICS

The concept of unit economics forms the underpinning of any venture's economic model: **you can make <u>one unit</u> of something for a price of X, and you can sell that unit at a price of Y.** If you're a bakery, your unit economics are pretty simple: every loaf of bread costs you X to make, and you can sell that loaf for Y. If you're a consulting firm, every hour of time costs you X, and a client is willing to pay Y for that hour. For hotels, the units are room nights. For airlines, the units are seat miles. Every venture distills down to unit economics.

For most companies, unit economics improve with scale. As your factory grows, your cost of producing one unit decreases, and maybe the price you can sell that unit for increases as your marketing and distribution improves. However, if your unit economics are fundamentally upside down (your cost of making a unit is hopelessly higher than you'll ever be able to sell a unit for), then scale just makes you go broke faster (which is not usually the desired outcome).

How to Calculate Your Unit Economics

The first step is to determine what you'll consider "one unit" for your business. For a taco shop, a unit is one taco sold. For a consulting firm, it's one billable hour. For a SaaS company, it's one monthly subscription. For a fertilizer company, maybe it's one ton of fertilizer. Everything distills down to Unit Economics, so think about what one unit is for your venture.

Now, what does it cost us to produce one unit? Don't include any general overhead, just the incremental cost of making one unit. For a widget factory, we don't include the cost of the factory, or the manager's salaries, just include the materials and labor to produce one single widget.

Taco Unit Economics

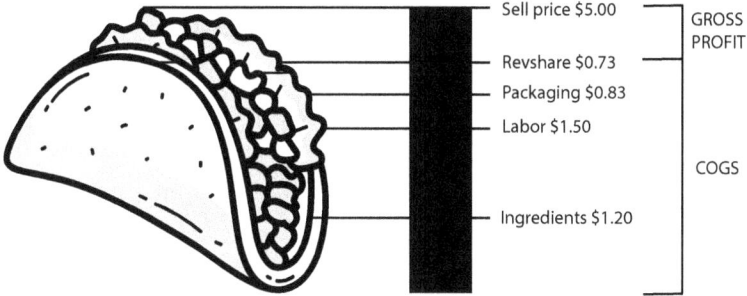

Sell price $5.00 — GROSS PROFIT

Revshare $0.73
Packaging $0.83
Labor $1.50

COGS

Ingredients $1.20

We sell each taco for $5.00. Each taco cost us $4.26 to make and deliver, yielding a gross profit of $0.74 per unit.

For our taco shop, each taco we make has several ingredients, so let's say those amount to $1.20 per taco, on average. We have some labor to assemble the taco ($1.50), some packaging ($.83), and we pay a revenue share to DoorDash to deliver the order ($.73). Adding those up, our cost-of-goods-sold (COGS) is $4.26 per unit, and if we sell that taco for $5.00, then our gross profit on one unit is .74—nice, easy unit economics.

The concept of unit economics is pretty simple, but of course, it gets more complicated in real life. What if we offer several different tacos, each at a different price point? In this case, the easiest approach is to think of one unit as an "average order."

The reality, of course, is that most ventures are more complicated than just "We make tacos for four dollars and sell them for five dollars." Unfortunately, many entrepreneurs make the fatal mistake of waving their hands and saying, "Well, unit economics doesn't really apply to what we do because what we do is new and different."

History says otherwise. Many startups have met painful demises because they didn't really understand the concept of unit economics. You can avoid one leading cause of startup death by taking the time to understand your venture's unit economics. Once you do, you can build a full economic model for your venture and go on to find great success (while eating some delicious tacos along the way).

The notion of unit economics even applies to nonprofits and social enterprises. You have fixed costs (overhead) for your nonprofit organization, and then maybe you run programs that help kids learn to read. Your costs for that work out to five dollars per kid per month, and the school district reimburses you at six dollars per kid per month. So there's your unit economics. Funders and donors will want to understand the unit economics of your social venture, and so should you. It's the key to creating sustainable impact.

Enterprise Economics

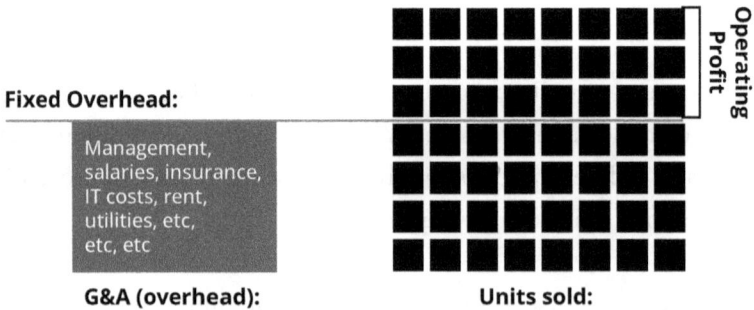

Fixed Overhead:

Management, salaries, insurance, IT costs, rent, utilities, etc, etc, etc

G&A (overhead):   **Units sold:**

Operating Profit

How this flows into Enterprise Economics

Unit economics then feed into enterprise economics. We need to sell a certain number of units every month to cover the enterprise's overhead. Once we've covered the overhead for the month, then additional units sold represent profit. Not only is this how a simple lemonade stand works, it's also exactly how nearly every business works.

Let's say the overhead for our taco shop is $2,000 per month. This includes the rent, utilities, insurance, etc. Since our unit economics say we make $.74 per unit sold, we need to sell 2,700 tacos in a month to cover the overhead. Each additional unit sold after that turns the whole operation profitable for the month, as the gross profit on each additional unit is pure net profit for our taco shop. Nice.

CAC < LTV:

One Equation to Rule Them All

Pay attention to the following eight pages because understanding this one equation will determine whether your startup venture flies or dies. Yes, I know you're just skimming this, but I guarantee you that if you don't take the time to understand these eight pages now, someday your venture will be going broke, and you'll be wondering why.

A business is an engine that attracts customers, delivers something of value to them, and then extracts that value in the form of profits. That's what a business is. It logically follows that the cost of attracting a new customer needs to be less than the value we can extract from that customer. If it costs fifteen dollars in advertising to get a customer, but we can only make seven dollars from that customer, then Houston, we have a problem.

Conversely, if it costs fifteen dollars to get them, and then once they are a customer, they make repeat purchases that yield seventy-five dollars in profit, then you are happy. **Ultimately, every venture of every kind has to have a Customer Acquisition Cost (CAC) that is less than the Lifetime Value (LTV) of a customer.** It's a simple, self-evident concept, yet failure to accurately project CAC:LTV remains a leading cause of startup death.

Customer Acquisition Cost (CAC) is a very simple concept—it's the amount of money we spend on customer acquisition activities during a given period, divided by the number of new customers acquired during that period. So if we spend $10,000 during the quarter on sales and marketing and we got 1,000 new customers during that period, then our CAC was $10. Easy peasy.

The Lifetime Value (LTV) of a customer is similarly simple in concept. Let's say we sell widgets for $20, and we make $8 in gross profit on each one we sell. Now let's say that the customer buys a widget from us, and then ends up coming back and buying an average of five more widgets from us before they disappear. This means that the average new customer buys a total of six widgets from which we make $8 each in gross profit, so our LTV on that customer is $48. Because math.

Given this example, our widget business is a pretty good one! We are able to get customers for $10, and make $48 from them, which gives us a LTV:CAC ratio of 4.8!

The fact is, a high percentage of startups die because their cost of getting customers turns out to be higher than they can make from them. This is partly just because we're all optimists—we all think our startup is so awesome that people will flock to become customers and will remain customers forever. Eventually, that optimism fades as we realize marketing is expensive and no customer stays forever.

Then the immutable laws of economics set in, and at some point, many startup founders find that their LTV:CAC ratio is slowly draining the bank account. To paraphrase Ernest Hemingway, startups go broke two ways: gradually, and then suddenly.

Investors tend to obsess over LTV:CAC

Investors care a lot about your LTV:CAC ratio because it's the essence of a successful business. It's also a proxy for their potential ROI. If you have proof that you can spend one dollar on customer acquisition activities and get five dollars in value back (an LTV:CAC ratio of 5.0), investors will want to shovel as much money as possible into that engine. Having a business with a LTV:CAC ratio over 5.0 looks like a just-add-money opportunity to investors.

It's a blunt tool that is better when sharpened

Let's say that during one quarter, you spent ten thousand dollars on sales and marketing and got one thousand new customers for a CAC of ten dollars. Some of those customers probably came through word of mouth, some as referrals, some from your PR efforts, and some from paid advertising. You had a blended CAC of ten dollars, but that doesn't tell you anything about the relative effectiveness of each of your different customer acquisition efforts, which leads to the next point:

Not all customers are created equal

With every business I've ever run, I've realized at some point that eighty percent of our profits were coming from twenty percent of our customers. It's incredible how this tends to be true with almost all businesses. If you look at the LTV of your entire universe of customers, you'll probably see that twenty percent of them have a much higher individual LTV than the rest. Wouldn't you want to focus your CAC efforts on getting more of the high-LTV customers? Yes, you would.

Therefore, cohorts matter

The two points above would suggest that you really want to track your LTV:CAC ratio by customer cohort. For example, what's the ratio for customers acquired through Facebook advertising versus those acquired through Google advertising? Knowing that would tell you a lot about allocating advertising dollars. What's the LTV:CAC ratio for customers acquired through our referral program? Knowing that would tell you how much you can afford to offer in a referral fee. **Your company's blended LTV:CAC indicates the health of the overall engine, but it doesn't tell you how to optimize the engine's performance for the next quarter.** Tracking customer cohorts tells you that.

Also, velocity matters

One afternoon, I sat in the backyard of longtime Silicon Valley venture capitalist Tim Connors as he drew graphs for me on his whiteboard (only VCs have whiteboards in their backyards). He explained that he doesn't care about the LTV:CAC ratio, per se; what he cares about is the velocity with which invested CAC comes back in the form of LTV. He's developed a metric he calls CACD (the D is for "doubled"). CACD answers the question, "If we spend twelve dollars in customer acquisition activities, how long does it take for us to get twenty-four dollars' worth of gross profit back?" As an investor, he wants to see a business with a CACD of less than eight months. Tim's formula gets to the heart of an inherent flaw in the LTV:CAC ratio: it doesn't include a time factor. A business with an LTV:CAC ratio of 5:1 might seem good at first, but if you have to service a customer for ten years before you make back the money you spent getting that customer, then it doesn't seem so good, right? Velocity matters, so think about how you can measure CACD for your business. Spending twelve dollars where it returns with a high velocity will accelerate your engine of growth (and make Tim happy).

Common Mistakes in Calculating CAC:LTV

At its essence, it's a straightforward concept, so why is getting the CAC:LTV ratio wrong still a leading cause of startup death? From my experience, here are the mistakes that many startup founders make:

- **Not adding in staff costs.**
  I've had entrepreneurs proudly tell me that they spent five thousand dollars on advertising in one quarter and got five thousand new customers, so their CAC was just one dollar! But then I look at their financials, and they have a full-time marketing person, two marketing assistants, a fancy graphic designer, an inside salesperson, and someone handling inbound

web leads. Their actual all-in customer acquisition costs were way more than a dollar—because math.

- **Thinking your time is free.**
  I've had entrepreneurs tell me that their customer acquisition cost is zero because they do all the selling themselves! That's only if you think your time is worthless. Also, it's not scalable. When you are calculating CAC, make sure you ascribe a reasonable value to the time you personally spend selling.

- **Thinking CAC is always a marketing problem.**
  I met with a startup recently that said they fired their marketing person because the customer acquisition cost was just too high, clearly because the marketing person was doing a crappy job. We dug into the funnel metrics together and found that plenty of customers were entering the top of the funnel on their e-commerce website, but very few were completing a purchase. In fact, most got all the way to the payment screen and then left. It turns out that the payment gateway they were using was a really crappy user experience. They switched to a new payment gateway, and the number of people completing purchases doubled, which cut the CAC in half. Bingo. It wasn't a marketing problem, it was a crappy payment gateway problem.

- **Overestimating repeat purchases.**
  Every entrepreneur thinks their product is so excellent that customers will come back and buy more and more. Every startup with a subscription model thinks no one will ever cancel their subscription. This isn't reality. Be conservative with how you calculate repeat purchases in order to come up with your LTV. It's better to be surprised in a good way than to end up in surprise bankruptcy.

- **Not factoring in promotions.**

  Let's say you find that offering a "no questions asked" return policy increases your sales. That's great! But if fifteen percent of all purchases get returned, then you need to either reflect this as part of your customer acquisition cost or within your gross profit/LTV numbers. Don't just wave your hands and pretend those economics don't apply to you. They do.

- **Not benchmarking.**

  If you show me your pitch deck, and it says that your LTV will be seventy-two times your CAC, I'm going to laugh and ask you whether pigs can fly. I've never seen anything anywhere near that high, and the chances that you will be the first person ever to overcome the laws of physics seem very unlikely. Look up the LTV:CAC ratio for similar businesses. Generally, you want to have an LTV:CAC ratio higher than 3:1. Seldom have I seen anything more than 10:1. If you're way outside that range, you probably have some assumptions wrong. Find a similar business you can benchmark to.

- **Using gross revenue instead of gross profit!**

  It seems silly, but I've seen entrepreneurs get confused by this. If we sell widgets for $20 (gross revenue), and those widgets cost us $12 each to make, then the gross profit is $8, so that's what we're actually making from the customer!

Let's face it—as entrepreneurs, we are naturally optimists. We all underestimate what it will cost to get a customer, and we all overestimate how much we will make from customers. Sadly, this optimism drives a lot of startups to failure because they realize too late that they have their CAC < LTV expression upside down. Do this math early, and do it with a solid dose of realism. You will dramatically increase your odds of growing a successful startup venture.

Some of Silicon Valley's worst failures have stemmed from the fact that the company (and its investors) thought that somehow the laws of economics had been suspended. An infamous example is pets.com, which raised $180 million with their great idea of selling bags of dog food at a loss and hoping to turn that model into a winner eventually, maybe, somehow. They went bankrupt in eighteen months, sending $180 million down the toilet.

Or take the much-hyped Y Combinator company, Homejoy. They were a startup marketplace for connecting consumers with home cleaning services, and they raised an impressive financing round of $38 million. Their cost of one house cleaning was $35, and they sold one house cleaning for $95 (unit economics). They ran a promotion offering the first cleaning for nineteen dollars, figuring that customers would come back for several more cleanings—except that people took the nineteen-dollar cleaning and never came back. Fundamentally, their CAC:LTV ratio was flawed, but they spent millions advertising their promotion, hoping that the economics would magically change at some point. Finally, they went bankrupt four years after founding, losing thirty-eight million dollars in investor money.

Most companies start with a CAC much higher than their LTV (see graph below). As you optimize your marketing and sales, hopefully, your CAC will come down, and as you build brand loyalty and happy customers, hopefully, your LTV will go up. The point at which those two lines cross is the notional point at which the company turns profitable.

The CAC < LTV concept applies to every business of every kind. Every venture must have a sustainable way to get customers at a cost less than the venture can make from them. It's an immutable law of economics. Ignoring the formula (or misunderstanding it) remains a leading cause of startup death. As the capitalist Bill Gurley once wrote in a post titled **The Dangerous Seduction of the LTV Formula,** "the formula can be confused, misused, and abused, much to the detriment of the business." So, don't do any of those things, or it will make Bill mad, and you won't like Bill when he's mad.

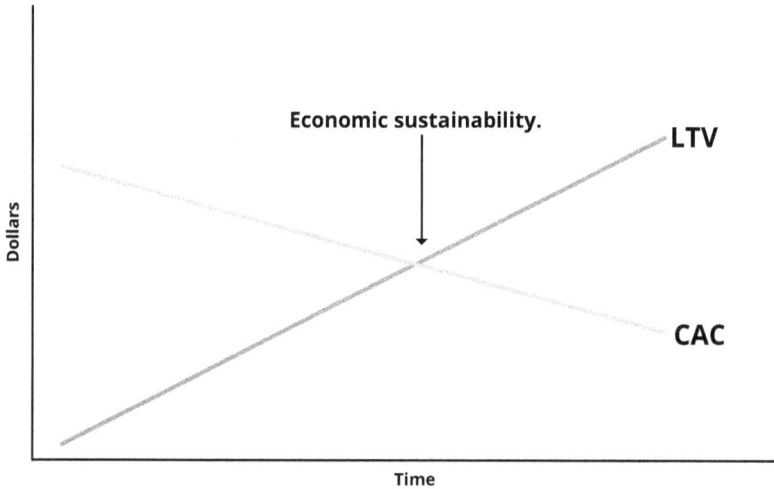

For most ventures, CAC starts off high, and LTV starts off low. Over time your sales and marketing gets optimized, and your CAC begins to come down. Meanwhile you're keeping customers longer, you're up-selling and cross-selling, and your LTV is going up. The point at which those two lines cross is notionally the point at which you have a profitable business.

Sharpen the tool by tracking customer cohorts, improve the formula by adding a time factor, and remember that not all customers are created equal, and you will have an engine of growth that makes you happy and investors eager.

Ultimately the success or failure of your venture will distill down to this one equation: CAC<LTV. Every business of every kind must have a way of getting a new customer at a cost less than they can make from that customer. It's a simple concept, yet getting it wrong remains a leading cause of startup death.

Case Study:
TUTORSPREE

In 2011, Tutorspree emerged from Y Combinator, calling themselves "like Airbnb for tutors." If you were a parent looking for a math tutor for your kid, you could find one on Tutorspree. Similarly, if you were a grad student looking to make some money tutoring, you could list your services on the platform.

It was a huge potential market—their research indicated that tutoring was a $5 billion market and growing. The revenue model was simple: Tutorspree would take a fifty-percent cut on each tutoring session booked.

The economic model Tutorspree presented to investors looked very solid, especially because the three founders were SEO experts, so they knew how to make the website show up at the top of Google searches for tutoring services without having to pay for any marketing or advertising. The recurring nature of tutoring sessions is such that Tutorspree expected the lifetime value (LTV) of a new customer to be reasonably high. They figured the average new customer would book a total of six tutoring sessions, so if they made an average of $25 on each one, then their LTV would be $150. Their CAC would be nearly zero (since the founders were SEO experts, they figured they'd get Google search traffic for free). What could go wrong?

They touted their "proprietary algorithm" that would match students and tutors based on various factors, including location, background, preferences, and style.

Based on their solid economic model, they raised $1.8 million in capital from leading investors, including Y Combinator, Sequoia, and Quora co-founder Adam D'angelo.

They signed up more than seven thousand tutors in the first few months after they launched, and soon customers began to appear, finding the site through Google and booking sessions with tutors.

However the tutors weren't pleased about giving fifty percent of their fees to Tutorspree, so at the end of the first tutoring session, they would often tell the student, "Hey, just contact me directly next time instead of going through the platform," so Tutorspree's estimate of a six-session customer lifetime value (LTV) turned out to be a bit off.

In March of 2013, Google changed its algorithm, and Tutorspree's SEO volume dropped by eighty percent overnight. It looked like they would actually need to spend money on paid advertising, and that wasn't in the economic model they had prepared.

By September, they had ceased operations. The investor money was gone in less than two years.

KEY TAKEAWAYS:

Fundamentally, Tutorspree story is a simple one: they underestimated their customer acquisition cost (CAC) and overestimated their lifetime value of a customer (LTV). It's a common issue in startup land.

◊ Every venture distills down to one simple mathematical expression: CAC < LTV. Every entrepreneur underestimates their customer acquisition cost ("We're SEO experts, so we don't need to spend any money on advertising!"), and every entrepreneur overestimates the lifetime value of a customer ("Once we have a customer, they'll come back and buy from us again and again and again!"). Finding out too late that your CAC is too high relative to your LTV will bring your startup to its knees faster than a tutor could have taught you the basic math you needed at the onset.

◊ As we explored in the Marketplace section of Chapter 4, one of the risks of a digital marketplace model is the threat of disintermediation. In other words, the marketplace model requires that you be in the middle of the transaction to take a cut—that's where your revenue comes from. If people want to go around you and transact off your platform, then the model fails. Successful marketplaces like Airbnb and Upwork have worked hard to provide benefits that discourage buyers and sellers from going around them. Tutorspree failed to do this.

Economics

What are the Unit Economics for this venture, what do we expect the CAC<LTV to look like, and what are out capital needs? (Link to full spreadsheet).

One unit = one average order: $15, on which our gross profit is $8.50.

Early tests indicate CAC of $11, and we expect an initial LTV of three orders per customer ($25.50), which will grow with time.

Our initial capital needs are $220K, which will get us through the pilot launch. We will propose to investors structuring this as a SAFE.

See full spreadsheet at this link.

The Launch Path Canvas
Lorem Ipsum

Name of Startup Venture: Fitaco, Inc

Prepared by: Bret Waters

Date: November 8, 2023

Iteration: 8

Problem ?
One clear sentence that articulates the problem your startup solves.

Consumers in the US spend $331 billion/year on fast food, and most of it is really unhealthy.

The paradox is that consumers today want to eat healthy, but also have a busy life that often drives them to resort to the convenience of fast food.

Solution
How does your venture solve the problem you have articulated? Keep this short and concise!

Fast food doesn't need to be unhealthy. Our startup is developing a new brand of health-conscious fast food (healthy tacos!), delivered directly to your home or office.

Why it matters
Why is this a problem worth solving?

The National Institutes for Health say that today a fast food diet may kill more people prematurely every year than cigarette smoking.

Alternatives
When a customer looks at alternative ways to solve the problem we solve, what will they see? This is a list of competitors and alternatives. Link to a graphic representation of the landscape.

There are many, many food delivery services, from Uber Eats to Doordash to Grubhub.

See visualization at this link.

Customer
It's all about understanding customers. Write a one-sentence description of key customer personas and the problem we solve for each. Circle the one that is most influential.

Adventurous Alex: A thrill-seeking foodie always on the hunt for unique and spicy taco creations to satisfy their daring palate.

Health-Conscious Haley: A fitness enthusiast looking for wholesome and fresh ingredient options that align with their nutritious lifestyle at the taqueria.

Path to PMF
What is our path to Product-Market Fit? Customer Development, MVP's, etc.

1. Farmers' markets where we can get input on our menu items.
2. One truck in the Palo Alto area for a pilot project.
3. Scale slowly to additional markets, based on our learnings.

Top 3 Benefits
What are the top 3 benefits that your product or services provides to customers?

1. Convenience. Use our mobile app to place a custom order and it's delivered directly to you.
2. Healthy food, designed by a nutritionist.
3. Tacos. Everybody loves tacos.

Distribution
What are our distribution channels? Direct to consumer, via resellers, or?

We intend to sell direct-to-consumer, via our mobile app and website, with delivery via our own vans.

In the future, we may be open to distribution partnerships.

Positioning
Within this landscape of competitors and alternatives, how is your venture positioned? Our positioning can basically be summed-up in two words: healthy, and delicious.

There are many food delivery apps that can deliver something that is delicious but not very healthy. Or you could eat a kale salad.

We serve delicious tacos designed by a nutritionist. That's our unique positioning.

Busy Ben: An on-the-go professional seeking quick, flavorful, and portable taco choices to enjoy during a busy workday.

Vegetarian Victoria: A plant-based eater in search of flavorful and creative vegetarian and vegan taco selections that cater to their dietary preferences.

Traditional Tony: A lover of classic flavors, Tony enjoys indulging in authentic and time-honored taco recipes that remind him of his cultural heritage.

Economics
What are the Unit Economics for this venture, what do we expect the CAC<LTV to look like, and what are out capital needs? (Link to full spreadsheet).

One unit = one taco. Sell price $5, on which our gross profit is 4.74

Early tests indicate CAC of $11, and we expect an initial LTV of three orders per customer ($25.50), which will grow with time.

Our initial capital needs are $220K, which will get us through the pilot launch. We will propose to investors structuring this as a SAFE.

See full spreadsheet at this link.

Team
What are the characteristics of the right team to make this venture a success?

The right team aligns with our target demographic - people who want to eat healthy and also enjoy the convenience of a quick taco meal.

The economics of our venture are such that we'll need drivers and cooks who are affordable, so we will work hard to make it an attractive part-time job for students, and a great evening second job for anybody.

Defensibility
What is your secret sauce that is difficult for competitors to copy?

The fact that we own the customer and customer data is a big part of our defensibility.

A restaurant selling through a 3rd-party like Doordash owns neither the customer nor the data.

Family-Oriented Felix: A parent looking for a family-friendly meal delivery with a variety of options to cater to the taste preferences of both kids and adults.

Budget-Conscious Bella: A student or frugal diner in pursuit of affordable yet flavorful taco choices that won't break the bank at the taqueria.

STEP 5, FOR YOUR STARTUP

For your startup to succeed, thrive, and scale, the numbers are going to have to work. Even for a very early-stage venture, it is helpful to begin to build an economic model which we can refine and expand as we get more clarity on what costs will actually be and how we will need to think about the revenue side.

On **thelaunchpath.com** you will find a complete economic model for our awesome fictional venture, Fitaco. You can make a copy of it, play around with it, and use it as a baseline spreadsheet to build your own.

▶ *For your Launch Path Canvas:*

In the box on the lower left of the canvas, put some of the key insights from your economic model, and link to the full spreadsheet. The key insights that should go on your Launch Path Canvas include:

- What are the unit economics for your business?
- What do we think our CAC:LTV will look like?
- What are our initial capital needs to get this venture off the ground?
- Realistically, how long will it take us to get to break-even?

Put those into the box on the canvas, with a link to your full economic model.

"Be so good they can't ignore you.

STEVE MARTIN

CHAPTER 6
CREATE A CAPITAL STRATEGY

There are more sources and structures of startup capital available today than ever before

I once pitched a venture capitalist a new startup, and the meeting went very well. The next day, I got an email from him saying that his VC firm was definitely interested but that, just as a formality, he'd like me to meet with one of the firm's other partners.

I walked into the second meeting fully expecting it to go as well as the first, but this partner hated everything in my presentation. He was skeptical of every slide, questioned my business model, and poked holes in my economic model. I was crestfallen but did my best to answer his questions and defend my thinking.

At the end of the meeting, he stood up, shook my hand, and said, "Great! We're looking forward to investing." It was the basic "good cop/ bad cop" routine, and apparently, I'd passed the test. A term sheet was issued, and I was the proud founder of a venture-funded startup.

While I was very excited that day, venture capital may not have been the best way to finance that particular startup. We raised more than we really needed, spent all of it, and two years later, we needed to raise more money in a challenging environment, on very difficult terms. When we finally sold the company, after all the liquidation preferences and dilution from the two rounds of venture capital, my final distribution check after five years of hard work was $84.75. That's right—eighty-four dollars and seventy-five cents.

But there are <u>many</u> ways to finance a startup

When people think of startup financing, they immediately think of venture capital, but in fact, there are many great ways to finance your new startup. My goal with this chapter is to open up the solution set a bit in your mind so you can choose the form of financing that makes sense for your particular venture.

I'm always amazed when new entrepreneurs tell me that their biggest hurdle is finding financing for their startup. In my own startup career, raising money has been the relatively easy part; the hard part is actually building a successful business.

Honestly, I think the startup world is too obsessed with venture capital as if it's the only way to finance and grow a startup venture. Too many wannabe entrepreneurs sit around fantasizing about the day they meet a VC who bestows upon them a wheelbarrow full of cash. Meanwhile, others just go out and build great businesses. In fact, ninety-nine percent of the world's successful businesses have never raised a single penny of venture capital.

Here's a rundown of just some of the many different sources and structures of capital you could consider for financing your awesome new startup:

- **Bootstrap It, Baby**
  The absolute best way to finance a startup, of course, is to simply grow it out of profits. This is the way most businesses have been built. Want a Silicon Valley example? See the Farmgirl Flowers case study in Chapter 7! Another remarkable example

is Mailchimp, which never raised any outside capital. The founders worked very hard on bootstrapping the company and then sold it to Intuit for twelve billion dollars. GitHub, the cloud-based platform that serves nearly every software developer in the world today, bootstrapped for the first four years, growing strictly from profits, and is now worth several billion dollars. Bootstrapping remains the absolutely best way for any entrepreneur to build a company.

- **Rich Uncle Bob**

  Many entrepreneurs have gotten their ventures off the ground with friends-and-family money. Borrowing from relatives has its pros and cons, of course (if you lose your mother-in-law's money, she'll never let you forget it), but if someone in your family has the capacity to help and believes in you, this is a very common way to raise initial funding.

  Structure: *Can be anything you agree upon; a simple promissory note can be family-friendly*

- **Bank Loan**

  Walk down to your friendly bank and ask the manager for a loan to get your startup off the ground. You'll get a reasonable interest rate, and you won't give away any equity. The downside is that you will almost certainly need to personally guarantee the loan (e.g., pledging your house), which can be a difficult conversation with your spouse. The amount you can borrow may be limited by your credit and personal assets.

  Structure: *Typically either fixed-term or revolving debt*

- **Venture Capital**

  Take a stroll down Sand Hill Road, hoping to show someone your pretty pitch deck! The purpose of venture capital is to allow companies to grow at an unnatural velocity in return for a large chunk of equity. Outcomes with a venture-financed business tend to be binary—home runs or strikeouts (e.g., IPO or bankruptcy). See the more lengthy discussion of venture capital starting on page 136.

  Structure: *Preferred equity.*

- **Angel Investors**

  While VC investors draw from funds of other people's money, angel investors are individuals investing their own money. This gives them more flexibility and the ability to make gut-level investment decisions (which early-stage investing usually is).

  Structure: *Typically, either convertible notes or simple agreements for future equity (SAFEs), both of which end up eventually as preferred equity. See glossary.*

- **Corporate Venture Capital**

  Many large corporations have corporate VC funds from which they make investments in startups that may have strategic value to the corporation. This fund is often allocated off of the business's balance sheet rather than as a standalone VC fund, causing CVCs to ebb and flow with the macromarkets and making them more or less active, accordingly. Many also look for a partnership to first be in place between the company and the startup or need it in conjunction with the financing in order to justify the strategic investment. Depending on the investment terms (e.g., customer exclusivity clauses), conflicts may arise in working with other customers deemed competitive, potentially limiting the growth of the startup. However, due to the strategic nature of the investment, CVCs tend to be more valuation-insensitive and flexible on the investment amount, since they are usually following other VCs rather than leading rounds and setting terms.

Structure: *Preferred equity but typically open to different investment vehicles since they are following rather than leading rounds (in most cases).*

- **Crowdfunding**

  Sites such as Kickstarter and Indiegogo primarily focus on creative projects (music, film, technology, art, design, etc.), not startup businesses, per se, because selling debt or equity gets into highly regulated territory. But product pre-sales on these platforms can be a great way to launch a startup. If you get ten thousand people to pledge to pre-purchase your product for one hundred dollars, boom! You've raised a million dollars and also proven market demand for your product! Meanwhile, sites such as AngelList can connect you with angel investors, and sites such as NextSeed provide platforms for entrepreneur fundraising,

  Structure: *Wide range, from term notes or revenue sharing notes to preferred equity.*

- **Equity-Based Accelerators**

  The most famous startup accelerator is Y Combinator, which offers a cash investment in return for around seven percent equity in your startup. There are many of these startup accelerators now, including several that are sector-specific. Alchemist is exclusively for enterprise-focused startups, and Miller Center is exclusively for social entrepreneurs (and does not take equity), for example. Not all come with cash funding, but all promise to accelerate your startup progress and introduce you to investors. A good list of accelerators can be found on AngelList.

Structure: *A very wide range, including SAFEs, an investment structure developed by Y Combinator.*

- **Revenue-Share Financing**
  I've seen several financing deals structured such that the startup pays a percentage of revenue to the investor, capped at a certain level. I recently participated in one as an investor, where I'll be paid five percent of the company's revenue until I've received 1.5 times my investment, and then the agreement terminates. This is especially well-suited to seasonal ventures since the payments are aligned with revenue every quarter.

  Structure: *A promissory note where the payment is defined as variable, based on revenue.*

- **Credit Cards**
  Don't do it. There is mythology about entrepreneurs who have launched a business by maxing out their credit cards and then gone on to be billionaires. It's pure bullshit. This approach will yield a 99.9-percent failure rate.

- **Customer Financing**
  Find a customer who wants your product so much they'll help finance your startup! Many software startups have financed themselves by finding a corporate customer to pay for custom-developed software implementation (which the startup then retains rights to productize and sell to others). In the defense industry, many startups have built an early prototype and then convinced the Department of Defense to provide the funding

to develop it further. This will look different for different sectors, of course, but customer financing is a tried-and-true way to launch and grow a startup.

Structure: *A statement of work and a purchase order, with IP rights clearly defined.*

- **Vendor Financing**

  I once started a business that needed some expensive capital equipment in order to get off the ground. I was stuck on how I was going to finance that until I met with the equipment vendors and realized they would finance it for me in order to get a new customer. It dramatically reduced my startup capital needs.

  Structure: *Variable.*

- **Venture Debt**

  Almost all venture capital is structured as equity, but there is a category called "venture debt" offered by certain banks and specialty finance firms. It is typically used alongside a venture capital equity round, with the venture debt component used to purchase capital equipment, for example.

  Structure: *Like a bank loan but with warrants added in to compensate the lender for the higher risk.*

- **Impact Funds**

  Are you starting up a social enterprise that will save the world? Great news—there are funds to pitch for that! Until a few years ago, social enterprises were difficult to finance—they weren't "nonprofit enough" for grant capital from foundations, but they were "for-profit enough" for venture capital. A whole new asset class has since appeared: impact capital, which typically comes from impact funds that have been put together partly for social impact in a particular sector and partly to provide an economic return on capital. Examples include New Schools Venture Fund (for startups working in the education sector) and Acumen (focused on global poverty).

Structure: *Wide variety (see Chapter 11).*

- **Social Impact Bonds**

  These are increasingly being used to finance social ventures. Despite the name, they aren't really a bond in the traditional sense. It's more of a pay-for-performance agreement. Let's say your startup has an innovative way to address homelessness in a particular city, and you'll need a million dollars to run the program. You draw up a social impact bond in which perhaps a private investor puts up the million dollars, and the city agrees to pay down the bond by $250,000 for each X-percent reduction in homelessness achieved, capped at a million dollars. If all goes well, the city is happy that the homelessness rate was reduced, the investor is pleased to have made a difference and also got their capital returned, and your social venture ended up with a million dollars.

- **SBA Loans**

  The US Small Business Administration can help you finance your business. They don't make the loans themselves but instead guarantee bank loans. The idea is that banks can make startup loans riskier than they would normally issue, and the SBA is helping US businesses to grow, succeed, and create jobs. Use their Lender Match tool to find SBA-approved lenders.

- **Non-Bank Business Lenders**

  Traditional banks are highly regulated, so they tend not to have much flexibility in their credit underwriting. Meanwhile, there are some new sources of business loans, including Kabbage, a non-bank lender that uses a variety of factors (including social media activity) in their credit decisions. Sites such as Fundera allow you to fill out one loan application, and then they shop around for deals among a variety of business funding sources. Peer-to-peer marketplaces such as LendingClub offer business loans up to five hundred thousand dollars from non-bank sources.

- **Alternative Growth Capital**

  There is a growing awareness that neither traditional venture capital nor traditional bank lending is well-suited to many online businesses today. A relatively new entrant, Clearco, addresses this with revenue-share financing specifically to fund the growth of businesses with positive CAC:LTV ratios. They deploy up to ten million dollars in capital in return for a revenue share capped at the capital infused plus six percent. I think we will see many more of these alternatives to venture capital emerge.

Here's the point: There are a lot of great ways to finance a startup venture today—more than ever before in history. It's not just venture capital, so expand the solution set in your mind and consider all the options. Venture Capital was an excellent fit for companies like Uber and Airbnb that needed to scale massively at an unnatural pace, with a billion-dollar IPO at the end.

For other kinds of startups, a different approach may be better. Ultimately what matters is alignment of incentives between investors, founders, and employees. The following pages will hopefully help you in making the right choice for your venture.

FLAVORS OF CAPITAL
(Grants, Debt, Equity)

All capital that goes into an organization is either **grants, debt,** or **equity**. It's essential to understand the differences between the three because they are very different animals.

Grants are largely associated with nonprofits and social ventures (see Chapter 11). A nonprofit working to alleviate poverty in East Africa might get a grant from the Gates Foundation to improve their distribution infrastructure, for example. Sometimes for-profit companies may qualify for government grants as well. Many state and local agencies provide grants to help small businesses grow in a way that helps local economies and employment. The distinguishing characteristic of a grant is that there is no expectation of it being paid back. It's not exactly free money because often there are a variety of strings attached to it, but it is neither debt nor equity on your financial statements.

Debt is an easy concept for anyone with a bank loan or a credit card to understand. If a company borrows money, they have an obligation to repay the lender—principal plus interest—incrementally over a specified amount of time. The lender has no claim to any ownership of the company nor to any future company profits beyond repayment of principal plus interest.

Equity is sort of the opposite of debt. An equity holder has claim to a percentage ownership of the company and a percentage share of all its future profits but no claim to any repayment of the capital they invested. When a venture capitalist invests in return for twenty percent equity, there is no repayment obligation, but they now own twenty percent of your company and a claim to twenty percent of all its future profits. The reason they invested is not because they expect you to pay the money back. They invested because when you sell the company for a billion dollars, they will get twenty percent of the money!

Debt vs Equity, Pros and Cons

Your parents probably told you that debt is evil and you should avoid it. They're not wrong, of course, but for companies, debt is actually cheaper than equity.

Say you had one source of capital offering you five hundred thousand dollars in debt financing at a six-percent interest rate amortized over five years. You also have another source of capital whispering in your ear, "Don't take that! I'll give you the same amount, but I'll structure it as twenty percent of your company's equity—no loan payments at all!"

Before you choose which one sounds better, let's look at the math. The debt capital will cost you $79,984 in interest, spread over five years (and that interest is fully tax deductible for the company to the extent it offsets earnings). If you think $79,984 is more expensive than twenty percent of all the company's future profits and equity, then I have some pretty serious concerns about your expectations for the venture.

The problem, of course, is that most startups don't have the creditworthiness to get the loan, nor do they have the cash flow to service the debt. That's why the venture capital industry was created: to make a ton of money from equity financing for companies that can't qualify for debt financing.

You may end up choosing equity financing for your startup, but don't fool yourself into thinking it's a better economic deal than debt financing; it's probably not.

VENTURE CAPITAL

As I've emphasized, venture capital is not right for every startup. But if you decide you want to go hiking along the venture capital trail, here is everything you need to know for your journey! Wear good boots for this hike; it may get muddy.

The standard Silicon Valley progression

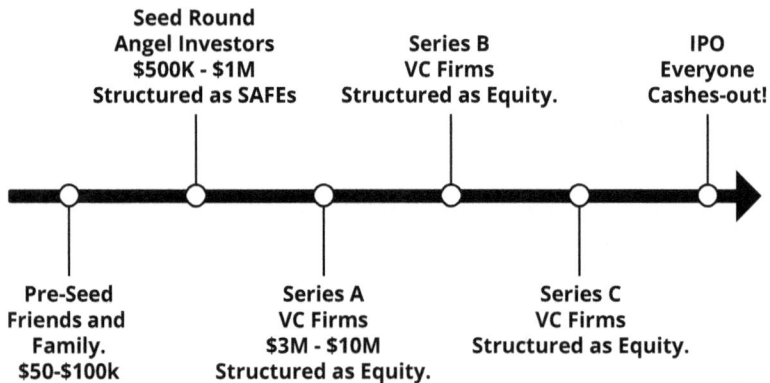

Seed Round
Angel Investors
$500K - $1M
Structured as SAFEs

Series B
VC Firms
Structured as Equity.

IPO
Everyone
Cashes-out!

Pre-Seed
Friends and
Family.
$50-$100k

Series A
VC Firms
$3M - $10M
Structured as Equity.

Series C
VC Firms
Structured as Equity.

It's typically a series of financings

The illustration above shows the typical financing progression of a venture-funded company. It usually begins with a little bit of pre-seed money from friends and family, then a seed round from angel investors structured as either convertible notes or SAFEs, and then the first round from a venture capital fund, then maybe additional rounds of venture capital, and then eventually an IPO (where stock is sold to the public), and all the equity holders get rich. Venture capital financings are typically called Series A, Series B, etc., because in the old days would print out a series of stock certificates after each equity financing round. Today, stock certificates are typically digital and managed by a service like Carta, but the naming convention lives on.

These are equity financings

Venture capital financing is nearly always structured as equity. Seed-stage financing might be structured initially as a convertible note or a SAFE, but those instruments eventually turn into equity.

Equity holders are looking for eventual liquidity and exit

The whole reason an investor would want to buy equity in your company is so that when you sell the company to Google for a billion dollars or have an IPO, they will be able to sell their equity at a large premium over what they paid for it. Remember that venture capital is not debt; there is no repayment obligation, so they are looking to sell their equity at some point in order to get liquidity.

Lawyers will love you

In venture capital financing, you are selling stock to private investors, which is tightly regulated by the US Securities and Exchange Commission (SEC). You will need a good law firm for this process, and it will be very expensive. One of the reasons that early (seed-stage) financing is done as SAFEs is that you're not actually selling stock; you're selling an instrument that can be redeemed for stock later, so the legal fees are much lower. Eventually, you have to pay the piper, and in the Series A financing, everything goes to equity, and you will need a good law firm. Don't be surprised if the term sheet from the venture capital firm says that your startup will pay their legal fees as well as your own. As unfair as that sounds, it's their way of having all the costs of the financing transaction come from the fund.

First, dance with angels

Seed-stage financing typically comes from angel investors (individuals investing their own money), not VC funds. Because angels are investing their own money, they can make the sort of gut-level investment decisions an early-stage startup needs. You don't yet have any operating history, you don't have any technology, you're just a passionate entrepreneur, certain they can be successful. You need someone who just believes in you and that will typically be an angel investor rather than a venture capital fund.

Then, the venture capital ball

Venture capital firms typically invest after there's some operating history, the idea has been proven, risk has been mitigated, and your company is ready to scale. As a VC friend of mine says, "I'm looking for just-add-money opportunities." Most VC firms don't come in at the idea stage, they come in at the ready-to-scale stage.

There will be math

Equity Financing Math:

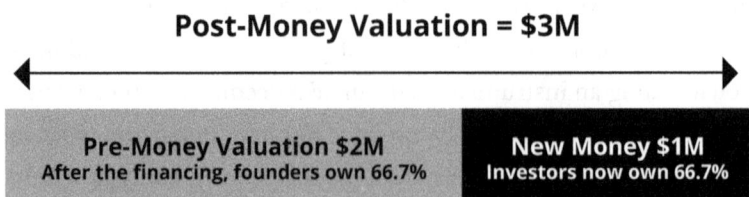

Post-Money Valuation = $3M

Pre-Money Valuation $2M	New Money $1M
After the financing, founders own 66.7%	Investors now own 66.7%

Equity financing always follows one simple formula: the percentage of the company owned by the investors equals the amount they invested divided by the post-money valuation of the company. Let's say we have a company currently valued at two million dollars (pre-money valuation), and the investors are dropping one million dollars in cash into the company (new money). After the financing, the company is worth what it was worth before, plus the new cash in the bank, a total of three million dollars (post-money valuation), so the investors now own 33.3 percent of the company. Because math.

Valuation matters

In the formula above—which applies to every single equity financing—the math is very easy. The hard part is determining the company's valuation before the financing (the pre-money valuation). This is especially true of early-stage companies with no operating history. It's just a passionate team and a bunch of optimistic slides—how do you objectively put a dollar value on that? Sometimes founders and investors will back into the formula; in other words, if the investor says, "If I put a million dollars in at this point, I would expect to own a third of the company," and the founder ponders that and responds, "I think that's reasonable, a million dollars for a third of the company's equity," then you have just implicitly agreed upon a pre-money valuation of two million dollars. It's the exact same math.

Liquidation preferences rule

Equity investors want to be first in line when the company is sold or wound down, so they will ask for preferred stock to represent their equity. This stock has a liquidation preference, meaning that when the company is liquidated (either through a sale or a wind-down), they get money before common shareholders (you and your employees). This preference will typically be an amount equal to their investment. In other words, if they invested a million dollars, when the company is liquidated they will get the first million, and then the rest of the money is evenly distributed amongst all the shareholders. In some instances, they may ask for 2x liquidation preferences, meaning they're putting a million in, but if the company is liquidated, they get the first two million before anything goes to you and your employees. This is a crucial point to understand.

Understanding voting rights

Some entrepreneurs fear that VCs just want to take over your business and fire you. Actually, this is pretty much the opposite of what they want to do. Their whole model depends on you doing all the hard work to run the company while they relax and make money! But it's essential to understand how corporate governance works and what rights they are requesting as part of their investment. The standard corporate governance is that shareholders elect a board of directors, and the board hires and fires the CEO. So, if the investors own thirty percent of the company, and you own seventy percent, then you still control the board, which means you still control the CEO. But the term sheet they present to you when offering financing may have slightly different rules. A typical term sheet might say there will be a five-person board with three members chosen by the common shareholders (you) and two members chosen by the preferred shareholders (them). Just pay attention to what you are agreeing to, and make sure it keeps everyone's interests well-aligned!

Get familiar with how the VC business works

If you're gonna pitch to VCs, it's important to understand how their business works. Venture capitalists manage other people's money, much like a mutual fund. When the general partners decide to raise a fund, they go out and pitch individuals and organizations on putting money into that fund; these are called limited partners. Two percent of the fund annually goes toward operating expenses (like fancy offices on

Sand Hill Road) every year. After ten years, the fund is dissolved, and eighty percent of the profits are paid out to the limited partners, while twenty percent go to the general partners who managed the fund and made the investment decisions. This is called the "two and twenty" system and is used by nearly every VC firm.

Most of the money in venture funds comes from pension plans, university endowments, and other large institutional investors. It is a business about high-risk/high-return investments with binary outcomes: each investment ends up either bankrupt or worth billions. Historically, about seventy-five percent of a venture fund's investments fail, but the other twenty-five percent succeed wildly and make the whole fund a success. The average partner at a VC firm will look at somewhere around 400 startups a year and invest in 4 of them.

What does all this mean for you?

As with anything else, you'll always do better in negotiations if you understand the other party's world. In that context, here are what the above points mean to you:

- Because they're not investing their own money, a VC firm has a fiduciary responsibility to its investors (limited partners). This is a key concept to understand. Angel investors, on the other hand, are investing their own money and so have a wider latitude in their investment decisions.
- If you're looking for a little bit of money to create a nice little business, it's just not a fit for traditional venture capital. Their model depends on finding billion-dollar unicorns. Because they are buying equity, the only way they make money is from eventually selling the company (either to an acquiring company or through an IPO).

- A fund's lifespan is typically ten years, and a venture firm typically has several different funds under management at any given time. The first two to three years of a fund is spent making investments, the next three to four is sitting on boards and managing those investments, and the final two to three is trying to get liquidity on those investments by selling the company or aiming it toward an IPO. You should always ask which fund they might be investing from and what the current life-cycle stage is for that fund.

- As with any asset class, venture capital firms want to put together a diversified investment portfolio. They may say "no" to you just because they already have some investments like your startup and are now trying to round out the portfolio with some different sorts of startups.

Cap Tables (avoid my mistakes!)

In the world of venture-funded startups, few documents are as consequential as the capitalization table (commonly called a Cap Table). Conceptually, it's just a list of who owns what percentage of the company. But it can get complicated in a hurry, with co-founder agreements, stock options issued, lawyers who hold stock warrants, investors who own preferred shares, advisors who were promised equity, and many other twists and turns.

It becomes a sacred document, and every investor you talk to for each round of financing will ask for a current cap table. Your lawyers will need it. The bank will ask for it. Contracts with large customers will sometimes require that you provide a copy. You will be asked to sign affidavits attesting to its accuracy. It's the Rosetta Stone for your company's equity structure.

One of the most embarrassing (and expensive) experiences in my career was when I sold a company; everything with the transaction was going great, and we all felt great about it. Suddenly, an angel investor from many years earlier said, "Hey, remember, you said you'd give me some extra shares for that additional help I gave you?" I had no memory of it, and it wasn't represented on the cap table, but he produced documentation that I had indeed promised him those shares. When I brought this up to the other shareholders, they shrugged and said, "That's not our problem; it's not on the cap table." In the end, I had to pay the guy $130,000 out of my own pocket to make good on the promise I had made but never entered on the cap table. Ouch. Be smarter than me.

The good news is that what was once a hairy Excel file being forwarded around is now typically kept centralized in an online service like Carta. Pretty much everyone is doing it this way these days, which at least makes the cap table easier to manage (and there's one canonical copy).

Dilution Happens (here's how to mitigate)

Each round of financing dilutes everyone on the cap table, so a series of financings can result in pretty substantial dilution for the founders. Today, Mark Zuckerberg only owns 12.8 percent of the company he founded (but let's not cry too much for him).

Dilution also happens every time you create stock option plans for your employees, give stock warrants to key partners, and give stock options to advisors. Every startup founder wants to preserve equity for themselves but also wants to use equity to drive the venture's success. Here is some advice to keep in mind with regard to dilution of your founder equity:

Make sure everything is carefully documented! In the embarrassing story I told you above, I gave out some shares and then forgot to record it on the cap table. This is surprisingly common and can be an expensive mistake (it certainly was for me).

Don't raise more money than you need. In another one of my many mistakes, I was once shopping for a five-hundred-thousand-dollar seed round and got talked into five million. It's seductive to be offered more than you were looking for, but you're also giving away more equity in the company than you need to.

Use SAFEs cautiously. SAFEs are a commonly used lightweight seed-stage investment instrument that isn't equity today but turns into equity in the future based on pre-defined terms (see the glossary in the reference section of this book). I've seen founders hand out SAFEs like tissue paper, then two years later when the SAFEs convert to equity, they are horrified at the dilution (see glossary at the back of the book).

Do cap table modeling. Use a good tool like Carta to model different cap-table scenarios so that you choose a financing path (through multiple financing rounds) that yields an optimized equity outcome for you and your co-founders.

Beware the full ratchet. Make sure you have a really good attorney to consult with before you accept any term sheet from an investor. They may well be asking for terms that sound reasonably innocuous on a term sheet but have the potential of being painfully dilutive in the future.

Vesting schedules are your friend. A vesting schedule simply means that when you give stock to an employee, they have to stay with the company for a certain number of years in order to get the full amount. Make sure that any stock you give out is on a vesting schedule, even for co-founders. The Silicon Valley standard is four years. I've seen cap tables show that the company is twenty percent owned by a co-founder who quit two weeks into the venture and whom nobody has heard from in five years. That's not a good look.

These are just a few of the steps you can take to optimize your founder equity as you grow your company. There are many other considerations, including a right of first refusal associated with stock agreements. Having a good corporate attorney is key.

Underrepresented startup founders

There has been a lot of attention focused in recent years on the fact that less than three percent of all US venture capital has historically gone to startups led by women and even less to founders of color.

That is a troubling fact. I would like to think it's much different now, moving forward, but we'll have to see where the numbers sit in a few years.

There was a time when almost all the venture capitalists on Sand Hill Road were middle-aged white guys who went to business school at either Stanford or Harvard. Human nature is such that after you've been successful, you tend to think that success looks like you, so you (consciously or unconsciously) find people who look like you to invest in.

Fortunately, today, if you look at any VC firm's investing partners, you will see more diversity than ever before. The past twenty years have seen people of all stripes develop very successful careers and then go into venture capital. While the problem still exists, to be sure, we now have a generation of diverse people making investment decisions, and we're seeing more diversity in the founders they invest in. Hopefully, this is a trend that continues.

I've been seeing an increasing number of venture capital firms put a diversity rider into their term sheets with text similar to this:[1]

> *"In order to advance diversity efforts in the venture capital industry, the Company and the lead investor, [Fund Name], will make commercial best efforts to offer and make every attempt to include as a co-investor in the financing at least one Black [or other underrepresented group including, but not limited to LatinX, women, LGBTQ+] check writer (DCWs), and to allocate a minimum of [X]% or [X] $'s of the total round for such co-investor."*

There is still much work to be done in order to create true diversity and equity. There are many great organizations out there helping to support underrepresented founders, including All Raise, How Women Invest, Project W, and many more. I keep an updated list of all these, with links, on thelaunchpath.com

Venture Capital Summary

Venture capital is the most expensive possible sort of capital, so you need to be sure that it's worth the price, for your venture. Many startups have decided that it's worth the price to be able to scale at a pace faster than you could ever scale organically. For companies like Uber and Airbnb, this turned out to be a good choice. For others, it may not be. Make sure it's the right choice for you and your venture before you start down the venture-capital path.

With any financing structure, what you're looking for is alignment of interests. Successful financing occurs when the investors' interests are well-aligned with the founders' and employees'. Make sure you review term sheets carefully and make sure you have a good attorney (one who

---

1: I got this one from cooleygo.com—they have an excellent set of tools and document generators.

knows the startup and venture capital worlds) who can advise you and help you think through various scenarios.

Many great companies have been scaled using venture capital with satisfying outcomes for all. Many others have crashed because venture capital wasn't really the right choice. Make sure you look at all the different ways to finance your startup, then choose the one that's the best fit for you and your venture.

RUNNING A FUNDRAISING EFFORT

So you've decided you want to go find some equity investors for your startup? Excellent! Be aware that it will take you longer than you think, and it will be hard on your ego because you will experience a lot of rejection, so it's important to use a structured process and approach it with intention. Let me give you my top ten tips for hitting the equity fundraising trail:

1. **It's a numbers game.**

   I recently had a call with a founder who told me he'd just closed a nice round of capital. Over the past year, he had more than one hundred investor conversations. Of those, forty-two requested more information, twenty-three requested a third meeting, eleven submitted the deal to the partnership for an investment decision, four issued term sheets, and two invested. These numbers are actually pretty decent.

2. **Play the long game.**

   The same founder also said that he kept investors engaged for many months—even those who had said "no." Over the year, he sent out quarterly updates to every investor he talked to, circled back with them about concerns they had expressed, and kept them informed as milestones were achieved. Raising capital is a sales process, and the sell cycle can be long. You're not going to pitch on Tuesday and have a term sheet on Wednesday. Play the long game, and you will succeed.

3. **Don't visit devils if you're looking for angels.**

   Angel investors will invest at the idea stage; VCs typically will not. I've seen founders waste a lot of time pitching to the wrong people. Research the right investors and funds beforehand.

4. **Solid economics are more important than ever.**

Remove from your brain the mythology that investors will drop cash into crazy-ass ideas with no clear monetization. Investors today want to see opportunities where the founders have already proven the economic model, and it's ready to scale. It all comes down to CAC < LTV, baby (see Chapter 5). You may not have actual data yet, but you need to have a compelling story about how the economics will come together.

5. **Cold calls aren't efficient.**

Every investor I've ever had in my career was either someone I knew socially or referred to me by someone I knew socially. Most VCs I know say they've never invested in a deal that came in over the transom. Focus your energy on getting warm introductions, and you will be 100x more effective in your fundraising efforts. Sending out cold emails is lazy and ineffective. Building relationships is difficult and takes longer but is far more effective.

6. **Ask for introductions.**

Here's a secret hack: Let's say you hear of an investor you think would be a perfect match for your startup, but you don't know them and would like an introduction. Find out what other startups they have invested in (use Crunchbase or PitchBook), and then reach out to one of the founders and see if they'd be willing to have a call just to get input on your startup idea. At the end of the call, assuming they seem friendly enough, ask whether they'd be willing to make an introduction. The point is that, as I mentioned, warm introductions will always be more effective than cold calls, so find ways to get them.

7. **Ask for advice (get money).**

There's an old expression: "If you want advice, ask for money. If you want money, ask for advice," and this maps pretty well to my own experience. When you pitch an investor for money, they are likely to say, "No," but then give you a whole lot of unsolicited advice that may or may not be helpful. Conversely, if you flatter an investor by asking whether they'd be willing to have a call with you so you can get their sage advice, they may well end the call by saying, "I like this thing you're working on; are you looking for investors right now?" Human nature is what it is.

8. **Don't look for peaches in the berry store.**

Don't pitch your early-stage SaaS startup to a growth-stage biotech investor. Every investor has a stage and sector focus. If you have a social venture, focus on impact funds, not traditional venture funds. If you have a digital health startup, find investors who focus on that niche. Taking the time to understand an investor's stage and sector focus will make your fundraising much more effective.

9. **Double down on storytelling skills.**

Every great entrepreneur has the ability to tell a crisp, clear, and compelling story about what they're working on and why it matters. The more you pitch, the better you get. The more you pitch, the more you learn. The more you pitch, the more opportunities you have to get a referral. It has always been thus (see Chapter 8).

10. **It's a sales process. Use sales tools.**

The fundraising trail is like any other sales process, so utilize the great sales tools available to you. Use customer relationship management (CRM) software for tracking every touchpoint, consider upgrading to LinkedIn Sales Navigator for research, use DocSend when you send out your deck, and then HubSpot for sending out updates and tracking opens. Treat your fundraising like a professional sales process—because that's precisely what it is.

You are going to hear a lot of no's, and you need to refrain from taking them personally. Startup investors want a diversified portfolio, so they may say "No," just because they already have a SaaS startup in their portfolio and now they are looking for an AI chatbot. Or a thousand other reasons, so don't ever take it personally.

As I was writing this chapter, I reached out to my friend Gleb who recently completed a successful seed-stage fundraising effort. I asked him what advice he would give new founders. He responded: "There's only one answer: do the damn work. Research plus execution equals success. There are no shortcuts, unfortunately. Increase the number of shots on goal to maximize opportunity." Be like Gleb.

Conventional wisdom once dictated that you should set a minimum investment threshold for seed-stage fundraising from angel investors. For example, you might say, "We're raising a six-hundred-thousand-dollar round, and we're looking for investors who would like to join with a minimum of fifty thousand dollars." Today, however, seed financing rounds are typically done with SAFEs, so transaction costs are low—an investor sends you the money, and you just send them back a SAFE. This means that there's really no reason to set a minimum. In fact, there are lots of upsides to having a bunch of excited investors at any monetary level. So, if someone is really excited about investing and they want to put in five thousand dollars, take it. You never know who they might introduce you to.

Running a startup fundraising process requires dedication and intention, and it will probably consume more of your time than you expect. Treat it like any other sales process: make sure you have the right tools, are pitching the right people, remain diligent in your follow-ups, and track every touchpoint. Play the long game, and build strong relationships. If you do that, you will succeed.

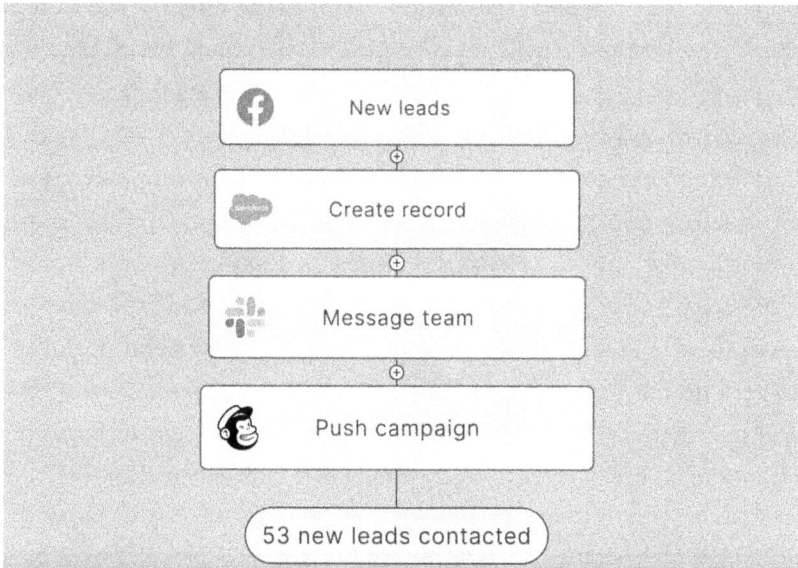

Case Study:
ZAPIER

When Wade Foster, Bryan Helmig, and Mike Knoop attended the 2011 Missouri Startup Weekend, they hacked together a way to automate the transfer of data from one web application to another. For example, maybe every time a new lead was entered into a Google spreadsheet, you also wanted it automatically added to your Salesforce database. It was a cool piece of code, but it wasn't yet clear that this could grow into an actual company. By the end of the weekend, they had, as co-founder Wade Foster said, "a barely functioning prototype and no clue what people wanted."

They started trolling online forums in search of the integrations people were looking for. For example, they would find a post from someone hoping to import PayPal transaction data into the Highrise CMS, and they'd add that to their list of integrations they could build. One day, they saw that a guy named Andrew Warner was looking for a particular integration, and they contacted him directly. As Foster said later, "I hate being cold-emailed with a sales pitch, so I intentionally try to avoid selling him on anything. I was just trying to find out if this is still a problem for him." It was, so the Zapier co-founders wrote a custom integration and sent it to Warner. He loved it and asked how much he owed them. Thinking quickly, they responded, "It's one hundred dollars to get into our beta program." Andrew Warner was pleased with that and sent them the money, but they had no company bank account and no way to accept payments, so they took care of both quickly.

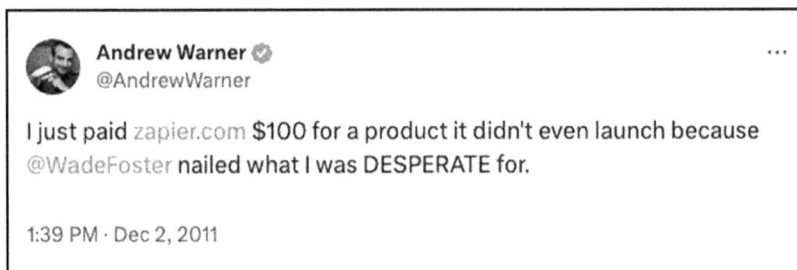

Andrew Warner ✅
@AndrewWarner   ...

I just paid zapier.com $100 for a product it didn't even launch because @WadeFoster nailed what I was DESPERATE for.

1:39 PM · Dec 2, 2011

The team continued to scour online forums for several months. If they saw several posts on Stack Overflow from users looking for a way to automatically transfer data between Stripe and a Google Spreadsheet, for example, they would write a script that would do that. They applied to Y Combinator, were rejected, but then tried again and were accepted into the next batch. Later that year, they raised a seed round of 1.3 million dollars from a total of six investors, including Y Combinator.

Today, Zapier has more than five hundred employees, is very profitable, and supports over four thousand different integrations, allowing users to connect all sorts of web applications without needing to write a single line of code. The best part of this story? They never raised any capital other than that first seed round. Sequoia, the legendary Sand Hill Road venture capital firm, has tried desperately to invest and has repeatedly been rebuffed by the founders. Finally, in April of 2021, the founders agreed to sell a few of their own shares to Sequoia—at a company valuation of more than five billion dollars.

KEY TAKEAWAYS:

I am a fan of Zapier. It's a great product, I use it all the time, and I love some of the lessons that are embedded in their story of success.

◊ Founders need to be awesome salespeople. The fact that Foster trolled posts reached out directly, and sold a deal was what got them rolling. Nothing is going to work if the founders can't sell.

◊ You're looking for a problem that people are willing to pay to have solved. Foster could have easily given that first integration away for free, but by naming a price—and having the customer eagerly accept—they knew they had something worth pursuing.

◊ Zapier could have easily raised wheelbarrows full of additional capital—they had the big-name VC firms begging to get in— but they preferred to grow the company organically, solving real problems for real customers and building one happy customer on top of the next. As a result, the founders are still majority shareholders of a profitable company with a valuation of five billion dollars.

Economics

What are the Unit Economics for this venture, what do we expect the CAC<LTV to look like, and what are out capital needs? (Link to full spreadsheet).

One unit = one average order: $15, on which our gross profit is $8.50.

Early tests indicate CAC of $11, and we expect an initial LTV of three orders per customer ($25.50), which will grow with time.

Our initial capital needs are $220K, which will get us through the pilot launch. We will propose to investors structuring this as a SAFE.

See full spreadsheet at this link.

The Launch Path Canvas
Lorem Ipsum

Name of Startup Venture: Fitaco, Inc

Date: November 8, 2023

Prepared by: Bret Waters

Iteration: 8

Problem
One clear sentence that articulates the problem your startup solves.

Consumers in the US spend $331 billion/year on fast food, and most of it is really unhealthy.

The paradox is that consumers today want to eat healthy, but also have a busy life that often drives them to resort to the convenience of fast food.

Solution
How does your venture solve the problem you have articulated? Keep this short and consise.

Fast food doesn't need to be unhealthy. Our startup is developing a new brand of heart-conscious fast food (healthy tacos!), delivered directly to your home or office.

Why it matters
Why is this a problem worth solving?

The National Institutes for Health say that today a fast food diet may kill more people prematurely every year than cigarette smoking.

Alternatives
When a customer looks at alternative ways to solve the problem we solve, what will they see? This is a list of competitors and alternatives. Link to a graphic representation of the landscape.

There are many many food delivery services, from Uber Eats to Doordash to Grubhub.

See visualization at this link.

Customer
It's all about understanding customers. Write a one-sentence description of key customer personas and the problem we solve for each. Circle the one that is most influential.

Adventurous Alex: A thrill-seeking foodie always on the hunt for unique and spicy taco creations to satisfy their daring palate.

Health-Conscious Haley: A fitness enthusiast looking for wholesome and fresh ingredient options that align with their nutritious lifestyle at the taqueria.

Busy Ben: An on-the-go professional seeking quick, flavorful, and portable taco choices to enjoy during a busy workday.

Vegetarian Victoria: A plant-based eater in search of flavorful and creative vegetarian and vegan taco selections that cater to their dietary preferences.

Traditional Tony: A lover of classic flavors, Tony enjoys indulging in authentic and time-honored taco recipes that remind him of his cultural heritage.

Path to PMF
What is our path to Product-Market Fit? Customer Development, MVP's, etc.

1. Farmers' markets where we can get input on our menu items.
2. One truck in the Palo Alto area for a pilot project.
3. Scale slowly to additional markets, based on our learnings.

Top 3 Benefits
What are the top 3 benefits that your product or services provides to customers?

1. Convenience. Use our mobile app to place a custom order and it's delivered directly to you.
2. Healthy food, designed by a nutritionist.
3. Tacos. Everybody loves tacos.

Distribution
What are our distribution channels? Direct to consumer, via resellers, or?

We intend to sell direct-to-consumer, via our mobile app and website, with delivery via our own vans.

In the future, we may be open to distribution partnerships.

Positioning
Within this landscape of competitors and alternatives, how is your venture positioned?

Our positioning can basically be summed-up in two words: healthy, and delicious.

There are many food delivery apps that can deliver something that is delicious but not very healthy. Or you could eat a kale salad.

We serve delicious tacos designed by a nutritionist. That's our unique positioning.

Family-Oriented Felix: A parent looking for a family-friendly meal delivery with a variety of options to cater to the taste preferences of both kids and adults.

Budget-Conscious Bella: A student or frugal diner in pursuit of affordable yet flavorful taco choices that won't break the bank at the taqueria.

Economics
What are the Unit Economics for this venture, what do we expect the CAC<LTV to look like, and what are out capital needs? (Link to full spreadsheet).

One unit = one taco: Sell price 45, on which our gross profit is 4.74

Early tests indicate CAC of $11, and we expect an initial LTV of three orders per customer ($25.50), which will grow with time.

Our initial capital needs are $220K, which will get us through the pilot launch. We will propose to investors structuring this as a SAFE.

See full spreadsheet at this link.

Team
What are the characteristics of the right team to make this venture a success?

The right team aligns with our target demographic - people who want to eat healthy and also enjoy the convenience of a quick taco meal.

The economics of our venture are such that we'll need drivers and cooks who are affordable, so we will work hard to make it an attractive part-time job for students, and a great evening second job for anybody.

Defensibility
What is your secret sauce that is difficult for competitors to copy?

The fact that we own the customer and customer data is a big part of our defensability.

A restaurant selling through a 3rd-party like Doordash owns neither the customer nor the data.

See full example at **thelaunchpath.com**

STEP 6, FOR YOUR STARTUP

Choosing the right capital strategy is a key to startup success. Fortunately today there are many different sources and structures of capital available to startup founders.

Assignment:

From the Economic Model that you created in Step 5, hopefully you have an idea of what the capital needs will be for the business. What are the total one-time expenses required even before operations begin? What's the total cash need for the first year? What's the point at which, realistically, the venture will turn cash-flow positive? Now, after reading thorugh Chapter 6, what financing structure that makes most sense for your startup?

Example:

For Fitaco, we will have $50K in one-time expenses before operations begin, and we'll likely be operating at a loss for the first 12 months (see spreadsheet). Equity financing may be the right structure, as we think this is the sort of company that could be sold in a few years to one of the large on-demand food brands. So with an equity structure we will have no debt payments, allowing us to reinvest all the profits, and investors will get liquidity in the future when the company is sold. Usually an equity financing requires agreeing on a current valuation of the company, but we'll suggest to investors that the financing be documented as a SAFE, which will then convert to equity later, a structure that deferrs the valuation question until we have some operating history.

"The purpose of a business is to create and keep a customer.

PETER DRUCKER

CHAPTER 7

FRAME A FUNNEL

Sales, marketing, advertising, and PR are all part of the most important function of all: getting customers

Most startups die from a lack of customers. Others die because they realize too late that the economics of their customer acquisition process are impossible to survive. Both are painful deaths, so let's try to avoid them.

As entrepreneurs, we're all optimists and so we tend to dramatically underestimate the effort that will be required to get customers. We all think our new product or service is so amazing that customers will just be lining up with cash in their hands, but it never works out that way.

And so my purpose with this chapter is to get you to start building and testing your customer acquisition process now, long before you have an actual product ready to sell. As with everything else on the **Launch Path** process, it's about continuous learning, optimization, and improvement.

Every venture is different, but customer acquisition is always a funnel.

You may have a business where getting customers is mostly old-fashioned sales calls, or maybe you're an e-commerce startup where it's all about online advertising, or maybe your new bakery is going to rely on local ads and neighborhood word-of-mouth. However, customer acquisition can always be visualized as a funnel. You need a whole bunch of leads coming in the top of the funnel, and then you slowly work those leads down through the funnel, and a certain percentage of them end up coming out of the bottom of the funnel as paying customers.

Let's say you're doing direct sales. You need to knock on 1,000 doors (top of the funnel) in order to get 35 people to invite you in. Of those, 18 ask you to send follow-up information (now they're in your funnel).

Awareness:
PR, podcasts, SEO, events, advertising, trade shows, content (blog posts, infographics, etc.), webinars, direct mail, viral campaigns, social media, search, media mentions

Interest:
emails, content that is more targeted around industries and brands, classess, newsletters

Consideration:
automated email campaigns, while continuing to nurture them with targeted content, case studies, free trials

Purchase:
Sign contract/enter credit card

Repeat:
Referral programs etc.

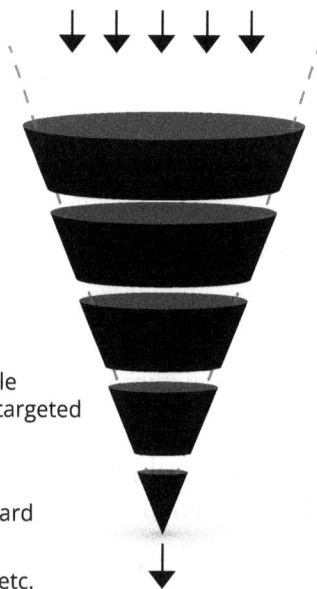

You follow up with them, giving them more information, and of those six end up making purchases (they come out the bottom of the funnel). So now we know that every 1,000 doors we knock on will result in 6 sales, and we can figure out ways to optimize that process. For any business, the customer acquisition process can be visualized as a funnel.

The illustration above shows the activities that companies today typically use for each stage in the funnel. The top of the funnel is all the stuff that makes people aware of your company—events, ads, podcasts, articles, etc. Hopefully, they will check out our website and enter their email address, and then we will follow up with them and give them more information. Hopefully, they'll come out the bottom of the funnel as a new paying customer.

Let's look at how the math works for a typical funnel. We run some ads, and 100,000 people visit our website, entering the top of our funnel. 20% of those give us their email address and enter the "interested" section of the funnel. 10% of those respond to our follow-up emails, converting to the "consideration" phase, and then 5% of those convert to "purchase." If you do the math, our ad campaign yielded 100 new customers. But what if we worked to optimize each conversion by just two percentage points (to 22%, 12% and 7%)? Now our yield is 185 new customers—an 85% increase in new customers! Optimizing each conversion point in the funnel is the key to success.

Now let's look at the economics. If we spent $1,000 on this campaign and got 100 new customers then our customer acquisition cost (CAC) was $10.00 each, right? But in the example above, if we optimize each funnel conversation point by two percentage points, then with the optimized funnel, our CAC is $5.41—that's a huge difference!

As we discussed in Chapter 5, in the end, the success or failure of any startup venture distills down to one equation—CAC < LTV. Read that sentence two or three more times, just to make sure you have fully internalized it.

SOME HIGH-LEVEL THOUGHTS ON MARKETING FOR STARTUPS:

While the particular marketing mix for your startup will depend on your particular type of business, here are some high-level thoughts that nearly always apply to startups everywhere.

Not all customers are equal

Two years from now, when you sit down and look at the numbers for your profitable startup, you will find that 80% of your profits are coming from 20% of your customers. It is nearly always true. And so, the sooner we can identify the high-value subset of customers for your venture, the better off we'll be. In Malcolm Gladwell's excellent book, *The Tipping Point*, he talks about how some members of any social structure are more influential than others. And so it is with the universe of potential customers for your startup. Some are more influential because they are respected by the community or because they are well-connected or because they are considered thought leaders that everyone looks to. So think about who the most influential people are for your product or service and target them. Targeting the right people can dramatically improve the efficiency of your customer acquisition effort.

Think about scaffolding customer segments

A few years ago, Geoffrey Moore wrote a book called Crossing the Chasm. In it, he discusses the fact that most startups can get an initial set of customers, but very few are able to "cross the chasm" and be able to get thousands (or millions) of customers, and he suggests a set of strategies that can help. His suggested methodology distills down to this straightforward concept: Start with a "beachhead" market, nail that one, and then add additional markets one at a time, using each one as a scaffold to the next. Many successful companies have done exactly this.

Owned Media, Earned Media, Paid Media

Your top-of-the-funnel will largely be people who heard about your startup from somewhere in the media landscape and are interested in finding out more. It's useful to think of the media landscape as having three components:

1. **Owned Media** is the stuff you own and have complete control over—your social media posts, your blog posts on Medium, your website, your landing pages
2. **Earned Media** is the added exposure you get because you've "earned" it, not because you've paid for it. These include social media likes, shares, and retweets of your owned media. Newspapers, magazines, and blogs who write about you because you're so awesome. Mentions on LinkedIn also count. And don't forget speaking slots you're offered at conferences because you are considered a thought leader.
3. **Paid Media** is all of your paid advertising. Here we have your paid search campaign on Google, your display ads on social media, your magazine ads, sponsored content, and the "influencers" you've paid to post about your product on Instagram.

You will need to generate activity in all three of those media types, and if you do, the media mentions will all help to drive each other. Remember, metrics matter, so you'll want to have a way of measuring where the leads into the top of the funnel are coming from, so that you can optimize, optimize, optimize.

Summary

Every venture will require a slightly different process for acquiring and keeping customers. For some, it will be more about a direct sales team that goes out making sales calls; for some, it's more about Instagram influencers; for others, it's more about Google search ads. But the funnel metaphor always applies, so think about how you will bring leads into the top of the funnel and how you will move those leads down through the funnel and turn them into paying customers. Most importantly, have processes in place by which you can measure and optimize each step of the funnel process, and make sure you use and optimize those processes too. In the end, your venture comes down to one simple equation: CAC < LTV. Focussing on the continuous improvement of your CAC is likely the single most important factor in making your startup a success.

THE NAME AND LOGO DILEMMA

Most entrepreneurs are passionate perfectionists who tend to have a lot of self-identity tied up in their new startup idea. So they **really** want to get their startup's name and logo right. My advice is not to get too hung up on this because the name and logo are probably less important than you think.

If you make a list of the top ten things that will make or break your startup, the name and logo aren't on the list. Plenty of companies with beautiful logos have failed miserably, and plenty of companies with terrible logos have succeeded brilliantly.

Similarly, many new entrepreneurs try too hard to come up with a company name that is meaningful. They spend endless hours trying to come up with a name that really expresses the essence of what the business does. And yet history indicates that a **short and meaningless** name is actually what usually wins. If you look at the most successful brand names throughout history, the vast majority of them are **two syllables and meaningless:** *Pepsi, Nike, Starbucks, Apple, FedEx, Yahoo, Google, Target, Nikon, Canon, Kodak, and Lego.* All of those billion-dollar brand names are **two syllables and meaningless.**

And yet some entrepreneurs agonize about coming up with a meaningful name for their startup. Just choose a name and push forward—it ain't that big a deal.

And whatever you do, **do not get paralyzed by the logo decision**. I've seen so many founders spend months and months agonizing about the logo until the entire startup opportunity has passed them by. Don't be one of those founders, either.

So focus on the things that will actually make or break your startup idea: **unit economics, Product-Market Fit, a sustainable economic model, a high-performing team, and a customer acquisition plan that works.** Thousands of startups have failed because they didn't get those things right. **No startup has ever failed because of the logo.** Focus on the things that matter. The beautiful logo can come later.

CUSTOMER PERSONAS

One of the most important things for any startup to do is to develop personas—descriptions of fictional people who represent typical customers for your venture. Some founders think this is a marketing exercise that some intern can do later after the product is built. Those founders are probably now broke and looking for a job. Don't be one of those.

Everything we know about successful product development is that it should be customer-centric in every way. Great products are developed by teams who **really understand customers, empathize with the problems they have, understand the ways customers currently solve those problems, and obsess about how our product can solve them better.** Writing personas is a critical part of this product development (and later on, personas will also be a big part of the successful marketing of that product).

Let's take a look at a very simple example. Let's say our new venture is an **on-demand service delivering healthy breakfasts.** We will likely have a few different customer segments, but let's start by writing personas on just two of them:

- **Single Sam** *is 25, lives alone, and hates cooking. Sometimes in the evening, he'll use DoorDash to get some dinner, but in the mornings, he usually just skips breakfast. A hot cup of coffee is all he needs to get him going. He's got a busy professional life, so he tends to just get up in the morning and jump right into work. He knows his mom says that breakfast is important, but who's got time for that?*

- **Mary the Mom Warrior** *is 36 and has two kids, 6 and 8. She's all about healthy living—she doesn't let her kids drink soda, she forces them to eat their vegetables, and definitely has a no-candy rule. But breakfast is a struggle. She's a working mom, so between getting the kids up and ready for school and getting herself ready for work, there just isn't much time for preparing a healthy fresh breakfast for the family.*

The point is to bring to the surface the fact that different customer segments care about slightly different things. In this example, **Single Sam** just really cares about time and not wanting to cook, whereas **Mary the Mom Warrior** is very much driven by wanting healthy meals for her kids.

Over time, you'll develop these further, add demographic and income data for each persona, add cute little illustrated portraits for each one, and more. If you Google "persona template," you will find many detailed examples of the ways to do this. Or, of course, you can just ask ChatGPT to write personas for you.

But for me, it starts by just writing a paragraph on each which you can then expand and iterate upon. Keep your personas in a shared doc where everyone on the team can refer to them. Most importantly, update them regularly as you continue to learn more about your customers and what they care about.

Like everything else in building a successful startup, it's about being customer-centric and iterating regularly based on what you learn. Start that process early by developing personas and referring to them obsessively.

BEGIN MARKETING NOW

There are many benefits to starting marketing operations for your startup long before you are actually ready to start selling products and services. Customer acquisition always ends up being harder than you think it's going to be, so begin the process of building a marketing foundation now.

Here's my quick list of (nearly free) things every startup should do long before you are actually ready to start selling products and services:

Landing Page. Don't put off building your startup's website, thinking that you need time to develop content and hire a designer. Just get a quick landing page up! Use one of the many DIY platforms such as Wix, Squarespace, WordPress, etc. Get a nice photo for free from Unsplash, write a few sentences about your startup, and say, *"Launching soon- sign up here to find out more!"*. While you're at it, make sure you install Google Analytics on your landing page. It's free. You can get all of this done in less than an hour.

Collect Emails. Growing an email list of followers is essential, so when people arrive on your landing page, you want to make it easy for them to enter their email address for future updates. You can use the free versions of MailChimp or HubSpot to create a sign-up form on your new landing page and keep your email list in a way that is fully compliant with all the privacy and spam laws. **Get on the Socials.** It costs you nothing to create accounts for your startup on Facebook, Instagram, LinkedIn, Twitter, TikTok, etc. Start posting things that are relevant to the sort of customers your startup will be targeting, with links to your landing page. For almost all startups today, a social media presence is important for getting awareness.

Be in the news. As the founder of a new startup, you want to start building your personal brand around being an expert in the field. Write an interesting article on Medium and then post it to all your socials. Publish a LinkedIn article and share it with your network. Find online magazines that are looking for contributors and submit an article to them (here are the submission guidelines for Business Insider, BuzzFeed, Fast Company, TechCrunch, and the New York Times). Always make sure anything you publish has a link to your startup's landing page, of course. Also, get yourself signed up on Help a Reporter Out (HARO)—if a Wall Street Journal reporter is writing an article about your sector, you want them to contact you for a quote to include in the article!

Find out what people are searching for. Free tools such as Google Trends, Answer the Public, and UberSuggest will give you insight into what people are searching for online. This will help you craft articles and posts that will align with current search traffic, plus it will give you market visibility that will help inform all of your marketing efforts.

Be active in online communities. If you've developed a new brand of ice cream, you'll want to join all the different online groups for ice cream lovers. Check out Facebook Groups, Reddit, Slack groups, and Quora, and find groups that are relevant to your venture. Join the conversation. It costs nothing, you'll learn a lot, and you'll develop leads that will end up being valuable for your startup.

Create content that performs well. Ultimately what matters is not just generating content; it's generating content that engages well and ultimately drives traffic to your startup's landing page and email signup. Tools like BuzzSumo can help you to find what sort of content performs best.

Stalk your competitors. Browsing review sites such as G2, Captara, and Product Hunt will give you insights into what consumers are saying about your competitors. This will not only help you to understand the competitive landscape, it will also give you ideas on the sort of messaging, and content that will resonate well with your audience.

A "sweet" example of early marketing:

One year in my Stanford course, our fictional venture was "Uber for fresh-baked cookies." Just push a button on your phone, and fresh cookies will arrive at your doorstep. Our assumption was that young men would be our typical customer persona—they get the munchies at midnight, and don't know how to make cookies, so they will order some from us. We spent $50 on some social media ads just to test the idea, and upon looking at the demographic that was responding to our ads, and were surprised that the core demographic clicking on our ads was women over fifty. So we reached out to some, and they told us the reason they had responded to the ad was that freshly delivered cookies looked like something they would like to give as a gift to someone. So, for $50, we uncovered a key insight: we thought men in their 20's would be our early customers, but it turned out that women over 50 loved the idea of giving our product as a gift to someone!

Not only that, we gathered some key metrics because $50 in ad spend yielded 15,260 impressions, 235 clicks, and 17 direct inquiries. Now we can start to project what our Customer Acquisition Cost will be, based on some actual data instead of just wild-ass guesses.

The point of this "sweet" story about cookies is that we live in an era where some initial marketing is incredibly inexpensive, and the data gathered can be incredibly informative. Don't wait until your product is complete before beginning some marketing activities.

Summary:

Even if your startup is many months away from actually having a product or service to sell, executing on some of the ideas listed above will give you insights, data, leads, and online equity that will dramatically improve your odds of success.

Great entrepreneurs know that successful startup methodology means doing <u>customer development</u> while doing product development.

Case Study:
FARMGIRL FLOWERS

I first met Christina Stembel when she was a twenty-something staff member at Stanford, organizing alumni events for the law school. As part of her job, she would buy thousands of dollars worth of flower arrangements for events and was dismayed at how expensive they were, how crappy the quality was, and the fact that after the event, the flowers all got tossed into the trash. Eventually, she became passionate about creating a better solution for the cut-flower business and quit her job at Stanford to found Farmgirl Flowers.

Excited about her new startup, her plan for the new venture had some specific ideas based on several assumptions:

- **Most customers would be men buying for women.**
  Christina assumed most customers would be men buying for women, and so she shaped the offering around an ordering process that would appeal to men, with arrangements that would be loved by the women who received them.

- **One featured arrangement each day.**
  Her belief was that people (men, especially) didn't like scrolling through the huge selections of the big floral companies but instead would like the idea of one easy choice that changed daily.

- **Priced well below competitors.**
  Christina wanted to be the low-cost leader in a field filled with expensive floral companies. She believed that the inherent efficiency of one arrangement per day would give her the dramatic cost savings to drive her positioning of offering a lower price point than her competitors.

- **Strong commitment to environmentalism.**
  Combining her personal belief set with what she saw as a positioning opportunity, Christina wanted to be the floral delivery company with the smallest carbon footprint. She'd source only locally-grown flowers, delivery would be by bicycle, and the one-arrangement-per-day model would dramatically reduce the flower industry's notoriously high wastage.

With those assumptions, she went about the process of getting the business ready to launch. Christina wanted to create a unique brand that was in keeping with her eco-friendly vibe, so she wrapped each flower arrangement in fabric from discarded burlap sacks that had been used to transport foods like potatoes and coffee beans.

With excitement, she launched the initial version of the Farmgirl Flowers website. As orders came in, Christina would build the arrangements in the dining room of her San Francisco apartment and then have them delivered by bicycle. By personally fulfilling each other, she was able to keep costs very low as she learned about her customers and tested her assumptions.

She found out pretty quickly that most of her assumptions were wrong. Nearly three-quarters of her orders were women buying for other women (not men buying for women). Buyers didn't care as much about her low price point; they cared far more about the quality of the flowers and the aesthetic of the arrangements. While they generally liked the eco-friendly positioning, they really wanted to be able to choose from more options.

She quickly adjusted the product offerings based on those early learnings, and the business grew fast. Eventually, Christina was able to move the operation out of her apartment and into actual commercial space in San Francisco. She hired employees to help make the arrangements and contracted bicycle messengers to deliver them.

Christina wanted to put her foot on the marketing pedal, but she quickly found that advertising in the flower-delivery sector was very expensive. The big flower companies really drove up the cost of keywords on Google, so a keyword like "flower delivery" was going to cost her $7 per click. If you assume that 9% of the clicks make a purchase (fairly typical), then $7 per click equates to a customer acquisition cost of $78—way more than she could make on an order.

So Christina switched to guerrilla marketing tactics. She provided San Francisco coffee shops with free arrangements to display on their front counters with a stack of her business cards. Instagram's popularity was just beginning to rise, and flower arrangements are the perfect sort of visual product for Instagram. People were soon taking pictures of arrangements they had received and tagging them with #farmgirlflowers. Her Instagram followers grew to almost half a million people.

With a solid following in the Bay Area, the next logical step was nationwide shipping. It would not be easy to scale from a perishable product delivered locally by hand to a perishable product that could be shipped nationwide and arrive in great condition, but Christina worked closely with a packaging design company and came up with a way to do it.

Having proven out the business by building it from an initial incarnation run out of her apartment into a nascent national operation, Christina then set out to raise some venture capital. She knew would face challenges—Sand Hill Road held a preconceived idea of a scalable venture-funded business, and it certainly didn't look like a woman selling flowers. But she set out on the fundraising trail with resolve and a pitch deck full of data.

Over the next couple of years, she pitched to a total of 104 venture capitalists and received 104 rejections. Some of the feedback she received included:

- "Sorry, this isn't a tech business to us."
- "It's just inherently unscalable."
- "There's no economic leverage."
- "Team seems weak."
- "Your slides are too pretty." (Really).
- "Maybe next time you can bring your husband?" (Seriously?)

Frustrated, Christina decided she'd continue to bootstrap the company, growing it organically (pun intended) without outside capital.

Her personal charisma and a great feel-good story got her lots of press attention, from *Forbes, the New York Times, Vanity Fair, Vogue, and Inc. to NPR's Marketplace and The Today Show* (Several times. If you go to *The Today Show* website, you'll see bunches of videos of her).

A low point in her entrepreneurial journey came when she found out that a new startup called BloomThat, founded by three guys with MBA's, raised $7.5 million in venture capital to copy pretty much every aspect of Farmgirl Flowers, from the messaging right down to the burlap wrap. The fact that Sand Hill Road investors had turned her down and then invested in men who stole her idea was a pretty hard pill to swallow.

Happily, the three dudes failed. BloomThat burned through all their money and had to cease operations, selling to FTD at a fire-sale price, while Christina kept building Farmgirl Flowers the old-fashioned way: **profitably, with no outside capital.**

Her nationwide shipping business did so well that soon she was facing a new problem: she couldn't source enough flowers to keep up with demand. Her commitment to only using local flowers sourced from the Bay Area had become a constraint on growth. So she bit the bullet and started sourcing internationally, including establishing a new facility in Ecuador.

Today, Farmgirl Flowers is an extensive operation, shipping from twenty-two facilities across North and South America. Originally launched as a one-woman operation in her San Francisco apartment, Farmgirl Flowers now profitably generates more than $35 million dollars per year in revenue.

And here's the best part: because all those venture capitalists turned her down, Christina and her team still own 100% of the business.

KEY TAKEAWAYS:

The Farmgirl Flowers story is one of my favorite case studies because it illustrates several important points:

◊ Like most entrepreneurs, Christina's original assumptions turned out to be wrong. Unlike some entrepreneurs, she tested her assumptions early and iterated on her product offering in order to quickly reach Product-Market Fit. By doing an "MVP" of the business out of her dining room, using local bicycle couriers, she was able to learn which of her assumptions were right, which were wrong, and how the offering could be refined while it was still small and agile.

◊ Early testing with ads indicated that her CAC:LTV was out-of-whack. A CAC of $77 was more than she could make back. So she worked on both ends—finding ways of getting customers more efficiently and increasing the price in order to get more lifetime value.

◊ As angry as she was at a new competitor copying her model, it ain't competition that kills startups. By just focusing on making her own business better, she got the last laugh as the competitor burned through their venture money and shut down.

◊ Bootstrapping wins. Many entrepreneurs would have quit after receiving 104 rejections from venture capitalists, but Christina didn't. Now she and her team own one hundred percent of a profitable $35 million-a-year business.

Customer

It's all about understading customers. Write a one-sentence description of key customer personas and the problem we solve for each. Circle the one that is most influential.

Adventurous Alex: A thrill-seeking foodie always on the hunt for unique and spicy taco creations to satisfy their daring palate.

Health-Conscious Haley: A fitness enthusiast looking for wholesome and fresh ingredient options that align with their nutritious lifestyle at the taqueria.

Busy Ben: An on-the-go professional seeking quick, flavorful, and portable taco choices to enjoy during a busy workday.

Vegetarian Victoria: A plant-based eater in search of flavorful and creative vegetarian and vegan taco selections that cater to their dietary preferences.

Traditional Tony: A lover of classic flavors, Tony enjoys indulging in authentic and time-honored taco recipes that remind him of his cultural heritage.

Family-Oriented Felix: A parent looking for a family-friendly meal delivery with a variety of options to cater to the taste preferences of both kids and adults.

Budget-Conscious Bella: A student or frugal diner in pursuit of affordable yet flavorful taco choices that won't break the bank at the taqueria.

Name of Startup Venture: Fittaco, Inc   Date: November 8, 2023

Prepared by: ___ Waters   Iteration: 8

Why it matters
Why is this a problem worth solving?

The National Institutes for Health say that today a fast food diet may kill more people prematurely every year than cigarette smoking.

Alternatives
When a customer looks at alternative ways to solve the problem we solve, what will they how is your venture positioned? This is a list of competitors and alternatives. Link to a graphic representation of the landscape.

There are many, many food delivery services, from Uber Eats to DoorDash to Grubhub.

See visualization at this link.

Customer
It's all about understanding customers. Write a one-sentence description of key customer personas and the problem we solve for each. Circle the one that is most influential.

Adventurous Alex: A thrill-seeking foodie always on the hunt for unique and spicy taco creations to satisfy their daring palate.

Health-Conscious Haley: A fitness enthusiast looking for wholesome and fresh ingredient options that align with their nutritious lifestyle at the taqueria.

Busy Ben: An on-the-go professional seeking quick, flavorful, and portable taco choices to enjoy during a busy workday.

Vegetarian Victoria: A plant-based eater in search of flavorful and creative vegetarian and vegan taco selections that cater to their dietary preferences.

Traditional Tony: A lover of classic flavors, Tony enjoys indulging in authentic and time-honored taco recipes that remind him of his cultural heritage.

Family-Oriented Felix: A parent looking for a family-friendly meal delivery with a variety of options to cater to the taste preferences of both kids and adults.

Budget-Conscious Bella: A student or frugal diner in pursuit of affordable yet flavorful taco choices that won't break the bank at the taqueria.

Distribution
What are our distribution channels? Direct to consumer, via resellers, or?

We intend to sell direct-to-consumer, via our mobile app and website, with delivery via our own vans.

In the future, we may be open to distribution partnerships.

Positioning
Within this landscape of competitors and alternatives, how is your venture positioned?

Our positioning can basically be summed-up in two words: healthy and delicious.

There are many food delivery apps that can deliver something that is delicious but not very healthy. Or you could eat a salad.

We serve delicious tacos designed by a nutritionist. That's our unique positioning.

Economics
What are the Unit Economics for this venture, what do we expect the CAC+LTV to look like, and what are out capital needs? (Link to full spreadsheet).

One unit = one taco: Sell price $5, on which our gross profit is 4.74

Early tests indicate CAC of 41, and we expect an initial LTV of three orders per customer (425.50), which will grow with time.

Our initial capital needs are $220K, which will get us through the pilot launch. We will propose to investors structuring this as a SAFE.

See full spreadsheet at this link.

Team
What are the characteristics of the right team to make this venture a success?

The right team aligns with our target demographic - people who want to eat healthy and also enjoy the convenience of a quick taco meal.

The economics of our venture are such that we'll need drivers and cooks who are affordable, so we will work hard to make it an attractive part-time job for students, and a great evening second job for anybody.

Defensibility
What is your secret sauce that is difficult for competitors to copy?

The fact that we own the customer and customer data is a big part of our defensibility.

A restaurant selling through a 3rd-party like Doordash owns neither the customer nor the data.

See a larger version at **thelaunchpath.com**

STEP 7, FOR YOUR STARTUP

Ultimately, the success or failure of any startup will be driven by whether or not it can successfully get enough customers (and get them at a cost that makes economic sense). So even long before your startup is actually ready to start selling, you want to build and test a customer acquitition process.

Assignment:

On thelaunchpath.com you will find a funnel diagram to fill out with what you think the marketing mix will be for your startup venture. Then go back to Step 5 (the Economic Model) and make sure you have the costs for all of these marketing activities reflected on your spreadsheet. believe you should target as being early-adopter customers.

▶ *For your Launch Path Canvas:*

In the box on the far right side, list the personas that you believe will represent your key market segments. Circle the one that you think will be your beachead market (the one you can reach first, that will help you build toward reaching the others).

**"*In the modern world of business, it is useless to be a creative, original thinker unless you can also <u>sell</u> what you create.*"

DAVID OGILVY, 1964

CHAPTER 8

BE A MASTER STORYTELLER

Every great entrepreneur has the ability to tell a crisp, clear, and compelling story about what she's working on, and why it matters

Warren Buffett is probably the most successful businessman in the world. He started investing his newspaper delivery money at age fourteen, soon was investing other people's money, and today he manages over $950 billion worth of assets via his holding company, Berkshire Hathaway.

If you walk into Warren Buffett's office in Omaha today, you might expect to see his framed diploma from Columbia Business School on the wall. But you won't. Instead, you'll see a faded 1952 certificate for completing a $100 Dale Carnegie course on public speaking proudly displayed.

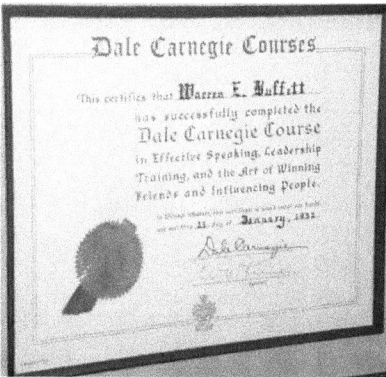

Buffett believes that learning how to be good at speaking and presenting changed his life, perhaps even more than his MBA. "In graduate school, you learn all this complicated stuff, but what's really essential is being able to get others to follow your ideas," he says.

And so it is for entrepreneurs everywhere. To be a successful startup founder, you must have the ability to tell a **crisp, clear, and compelling story about what your startup does and why it matters.**

Many people think of this as a skill required mainly for fundraising, but successful entrepreneurs are pitching all the time for all sorts of reasons: pitching for customers, recruiting employees, getting partners, rallying the team, and so much more. Also, when you win your Nobel Prize, they will expect you to give a speech. So there's that. As Warren Buffett tells us, entrepreneurial success requires being good at preparing and delivering great presentations.

Eric Bahn is a venture capitalist with Hustle Fund.

Eric Bahn 🤍
@ericbahn

My historical progression on what it takes to lead a great company:

In my 20s, I thought it was all about product.

In my 30s, I thought it was all about sales.

In my 40s, I'm realizing it's all about great storytelling.

10:46 PM · Apr 26, 2022

Eric Bahn is a venture capitalist with Hustle Fund.

Pitching is really all about <u>storytelling</u> skills

If you want to be an effective speaker, you need to learn how to be a good storyteller. All great startup founders are great storytellers. In fact, *all great leaders* are great storytellers.

Humans are hardwired to love stories; we told them around campfires for several thousand years before PowerPoint was invented. In fact, an excellent presentation doesn't need slides at all.

The most important thing to know about pitching, presenting, and speaking is that it's all storytelling. Here are a few storytelling tips and tricks.

Simple stories are the best stories

The key factor of storytelling is keeping your stories simple, which is much more difficult than many people realize. Avoid jargon, and keep your narrative easy to understand. As Paul Graham (whom I have already quoted several times) advises, "When you describe what your startup does, describe it in the most matter-of-fact way possible. Professional investors hate having to decode marketing speak. Describing your startup in grandiose terms is the mark of a noob." I laughed to myself when I first read that tweet, thinking of all the overwrought startup descriptions I've encountered over the years. It's common for inexperienced entrepreneurs to believe investors will be impressed by a lot of grandiose buzzwords. In fact, the opposite is true.

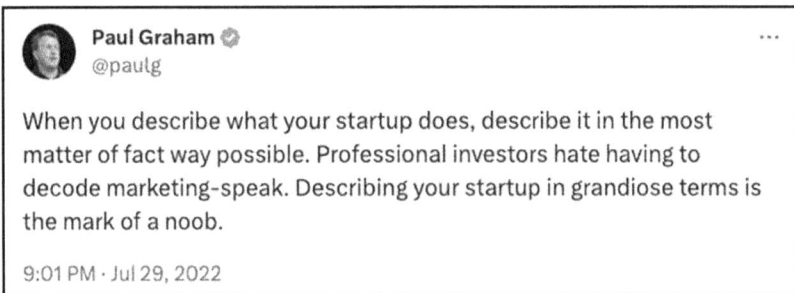

> **Paul Graham** ✓ ···
> @paulg
>
> When you describe what your startup does, describe it in the most matter of fact way possible. Professional investors hate having to decode marketing-speak. Describing your startup in grandiose terms is the mark of a noob.
>
> 9:01 PM · Jul 29, 2022

Uber's original pitch deck described the startup as "a fast and efficient on-demand car service"—nice, simple, and clear. I've met some entrepreneurs who would have described it as a "disruptive mobile-optimized GPS-enabled cloud platform that changes the entire personal-mobility paradigm." That startup never would have gotten funded.

The original Airbnb pitch deck title slide says, "Book rooms with locals, rather than hotels." It doesn't say it's a "peer-to-peer accommodations marketplace platform using an AI engine and a revolutionary new trust mechanism" because no one would fund that.

So, keep it simple and clear. **Focus on a simple sentence that makes it easy for someone to understand what problem your startup solves and how customers benefit.** That's what an investor cares about.

I once met an entrepreneur at a social event and asked him what he was working on. "Well," he said, "there are a lot of grocery stores in the country," pausing to take a sip from his glass of wine. "Their biggest facilities expense is cold storage," then another sip of wine. "We make a device that cuts that cost in half."

Boom! In three short sentences, he alluded to the size of the market, articulated the problem to be solved, and then suggested he had a product with a compelling ROI for its customers. I wanted to invest!

He went on to explain that it's an internet-of-things (IoT) device that goes into a store's refrigerators and freezers, monitors a bunch of data, connects to the cloud via WiFi, and sends back a bunch of data that helps to optimize energy usage.

An inexperienced entrepreneur might have described the exact same startup this way: "We've developed a cloud-powered IoT device that uses proprietary algorithms to analyze operational data for mercantile customers, generating paradigm-changing results." I would have walked away from that guy.

So, take Paul Graham's advice. Describe your startup in simple, matter-of-fact terms. Make it **easy for someone to understand the essence of what your startup does**—because why would you want to make it complicated?

First-person stories are the best stories

Telling your stories from your own personal perspective always makes them more interesting. Whenever you are giving a talk, make sure you weave in your personal insight. How did you come up with this startup idea? Why is it meaningful to you? What gets you up and moving in the morning? And most importantly of all—why are you exactly the right entrepreneur for this venture?

Practice, but don't memorize

You want to sound like a human delivering a great story, not a robot reading a script. There's a subtle but crucial difference. Don't memorize your pitch or presentation word-for-word. Instead, memorize your key talking points, then practice repeating them until they sound natural, like something an actual person might say in casual conversation. Practice by delivering it to your mom, your husband, your daughter, or your neighbor. Tell them the story. What's the problem you're trying to solve? Why does it matter? How did you get involved? Practice telling your story and keeping it real.

Know your audience

I was once in a pitch meeting with another investor, a woman with a PhD in artificial intelligence. As the young (male) entrepreneur was getting ready to give us his pitch, he turned to her and said, "I don't know how much you know about AI technology, so I'll try to keep this simple." I cringed. Needless to say, he didn't get the investment. Before you walk into any pitch meeting, make sure you understand who will be there, and then take the time to look them up on LinkedIn. Your presentation will be much more targeted, and you'll avoid some cringe-worthy moments.

Be clear on your desired outcome

I once worked with a guy who was the most disciplined salesperson I've ever known. Every time we were about to walk into a customer meeting together, he would turn to me and say, "What do we want the outcome of this meeting to be?" So it is with pitches and presentations—be clear on your desired outcome as you prepare. Maybe your desired outcome is to get invited back to meet with other partners, or maybe your desired outcome is a referral, or maybe you're already deep in the process, and your designed outcome is to get a signed deal that day. On a related note, research shows that people are only going to remember one or two points of your presentation, so decide in advance what you want those points to be, then highlight them several times.

What, What, and How?

Whenever you're telling an audience about your awesome startup, there are three simple things they need to understand easily: **What is it, what problem does it solve, and how does it make money?** I can't tell you how many pitches I've sat through without actually knowing what it actually was at the end. Is it a mobile app, a consulting service, or some sort of physical product? Again, don't make it complicated! Make your first sentence simple and clear, like:

> "We sell organic fertilizers that help small farmers grow more food without hurting the planet."

Then you can launch into the details, the ingredients, the distribution strategy, the carbon footprint, and everything else. All that will be much more meaningful for your audience if they first simply understand what this is, what problem it solves, and how it makes money.

No live product demos—ever

I once sat in on a pitch where a young entrepreneur was having his first VC meeting. He was building a software platform for consumer health. After brief introductions, the VC said, "I think this is an exciting space, and I'd love to hear your thoughts on the best monetization route for a product like this." As if he didn't even hear the question, the entrepreneur launched into a thirty-minute product demo—a really boring one that never actually answered the question asked. It was a live demo, so there were a few bugs and glitches. I knew after about five minutes that this pitch was lost.

I've seen this pattern happen many times. An entrepreneur is so excited by what she has built that she can't wait to give a demo of it. But ninety-nine percent of the time, an investor isn't worried about whether the product could be built; he's worried about the monetization model, the go-to-market strategy, the unit economics, the depth of the team, the competitive landscape, etc. A glitchy product demo doesn't address any of those. So, while you may be excited to show off what you've spent nights and weekends building, that's really not what an investor cares about.

Successful entrepreneurs are great listeners. Mediocre ones just want to show off what they've built.

Benefits > Features

When Apple launched the original iPod, there were many other portable music players on the market. The competitors' ads boasted long lists of features: specs about MP3s, megabytes of storage, kilohertz of audio playback, etc. In contrast, the iPod ads simply showed a photo of the product with the headline: "A thousand songs in your pocket."

Engineers develop features, but customers buy benefits. What an investor cares about is whether your startup will provide benefits that customers will pay for. You can talk later to the investor's team about the amazing technology features your engineers have worked hard to build, but keep your pitch focused on benefits for customers.

Look good on Zoom

As an entrepreneur today, many of your initial presentations will probably be conducted via video. Make sure you make the effort to look and sound good. If people are struggling to hear you through choppy audio, that's all they'll remember about your presentation. If your backlighting is bad, what they'll remember is how your silhouette made you look like you're in the witness protection program. So get a real microphone, get good lighting, unclutter your background, and make sure your slides are all set up and you know how to share them. Practice your pro-level Zooming with your cousin in Cedar Rapids. Early in the pandemic, we all suffered through a lot of bad Zoom meetings, but patience is thinner now, and our expectations for professionalism via video are higher.

Finally, some words from Einstein

I started this chapter with Warren Buffett, and I'll finish it with Albert Einstein. He said, "If you can't explain it simply, you don't yet fully understand it." So one of the many reasons why you want to get good at telling your startup story simply is that in the process you will get better clarity yourself on the essence of the startup you are building. I have often found it true for myself. The process of figuring out how to say something simply has helped me find better clarity on the essence of what I'm working on.

Great thinkers (and great entrepreneurs) are able to present their ideas in a crisp, clear, and compelling way. Keep practicing, and you'll become one of them.

PITCH DECKS

The startup world is pretty obsessed with pitch decks. A Google search will turn up thousands of templates and plenty of dubious advice on how to build a winning pitch deck that will land you a big pile of venture capital. The reality, of course, is that venture capitalists don't invest in slides—they invest in people. The ability to build a set of pretty slides is not a predictor of startup success, but the ability to deliver a crisp, clear, and compelling story is.

It shouldn't come as a surprise that the first piece of advice I have about pitch decks is: **don't use someone else's template!** This is your startup and your story. Do you think Steve Jobs copied a template he found somewhere? I don't think so, and neither should you. Here are my thoughts on preparing a great pitch deck:

Start by writing out the story
If I'm preparing a pitch deck, the first thing I do is write out the narrative. Once I'm happy with the story, then I start building some slides to go with it. Many people do it the other way around; they build slides first and then try to decide what story the slides tell. That's bass-ackwards.

Here are some of the things that might be part of the story you tell:

- What problem are you solving?
- Why does it matter?
- What's your "secret sauce"?
- What does the current competitive landscape look like?
- How big is the opportunity?
- How will you efficiently acquire customers?
- What are your initial capital needs, and what milestone will that initial capital get you to?

This is not a definitive list, of course. Every venture is different, but in three to four minutes, you should be able to tell an interesting story that incorporates most of these key points and leaves the recipient intrigued and wanting to hear more. And that's your desired outcome with a pitch deck—leaving the audience wanting to hear more. You're not going to sell the deal with one pitch deck, but hopefully, you'll leave them intrigued enough that they want to know more.

If you have a one-hour meeting scheduled with an investor, do not go in with an hour's worth of slides! No one wants to sit through that. Not only will they not invest, they will block you on all their phones so that you can never torture them again!

If I have a one-hour meeting scheduled with an investor, I like to walk in and say, "Let me give you the three-minute overview, and then we can dive deeper into whatever part of this you'd like." Some investors want to know more about the market size, some will want to focus on understanding the competitive landscape, and others will just want to learn more about you. Either way, I guarantee no one wants to sit through sixty minutes of slides.

Why you?

To me, nothing is more important to articulate in your pitch than **the reason why you are exactly the right entrepreneur for this venture.** Investors want to know that your passion for this startup is so deep it will carry you through good times and bad. They may even be looking at three similar startups, trying to decide which one to invest in. Their decision will be based on their perception of the founder every time. Make sure they understand why you are exactly the right entrepreneur for this venture.

Different decks for different purposes

Ultimately, you'll end up with different pitch decks for different purposes. Most startup founders use three decks or, more accurately, three sets of messaging. One is investor-facing, one is customer-facing, and one is for thought leadership (when you speak at a conference, for example). Great entrepreneurs are able to talk about one set of benefits when meeting with a potential investor, a different set of benefits when talking with a prospective customer, and yet another set of messages at a conference.

It's actually not about slides at all

One of the most valuable lessons I've learned as an entrepreneur happened when I took my carefully prepared pitch deck into a meeting with a grumpy venture capitalist named Rich.

I opened up my laptop, got ready to show him my awesome slides, and was taken aback when he said, "Close that damn thing up. I don't want to see your stupid slides. What I want to know is whether you can tell me—using words and words alone—why what you're working on is so interesting that I would want to invest."

I did, and he invested, but he never saw those beautiful slides I had worked so diligently on—because venture capitalists don't invest in slides. So, can you deliver a compelling story about your startup without slides? If not, go back and work on it some more.

Pitch Deck Resources

On thelaunchpath.com, you'll find resources for creating a great pitch deck, along with videos of some great pitches. Watching others pitch is a great way to learn, so look for pitch events near you. Go and watch: you'll notice aspects you like and others you don't. You'll see what seems to really resonate with an audience. Every time I've pitched, I've learned something new.

Successful pitching isn't about pitch decks. It's about telling a crisp, clear, and compelling story about yourself, your startup, and why it matters.

Allison Byers
@apbyers

I HATE it when investors tell founders to hire designers for their decks. Such a waste of time and money.

Focus on getting the right content, narrative flow, making slides easy to read, and confidently presenting. Hiring a graphic designer isn't getting you a check.

6:35 AM · Apr 13, 2022

SELLING CUSTOMERS > SELLING INVESTORS

I once asked my friend David to sit in as a guest judge during Pitch Night in my Stanford class on entrepreneurship. He has had a long and successful career as a Silicon Valley venture capitalist, and he's one of the smartest guys I know. I knew the students would appreciate his input.

Indeed, they did. Each student gave their three-minute pitch, and David provided lots of helpful insights. He was very supportive and encouraging to each of them.

Yet, as we walked to our cars afterward, I could tell David was troubled. "Their pitches were built around trying to impress investors, but the thing that impresses investors most is having actual paying customers," David pointed out. "That's the signal an investor is looking for, so that's really where any entrepreneur should be focusing their efforts."

This was a really good observation, and I began to think that maybe I should have given the students better guidance. It's easy to get caught up in the venture capital fantasy, especially here in Silicon Valley. My students often ask me questions like, "What sort of projected profit margin should I put in my slides in order to impress investors?" or, "What's the CAC:LTV ratio that investors want to see?"

This is an upside-down way of thinking about building a business. A founder really should think about creating a business that successfully delivers value to customers—a business with a sustainable economic model, a business that you will be passionate about running. That's what impresses investors.

So as you're building your pitch deck, make sure your focus is on selling customers, not selling investors. By doing that, you will impress investors.

STARTUP PITCHES AND NESTING DOLLS

Pitching tends to be a series of meetings of increasing length. First comes the proverbial elevator encounter, where you only have time for a sentence or two that will get you a contact, which might lead to an initial very short (maybe ten-minute) follow-up over Zoom. Then you might get an invite to actually come into the office for a half-hour in-person meeting. Then, hopefully, an invite will follow for an hour-long meeting with the other partners. In each case, your desired outcome is precisely the same: **to leave them intrigued enough that they want to have another meeting.**

You'll end up with a set of little pitches that function a bit like one of those Russian nesting dolls, a *matryoshka*. You need a one-sentence hook that opens up to a one-minute pitch that opens up to a three-minute hook that opens up to a ten-minute pitch, etc.

Let's look at our fictional venture, Fitaco. The one-sentence hook might be:

> *"Imagine a taco truck dedicated to delivering healthy food to you wherever you are."*

Now that I have your attention, I'll give you a three-sentence description:

> *"Here's the thing: Consumers in the US spend $331 billion per year on fast food, and most of it is really unhealthy. In fact, the National Institutes of Health say that a fast-food diet may kill more people prematurely than cigarette smoking. We're addressing that with a new brand of health-conscious fast food (tacos!), delivered directly to your home or office."*

Now you're interested enough that you tell me to call you sometime. On the call, I'm ready with my one-minute pitch:

> *"We all know that we should eat healthy, right? Our moms told us we should eat healthy. Yet all of us sometimes sacrifice eating healthy for the convenience of fast food. Americans spend over three hundred billion dollars per year on fast food, and now, with all the on-demand delivery apps, we can get unhealthy fast food delivered directly to our doorsteps, so we don't even have to burn any calories getting it!*
>
> *But what if we could get healthy meals fast, meals designed by a nutritionist? And what if they were tacos because everybody loves tacos! I'd like to tell you about Fitaco, a new startup that, as the name implies, delivers tacos that keep you fit. We're building a nationwide fleet of Fitaco trucks, efficiently delivering healthy, fresh tacos to you on-demand, directly to your home or office. I'd love a chance to tell you more about what we're doing and the very compelling economics we have baked into the plan."*

Now you invite me to come into your office to meet with your investment partners, and I'll start that meeting with a five-minute set of slides that give you the full overview (see full video on thelaunchpath.com).

Every great entrepreneur is nimble enough to tell that story **within the confines of the time available**, with the desired outcome always being to leave the audience wanting to hear more (i.e., get another meeting).

So, in your head (and on your laptop), you need to have a set of pitches that fit inside each other. Sort of like those Russian nesting dolls.

Case Study:
MAILCHIMP

In 2001, Ben Chestnut and Mark Armstrong were running a marketing agency in Atlanta. Many of their clients wanted them to manage their email marketing, and as a marketing agency they were frustrated with how bad the existing email management software was. So Ben Chestnut dug up some old code from a failed e-greeting card company he had founded a couple years earlier, and decided to reincarnate that code as a new product for managing email. Their most popular e-card featured a chimpanzee, and since they already had that art they used it for a logo for the new product and called it MailChimp.

Constant Contact was the leading brand in the email marketing space, having raised over $100 million in venture capital, and it was one of those products that everyone used and everyone hated. Chestnut and

Armstrong had no interest in trying to compete with a company that has raised that much money, so they mostly used MailChimp for their own clients, but slowly also offered it to others on a paid subscription basis.

They kept running their marketing agency as their primary business, with MailChimp as a side project. They ran lots of email marketing campaigns for clients, using their side-hustle app, and when a new client need came up they would add it as a new feature on MailChimp. This gave them, as Ben Chestnut would say, "a proximity to its customers that its competitors lacked."

The MailChimp user base of paying customers slowly grew, and they got lots of nice feedback on how much people loved it. One day in 2009 co-founder Ben Chestnut was in a Ben & Jerry's ice cream shop and they offered him free samples. He tasted several, chose one he particularly liked, and ended up being a loyal customer. "That, in a nutshell, was my inspiration and motivation in offering the freemium program at MailChimp", says Ben now. So they launched a free plan, and used data to tinker with the pricing on upgrading to a paid plan. "Ever since inception, I've been fascinated with the art and science of pricing. I've tinkered with pay-as-you-go and monthly plans for $9, $9.99, $25, $49, $99.99 and so on. We've changed our pricing models at least a half-dozen times throughout the years, and along the way we tracked profitability, changes in order volume, how many people downgraded when we reduced prices, how many refunds were given, etc. We're sitting on tons of pricing data. When we launched our freemium plan in 2009, you betcha we used that data to see what would happen if we cannibalized our $15 plan. If we had started with freemium at ground zero, the story would've been different".

Within a year of changing to a freemium model, MailChimp's user base had grown from 85,000 to 450,000.

Once the flywheel started spinning, the network effects were significant. Every email sent from the free plan had the MailChimp logo at the bottom, and a link to sign up for your own free plan. The monkey mascot became a big hit, and the MailChimp team distributed free branded merchandise to customers who were active evangelists for the product. By 2012, their customer base had grown from 450,000 to 1.2 million and they were adding 5,000 new users every day. Their all-in Customer Acquisition Cost (CAC) was less than $100, and with a $20/month subscription, the pay-back period on that CAC was excellent.

With the flywheel now spinning and optimized, they continued to grow both the customer base and the feature set. Spending $100 on CAC and having them come back in just a few months was a cash cycle they could finance themselves, so they were able to grow the venture organically, with no outside capital required. Eventually they shut down the marketing agency, as their "side hustle" required their full attention. What started as an email platform for small businesses at $20/month was soon gaining large enterprise customers who would happily spend several hundred dollars a month for premium plans.

By 2014 the MailChimp platform was sending 10 billion emails a month for customers. They acquired LemonStand, a smaller competitor, and as social media took off they expanded from simply being an email platform to a more comprehensive marketing platform that included lead tracking and retargeting on Facebook and Instagram.

The company was still completely bootstrapped—no outside capital. Their success got the attention of many venture capital and private equity investors who came knocking on the door of Ben Chestnut and Mark Armstrong, but they stood firm. They liked being a bootstrapped company.

Finally, in 2021, they decided to cash out. They sold the company to Intuit, who rebranded it as Intuit Mailchimp. The deal was $5.7 billion in cash and $6.3 billion in Intuit stock. That's right—founders who never took any outside capital and grew the venture organically, sold it for a total of $12 billion.

KEY TAKEAWAYS:

◊ The number one takeaway is they built a product they used themselves, for their own marketing clients, they weren't coming up with features in a vacuum. Every feature developed was one built to serve actual customer needs.

◊ Having data on which to make pricing decisions is huge. Too many founders are forced to come up with pricing out of thin air. The MailChimp founders announced the freemium plan after they already had lots of customers so they were able to see exactly to what extent it cannibalized paying customers, see upgrade/downgrade conversion data, etc.

◊ The viral nature of the product was huge (people who received an email from the free plan could click on the footer and sign up themselves), and the cash cycle provided by their LTV/CAC was very favorable. If it cost them $100 to get a $20/month customer, then CACD (the time it takes to make back 2x the CAC) was ten months. That's very solid.

◊ By staying close to customers, they knew when customer needs were changing. When they launched in 2001, it was all about email marketing. Today email is still part of the marketing mix for many brands, but social media, SMS, and other channels are more likely to be where the big dollars are spent. MailChimp was able to make that transition along with the customers. Today, if you go to the website of Constant Contact (the gorilla in the space when MailChimp originally launched), the website looks like it's stuck in 2008. They feature their "newly-launched" SMS platform.

MailChimp is probably the most extraordinary example ever of a bootstrapped company—from launch to a $12 billion exit. Something on this scale may never happen again, but the lessons are timeless ones that every entrepreneur should take note of.

You will find videos of example pitches for Fitaco at **thelaunchpath.com**

STEP 8, FOR YOUR STARTUP

Every entrepreneur needs to have the ability to tell a crisp story about their venture—short, medium, or long! No confusing acronyms, no long convoluted sentences, no dense marketing-speak filled with buzzwords. Just crisp and clear storytelling.

Assignment:

For your venture, create a series of "Nesting Doll" pitches:

- A nice, simple **one-sentence** description.
- **A three sentence version,** getting a little deeper.
- A paragraph that you can say in **60 seconds or less.**
- A slide deck that you can deliver in **less than 5 minutes.**

Now practice these until they come naturally to you. Remember, when someone asks you what you're working on you don't want to sound like you're a robot reciting something from memory; you want to give a crisp and clear answer that seems natural and enthusiastic.

Practice delivering your pitch deck (a set of slides you can deliver in less than give minutes), then watch a video of yourself (painful, but very helpful).

Don't just recite the features of your product—**tell a story** about the problem your startup solves, the benefits to customers, and why you are exactly the right entrepreneur for this venture.

"It's all in the mind, you know.

GEORGE HARRISON

CHAPTER 9

MIND THE MIND

What is an "entrepreneurial mindset"?

O f all the factors that tend to drive the success or failure of a startup venture, the CEO's mindset may be the most important. Looking back on my own career, I think my failures happened, more often than not, at times when I let my mindset slip.

People talk about an "entrepreneurial mindset," but what is that, exactly? I was asked to do a lecture on the topic recently, so I decided to do a mini research project and reach out to some successful startup founders and venture capital investors, asking what they thought were the components of an entrepreneurial mindset.

Here's what they said:

- Olivia (VC): "An entrepreneurial mindset includes excitement around building something new and **perseverance to navigate the many obstacles** that come up in that process."
- David (Founder): "An understanding that the world is both mutable and imperfect coupled with the **resolve to improve it.**"
- Jeremy (Founder): "A **relentless dissatisfaction with the status quo** that drives you to build novel solutions that others will value."
- Tim (VC): "Folks with outsized smarts, goodness, and grit who **can't imagine not spending their lives solving the unmet need about which they care most deeply**."

- Kent (Founder): You cannot have any fear. It doesn't mean you are oblivious to what can go wrong, but you have **confidence that you will find a solution**."
- Bob (VC): "An entrepreneurial mindset is one which **takes risks others won't take** to achieve a vision others don't share."
- Jason (Founder): "Seeing what others don't and having **an unstoppable will**."
- Danielle (VC): "The entrepreneurial mindset is one consisting of **grit and perseverance while being realistic enough to know when to adapt and change course**."
- Chris (Founder): "Entrepreneurial mindset is all about **efficient hypothesis testing** and grit."
- Thane (Founder): "I believe there is an entrepreneurial mindset or spirit: **creating shared value**."

Oh, there's some really great stuff in there. Let's explore the patterns in those answers:

- **Grit, perseverance, unstoppable will, relentlessness.**
  This is pretty obvious—being an entrepreneur is hard. The successful ones have a mindset that makes them relentless in pursuing their passions. Steve Jobs himself said, "I'm convinced that about half of what separates the successful entrepreneurs from the non-successful ones is pure perseverance."

- **Hypothesis testing, a willingness to adapt and change course.**
  This is a key point because the reality for most startups is that the original idea fails. Despite those odds, great entrepreneurs are constantly testing their assumptions and pivoting their way to success. Remember from Chapter 2 that the founders' plans for YouTube, Instagram, Slack, and Uber were dramatically different from what the companies grew into. In all of these cases, the original idea failed, but the teams were agile enough

to test their assumptions, realize where they were wrong, and pivot to success.

- **Driven by a desire to solve problems worth solving.**
  As we discussed in Chapter 1, the best way to get startup ideas is to look for problems. Great entrepreneurs fall in love with a problem worth solving, and that passion then creates the unstoppable will that drives a startup to success.

- **Creating shared value.**
  Entrepreneurship is a team sport. Successful entrepreneurs are great at recruiting team members, customers, and investors to join their value-creation mission. Not everybody I know is passionate about creating shared value—but every single successful entrepreneur I know is.

With this great input from my founder and VC friends, I felt like I was making progress on my lecture, but I still needed to weave this into a concise definition of the entrepreneurial mindset. You may remember the definition of entrepreneurship I used in Chapter 1: **"Entrepreneurship is the pursuit of opportunity, without regard for resources currently controlled."**[1]

When successful entrepreneurs see opportunity and decide to pursue it, they are never deterred by a lack of resources; they know they can pull the resources together. Therefore, the definition of an entrepreneurial mindset must fall along these lines:

An entrepreneurial mindset is a set of mental habits that tend to optimize the successful pursuit of opportunity. These habits include a

---

1: This definition is from Howard Stevenson, professor at Harvard Business School.

passion for solving problems worth solving, a willingness to test assumptions and change course, and a relentless desire to create shared value.

Boom! My lecture was a success. Now let's look more broadly at some tricks of the mind that entrepreneurs need to pay attention to:

Biases, blind spots, and echo chambers, oh my

As humans, we all have certain biases we may be blind to. Successful entrepreneurs need enough self-awareness to identify and examine their own unconscious biases so those biases don't jump up and bite them in the ass. Here are some normal human biases that can be especially dangerous for startup founders:[2]

- **Confirmation Bias**

  Our natural tendency is to notice all the things around us that confirm our beliefs, and we tend to undervalue that which might disprove our beliefs. As entrepreneurs, we tend to fall in love with our startup idea, and then all day long, we see evidence that confirms how brilliant our idea is (and ignore any evidence to the contrary). This is how bad products are built and how many startups fail.

- **Echo Chambers**

  As social animals, we tend to surround ourselves with people who share our beliefs and think like we do. When my friends come to dinner, and the conversation moves to politics, we all start pounding the table in agreement. This is why customer development interviews with your friends aren't effective—you

---

2: For more insights on human biases, I recommend Howard Ross's excellent book Everyday Bias: Identifying and Navigating Unconscious Judgments in Our Daily Lives.

are unlikely to get any unexpected insights from people who think like you! Get out of your echo chamber and get product feedback from people who are not your friends.

- **Pattern Recognition Bias**
  As what bias expert Howard Ross calls "the tendency to sort and identify information based on prior experience or habit," this one can be tricky in the startup world. You might discern a pattern of events that convinces you the world needs your app for frog owners to connect with potential frog-sitters (e.g., a spate of social media posts about cute frogs and a couple of articles about the difficulties of finding reliable pet care).

  This overlaps with other flavors of bias to some extent: confirmation bias, as described above, but also selective attention bias, where things you are focused on crowd out the things you're not paying attention to. I know that when I'm thinking about buying a sweet new car, I suddenly start seeing that model everywhere I go.

- **Commitment Bias**
  Sometimes an entrepreneur's most difficult admission is that the project we're pouring our heart and soul into isn't working. Ross describes commitment bias as an attachment "to a particular point of view, even when it may be obviously wrong, especially when it provides us a way to save face, appear right, or allow us to glorify ourselves." Amidst the necessity of remaining agile and pivoting as a founder, I've also seen commitment bias get in the way of an objective assessment and ultimately lead to startup failure. Humans have egos, and our egos want us to appear smart, even brilliant, to others (and ourselves). Startup founders sometimes get an extra dose of this kind of ego ("I see the opportunity that

nobody else sees!"), but the right move is always to take a hard look at the situation and see if commitment bias is at play.

- **Opinions Versus Facts**

  Humans have a tendency to believe that what we think is fact when it's usually just our opinion. When we act on a belief, and it turns out to be not only just opinion but also wrong, this is when things can often go spectacularly downhill. One of my favorite Mark Twain quotes is, "It ain't what you don't know that gets you into trouble; it's what you know for sure that just ain't so."[3] I have founded startups where I was very honest with myself about what I didn't yet know, but what tripped me up was that some of what I thought I knew for sure turned out to be wrong. So, test your assumptions. Some of what you consider obvious facts may actually turn out to just be wrong opinions.

Pour some mindfulness into your tea

Mindfulness was one of those concepts I was generally aware of but didn't know exactly what it meant. One day I had a conversation with a Stanford faculty member who really brought it into focus for me. "The great American mantra is **Oh, shit**," she said. "Mindfulness is shortening that to just **Oh**. When something happens, just acknowledge it without attaching judgment."

This explanation really resonated with me. The fact is that being a startup founder is a bit of a roller coaster—one day, you win a big new customer deal, and the next day you lose one. Staying on an even keel turns out to be critical to your success as a startup CEO. Personally, my emotions tend to be overly sensitive to exterior triggers. When something good happens, I tend to go on a high, and when something bad happens, I

3: This quote is usually attributed to Mark Twain but doesn't seem to actually appear in any of his known writings. So who knows. I like it anyway.

tend to mope. Neither of those states is productive. Learning to just say, "Oh," rather than "Oh, shit" has helped me become a more productive person and a more effective startup leader.

Cry like an entrepreneur; learn like a baby

Alison Gopnik is a professor of psychology at the University of California at Berkeley, and she's done extensive research on the evolutionary biology of human brains. It turns out that humans have an unusually long childhood—children aren't self-sufficient for around fifteen years after birth, much longer than any other species. As a result, our brain wiring is optimized for learning until our mid-teens, then the wiring switches to become optimized for the execution of what has been learned. To support the hyper-learning mode of a four-year-old, for example, the body routes sixty percent of its caloric intake to the brain, whereas in an adult, only about twenty percent of calories are routed there. In Gopnik's words, human childhood brains are optimized for "exploring," and then as we become adults, our brain wiring changes to optimization for "exploiting" (when my wife says I'm acting like a 12-year-old I just tell her I'm in learning mode today).

The Silicon Valley startup methodology presented in this book is all about agility, quick experimentation, soaking up market data, talking to customers, and rapid iterations. In other words, as a startup founder, you and your team have to be optimized for learning and exploring. Then, as you cross the magic threshold into Product-Market Fit, you and your team need to be optimized to execute upon the market opportunity you have found. As Steve Blank says, "A corporation is an organization built to <u>execute</u> a business model; a startup is an organization built to <u>find</u> a business model."

As a startup founder, you want your mind to be all about <u>learning</u> at the early stage of the venture and instill this state of mind into the team.

Prioritize your time

Perhaps you've heard the parable of the professor giving a lecture on time management. He places a giant glass jar in front of his class and fills it up to the top with large rocks. He asks the class whether any more can fit in there, and the students shake their heads—it seems pretty full. He then proves them wrong by pouring in some gravel, which fills in the space around the big rocks. Again he asks whether any more can fit into the jar, and again the students shake their heads. He then pours some sand in, which fills the space between the gravel and the big rocks. With a self-satisfied look, the professor asks, "So, in the context of time management, what can we learn from this demonstration?"

An eager student in the front row replies, "What we can learn is that no matter how crowded our calendar is, with good time management skills, you can always fit more meetings in!"

"No," the professor retorts. "What we can learn is that unless you get the big rocks in first, you'll never get them in. So, decide what the big rocks are in your life and put those on your calendar first. Work in everything else around the big rocks."

This is how I got through the period in my life when I was a startup CEO with young kids. Every month, I put my kids' stuff on my calendar first: the days I would pick them up from school, the afternoon soccer games, the field trips I had volunteered for. Those were my big rocks, and everything else got scheduled around them.

In the end, passion is what matters most

As I mentioned way back in Chapter 1, when a startup founder is pitching, I want to see their passion shining through. I want to see that they've fallen in love with a problem worth solving and are passionate about solving it. Running a startup is hard; all I really care about is whether the founder has the grit and tenacity to see their vision through to success. Investor Ben Horowitz has written, "Whenever I meet a successful CEO, I ask them how they did it. Mediocre CEOs point to their brilliant strategic moves their intuitive business sense, or a variety of other self-congratulatory explanations. The great CEOs tend to be remarkably consistent in their answers. They all say, 'I didn't quit.'"[4]

Be willful, intentional, and optimistic

I've seen a lot of startup founders fail because they just never put enough effort into succeeding. Maybe it was self-doubt, maybe it was just too much work, maybe rejection and failure just wore them down too quickly. Sam Altman once wrote an essay on success in which he wrote, "Ask for what you want. You usually won't get it, and often the rejection will be painful. But when this works, it works surprisingly well."[5] What I love about this quote is that it encapsulates the notion that if you are intentional and resilient, the universe will reward you. Entrepreneurs have to believe this—I have never met a successful pessimist.

In the end, be grateful

I once had a conversation with a business school classmate who has gone on to great success. Over a glass of wine, we talked about success patterns—the characteristics that high-achievers tend to have. I was surprised when he said that gratitude was an important characteristic. He said: "Some people spend too much of their day being mad at someone or resentful about something that happened in the past. If you wake up every morning feeling grateful for everything that you have, it

---

4: This quote is from his book The Hard Thing About Hard Things: Building a Business When There Are No Easy Answers (ISBN 978-0062273208), which I highly recommend.

5: You can find Sam's essay on success at blog.samaltman.com/how-to-be-successful

frees up your mind to just focus on being productive and getting things done".

Navigating the startup world is a tough challenge or rather a whole series of tough challenges. Success is often elusive, and you will be hit again and again by unforeseen setbacks and blows to your state of mind and emotions. As a founder, your ability to practice perseverance, mindfulness, practical learning, and balance will be a huge part of getting you to where you want to go.

In London, they say Mind the Gap. I say Mind the Mind, baby.

Case Study:
BE GIRL

I met Diana Sierra through my work with Miller Center for Social Entrepreneurship. She grew up in rural Colombia, earned a degree in industrial and product design, and ended up in NYC, where she designed and engineered products for some very large global brands. After watching how the big corporate world operated, she became interested in sustainability and worked toward a master's in sustainability management from Columbia University (she went from Colombia to Columbia!).

At Columbia, she met the renowned economist Jeffery Sachs and accompanied him and other students to Uganda. She was eager to put her product design skills towards projects that would deliver social impact, and on that trip, she found a problem she became obsessed with solving: menstrual health. All over the developing world, this frequently becomes a factor in the gender-driven academic achievement gap—girls who miss several days of school every month because of a biological function start to lag behind their non-menstruating peers.

Diana launched a social venture, Be Girl, with a mission of making sure that "being a girl does not stand in the way of opportunities, health, and success." She used her design skills to develop a reusable product that could deliver long-term performance and protection at a price point that made sense for women and girls living at the base of the pyramid in emerging economies.

She initially launched Be Girl from her home in NYC with a model like Toms Shoes—she marketed the product to American consumers, promising that each one purchased would result in one being given away for free to someone in Africa. Unfortunately, that model never really took off, and eventually, Diana decided that, to really achieve impact, she needed to actually be immersed in the world she was serving. She packed up her apartment and moved to Mozambique.

Diana continued to iterate on the product design, and the feedback was very positive—women and girls who tested it said they were very happy with the product. However she encountered an unexpected problem: she "realized that there was a big need but no market for reusable menstrual products." They just didn't fit into a typical Mozambique and African household budget. "Imagine trying to sell menstrual products in a country/continent where you're not even allowed to speak about your period at home. Now imagine at a school or government level.

No one was familiar with the importance of menstrual health and its benefits at all".

Diana then extended the design reach of Be Girl from menstrual products to education services, focusing on the development of educational materials and other tools to teach girls, parents, and communities about the importance of menstrual health and how it leads to girls becoming healthy, productive, well-educated women. She also worked with regulatory authorities to establish standards for menstrual products as part of establishing a market where there hadn't been one before. "As a product designer," she says, "I thought my product was so awesome that it would sell itself. I found out that the path is actually consumer awareness, education, advocacy, product standards, and then commercialization."

Mozambique eventually adopted Be Girl's menstrual health curriculum into official government programs. "As a social entrepreneur trying to achieve change at scale," she says, "when your own education material gets adopted by a government, that's when you really see numbers take off." Currently, the government of Angola is also working to adopt Be Girl's curriculum, and her advocacy efforts are being recognized by countries across the African continent. Be Girl has now raised more than three million dollars in capital, distributed over half a million products in thirty-five countries, and provided education to 360 thousand adolescents. Her twenty-one-person team is now expanding the Be Girl operation into West Africa. Reflecting back on her journey, Diana says, "I think that ignorance is bliss when it comes to social entrepreneurship, in a way, because if you know in the beginning how complex it will be, you may never do it."

KEY TAKEAWAYS:

Diana Sierra is an inspirational social entrepreneur, and her BeGirl story has several lessons in it that entrepreneurs of all stripes should take note of:

◊ Marry the problem, not the solution. Diana's north star remained the same—menstrual health leads to all sorts of positive outcomes for girls and women—but she needed to pivot several times with regard to the best way to solve that problem.

◊ Selling a product for which there is no existing market for similar products is a challenge. Many first-time entrepreneurs think that having no competition would be great, but in fact, creating demand where there isn't any requires twice the effort.

◊ It's difficult to design and deliver a product into a world you are not immersed in. Diana found that trying to run Be Girl from her NYC office wasn't going to work. She had to actually be on the ground in Africa to fully immerse herself in the people, governments, and markets that would become partners in her organization's success.

◊ Back in Chapter 2, we talked about how every startup needs to get to Product-Market Fit and that, ultimately, you'll need Product-Market-<u>Channel</u> Fit. Diana found out that having a great product with PMF doesn't do you any good until you also find the right channel through which to sell and distribute it.

"An idea can turn to dust or magic, depending on the talent that rubs up against it.

WILLIAM BERNBACH

CHAPTER 10

BUILD A GREAT TEAM

Nothing matters more than surrounding yourself with great people

In my years of founding and running companies, I've had some successes and some failures. But when I look back, the successes have always been because of the team I had assembled. Honestly, I think that success in business really just distills down to just that: **build great teams.**

At the beginning of this book, I gave you several examples of startups where the original idea failed, but the team was good enough to forge a path to huge success. And it's happened to me. In 2008 I co-founded a company, and the original idea failed miserably, yet we went on to great success, building a thriving global business with five offices around the world. We hit it out of the ballpark because we had a great team. Great teams figure out a way to win.

Here's an interesting observation: you would think that, in the technology world, most founders are tech geniuses. But there are surprisingly few examples of "technology genius" being the defining characteristic of a successful tech startup CEO. Steve Jobs didn't have a college degree, let alone any engineering experience. Peter Thiel was a philosophy major. Ben Silbermann of Pinterest was a political science major. Stewart Butterfield of Slack was a philosophy major. Marc Benioff of Salesforce has no engineering degree; he started as a customer service rep at Oracle. **But they were all great at building teams.** The ability to build high-achieving teams turns out to be one of the most essential skills of a successful startup founder.

I think probably my superpower throughout my own career has been building teams. I'm average with spreadsheets, I'm mediocre at sales, I know just enough about technology to be dangerous, but I've been great at building high-achieving teams. That's my personal superpower.

Question #1: Go solo or find some co-founders?

For you as an entrepreneur, one of your first questions may be whether you should find co-founders or go at it as a solo founder. Which is better? This is one of the longest-running debates in Silicon Valley.

I've been a solo founder, and I've also been part of founding teams. Honestly, I think my personality is better suited to solo-founder status (and my former co-founders would probably agree).

Up on Sand Hill Road, most of the venture capitalists I know still express a preference for founding teams. It has become commonly accepted wisdom, and the echo chamber is strong. Y Combinator pretty much sticks to that belief as well—only about ten percent of the startups they admit to their accelerator program are run by solo founders.

But does the data back this up? Are outcomes actually better for startups with multiple co-founders than for those with a single founder?

Three years ago, a research study came out of The Wharton School of the University of Pennsylvania that suggests that, no, the data does not seem to back this up. The study[1] looked at 3,526 startup companies. They found an interesting dichotomy: indeed, investors seemed biased toward teams, as the startups with multiple co-founders raised more

1: Greenberg, Jason and Mollick, Ethan R., Sole Survivors: Solo Ventures Versus Founding Teams (January 23, 2018). Available at SSRN.

money. But, in terms of outcomes, they found that **startups with single founders tended to last longer and eventually achieve higher revenue.**

The researchers suggest this may partly be because a solo founder is more agile in decision-making. Co-founding teams tend to make slower, more collaborative decisions and are less likely to take chances.

It's certainly true that running a startup requires multiple skill sets. Investor Dave McClure famously said that every startup needs a Hacker, a Hustler, and a Hipster (a tech person, a salesperson, and a product design person).[2] I like Dave's framework, and I think it's probably about right in terms of the skill sets required for many ventures. But every venture is different, and a solo founder can hire for the skill sets she/he doesn't have. So while the Hacker-Hustler-Hipster framework is a clever way of thinking about skill sets, it does not literally mean that every startup needs three founders.

Mark Zuckerberg had co-founders, but eventually, they drifted off. His company's real turning point was hiring a non-founder, Sheryl Sandberg, who brought the skill set Mark lacked—and that moment turbo-charged the company. Facebook isn't a success today because Zuckerberg had co-founders; it's a success because he made good hires.

When you objectively look at the factors that tend to drive startup success or failure, I honestly don't think "number of founders" is one of them. So choose what's best for you.

How to hire

Hiring is more art than science, and everyone has their own style. But I do think that hiring is the one thing that a startup CEO should never

---

2: Other people claim to have coined the "hacker, hustler, hipster" term, but I first heard it from Dave McClure.

delegate to others. I've heard it said that the CEO needs to personally hire the first 100 employees at a company, and I think that's probably about right. A CEO who delegates the hiring process to others too soon has been the death of many companies.

Your first ten hires are going to determine the culture of the company. As the CEO, it will be difficult to "fix" an underperforming team culture if you don't get the first ten hires right. So take some time to be clear on your values and objectives with those first ten hires.

In my career, I've done well looking for "diamonds in the rough"—people who don't yet quite have the resume credentials, but you spot something that makes you think they can do the job and blossom. In fact, I once hired a guy whose cover letter began with "I do not have the qualifications outlined in your job description" and then went on to tell me all the reasons why I should hire him anyway. I did, and he turned out to be one of the best hires I've ever made.

This is the one area where 1+1 does not equal 2

Team is the one place where 1+1 never equals 2. A great hire adds more than their incremental value. A bad hire subtracts from the rest of the team. Get your team math right by **hiring slow and firing fast**. As Richard Fairbanks, Co-founder of CapitalOne, says, *"At most companies, people spend 2% of their time recruiting and 75% managing their recruiting mistakes."*. Better to take your time and get your team math right.

Google did a study a few years ago called Project Aristotle, trying to figure out the characteristics of high-performing teams so that they could automate the selection of individuals for their teams. They were hoping for a nice recipe like "A good team has one senior engineer with >8 years coding experience, plus one recent CS graduate with a GPA >3.8, plus one PM who was a liberal arts major". Or something like that.

What they found was completely different —what they found was that the things that made for high-performing teams were common vocabulary, strong communication skills, cultural fit, and mission clarity from management.

Never let the financial guy run HR

I've never understood why the HR function sometimes gets assigned to the person who runs finance. It's just a huge mismatch of skills, and it's been the kiss of death for the culture of many organizations. What emerges is a spreadsheet-centric approach to evaluating people, a "competency matrix." That's a bit like thinking that a paint-by-numbers kit will help you create great art. As Ben Horowitz says, "Hiring based on checking boxes or looking for weaknesses is a guaranteed way to create a low-performing organization." I've seen it happen right before my eyes, and it's painful to witness.

Here's the problem: You want to hire someone who will add value to your JavaScript team. But that gets expressed in a job post as "Must have 5 years experience with JavaScript." **Those two things are not necessarily the same.** A good CEO knows the difference, but the crappy finance guy you put in charge of hiring doesn't.

In my experience, great leaders hire people based on their **future potential**, not on their past accomplishments. Leadership is about making others better.

Choose people you would like to have by your side in trench warfare. Choose smart over well-educated. Choose values over GPA. Hire people who ask good questions. Hire someone who tells you how much she doesn't know—that person knows a lot.

Steve Jobs didn't need to be an engineer because he had an innate ability to recruit and manage world-class engineers. Mark Zuckerberg didn't have to know how to build the world's most complex cloud application because he knew he could hire those guys. Elon Musk doesn't need to know how to fly a rocket or build a solar panel because he's great at recruiting brilliant engineers who can do those things.

Don't get me wrong—it's great to be a founding CEO who has deep knowledge is various domains. But the one skill to rule them all is being good at building teams and getting team members to achieve beyond their own expectations.

Case Study:
VENMO

Andrew Kortina and Iqram Magdon-Ismail met as freshman roommates at the University of Pennsylvania. In the process of helping a friend open a yogurt shop, they realized how awful traditional point-of-sale software was. Accepting and processing credit cards for a small purchase like a cup of yogurt was awkward and expensive.

Sometime later, they noticed a related problem: repaying each other for split dinner tabs. They'd go to dinner with six friends, the restaurants were often unwilling to split the check six ways, so one friend would pay for the dinner and then have to collect from the others. PayPal existed at the time but wasn't used by any of their friends because the PayPal user experience was a little clunky. "So we decided, let's just try to solve this problem and build a way to pay each other back that feels consistent with all of the other experiences we have in apps we use with our friends," says Kortina.

What they originally built was SMS-based. Kortina would text "iqram 20" to a number, and Iqram would receive a text that said, "kortina paid you $20". Dead simple. Then they added the ability to add a note so that the recipient's text would say, "kortina paid you $20 for tacos at sanchos".

Now they were onto something.

Like many first-time entrepreneurs, they were worried that someone out there may have the same idea. Kortina says, "We started googling and soon came across Obopay: a way to send money to anyone directly from your cell phone. They had recently raised $70 million from Nokia". Kortina and Magdon-Ismail were crushed, thinking there was no way they could compete with that. However, upon looking at Obopay's website, they were sure they could build something better.

And they did, eventually moving Venmo from being SMS-based to a native mobile app and watching their user base continue to grow. Young people were increasingly using their mobile phones for everything and loved the ability to split a dinner check on the spot or quickly pay rent to a roommate. Plus, Venmo had this unique social component, wherein the feed on your Venmo app, you could see your friends' activity. Venmo was quickly adopted by hundreds of people, then thousands, and eventually millions.

Kortina and Magdon-Ismail were confident in their technical skills, but they were very much aware that they knew nothing about running a company. So they convinced two friends to be company advisors—Sam Lessin, who was running a startup called drop.io, and Chris Stanchak, who had been Iqram's boss at a previous company.

In 2009 Facebook launched the "like button" and, as quaint as it seems now, that one feature really drove Facebook's growth. In September of that year, Sam Lessin sent a $3.33 Venmo payment to Magdon-Ismail with a note saying, "holy shit—you just built 'like' with money." Indeed, that's exactly what Venmo was—an app that made sending money to friends as easy as the new like button on Facebook.

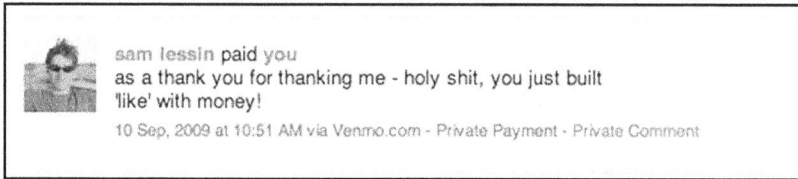

> sam lessin **paid you**
> as a thank you for thanking me - holy shit, you just built
> 'like' with money!
> 10 Sep, 2009 at 10:51 AM via Venmo.com - Private Payment - Private Comment

In December of that year, Sam and his father, Bob, led the first round of angel investment in Venmo. An investment that would eventually pay huge dividends.

And the brand name? Kortina says, "We were exploring the Latin root *vendere* which means sell and *mo* for mobile, but purely as a means to get to a name that (1) was short, 5-6 letters, (2) could be a verb, (3) didn't have an unintuitive spelling, and (4) was cheap. Venmo was available on GoDaddy for $12 and met the important criteria, so we grabbed it."

Today, Venmo is owned by PayPal, has over 78 million active users, and in 2022 processed over $224 billion in payments. I suspect Kortina and Magdon-Ismail aren't splitting many dinner tabs these days.

KEY TAKEAWAYS:

There are several great lessons in the Venmo story:

◊ As usual, it began with founders who noticed a problem worth solving.

◊ Don't worry about well-funded competition. As Richard Draeger said in Chapter 3, just focus on making your business better.

◊ The founders were self-aware about their own strengths and weaknesses and brought on advisors who were strong in areas the founders were weak.

◊ The funding didn't come through cold calls, it came through social connections after the idea had been proven and was ready to scale.

◊ Like most great brand names, Venmo is two syllables and meaningless (no one knows the name's Latin roots)! Two syllables and meaningless, just as most great brand names in history have been.

Team

What are the characteristics of the right team to make this venture a success?

The right team aligns with our target demographic - people who want to eat healthy and also enjoy the conveniece of a quick taco meal.

The economics of our venture are such that we'll need drivers and cooks who are affordable, so we will work hard to make it an attractive part-time job for students, and a great evening second job for anybody.

The Launch Path Canvas
Lorem ipsum

Name of Startup Venture: Fitaco, Inc
Prepared by: Bret Waters

Date: November 8, 2023
Iteration: 8

Problem
One clear sentence that articulates the problem your startup solves.

Consumers in the US spend $331 billion/year on fast food, and most of it is really unhealthy.

The paradox is that consumers today want to eat healthy, but also have a busy life that often drives them to resort to the convenience of fast food.

Solution
How does your venture solve the problem you have articulated? Keep this short and concise!

Fast food doesn't need to be unhealthy. Our startup is developing a new brand of health-conscious fast food (healthy tacos!), delivered directly to your home or office.

Why it matters
Why is this a problem worth solving?

The National Institutes for Health say that today a fast food diet may kill more people prematurely every year than cigarette smoking.

Alternatives
When a customer looks at alternative ways to solve the problem we solve, what will they see? This is a list of competitors and alternatives. Link to a graphic representation of the landscape.

There are many meal food delivery services, from Uber Eats to Doordash to Grubhub.

See visualization at this link.

Customer
It's all about understanding customers. Write a one-sentence description of key customer personas and the problem we solve for each. Circle the one that is most influential.

Adventurous Alex: A thrill-seeking foodie always on the hunt for unique and spicy taco creations to satisfy their daring palate.

Health-Conscious Haley: A fitness enthusiast looking for wholesome and fresh ingredient options that align with their nutritious lifestyle at the taqueria.

Busy Ben: An on-the-go professional seeking quick, flavorful, and portable taco choices to enjoy during a busy workday.

Vegetarian Victoria: A plant-based eater in search of flavorful and creative vegetarian and vegan taco selections that cater to their dietary preferences.

Traditional Tony: A lover of classic flavors, Tony enjoys indulging in authentic and time-honored taco recipes that remind him of his cultural heritage.

Family-Oriented Felix: A parent looking for a family-friendly meal delivery with a variety of options to cater to the taste preferences of both kids and adults.

Budget-Conscious Bella: A student or frugal diner in pursuit of affordable yet flavorful taco choices that won't break the bank at the taqueria.

Path to PMF
What is our path to Product-Market Fit? Customer Development, MVP's, etc.

1. Farmers' markets where we can get input on our menu items.
2. One truck in the Palo Alto area for a pilot project.
3. Scale slowly to additional markets, based on our learnings.

Top 3 Benefits
What are the top 3 benefits that your product or services provides to customers?

1. Convenience. Use our mobile app to place a custom order and it's delivered directly to you.
2. Healthy food, designed by a nutritionist.
3. Tacos. Everybody loves tacos.

Distribution
What are our distribuion channels? Direct to consumer, via resellers, or?

We intend to sell direct-to-consumer, via our mobile app and website, with delivery via our own vans.

In the future, we may be open to distribution partners.

Positioning
Within this landscape of competitors and alternatives, how is your venture positioned?

Our positioning can basically be summed-up in two words: healthy and delicious.

There are many food delivery apps that can deliver something that is delicious but not very healthy. Or you could eat a kale salad.

We serve delicious tacos designed by a nutritionist. That's our unique positioning.

Economics
What are the Unit Economics for this venture, what do we expect the CAC<LTV to look like, and what are our capital needs? (Link to full spreadsheet).

One unit = one taco: Sell price $5, on which our gross profit is $.74

Early tests indicate CAC of $11, and we expect an initial LTV of three orders per customer ($25.50), which will grow with time.

Our initial capital needs are $220K, which will get us through the pilot launch. We will propose to investors structuring this as a SAFE.

See full spreadsheet at this link.

Team
What are the characteristics of the right team to make this venture a success?

The right team aligns with our target demographic - people who want to eat healthy and also enjoy the convenience of a quick taco meal.

The economics of our venture are such that we'll need drivers and cooks who are affordable, so we will work hard to make it an attractive part-time job for students, and a great evening second job for anybody.

Defensibility
What is your secret sauce that is difficult for competitors to copy?

The fact that we own the customer and customer data is a big part of our defensibility.

A restaurant selling through a 3rd-party like Doordash owns neither the customer nor the data.

See full example at **thelaunchpath.com**

STEP 10, FOR YOUR STARTUP

Putting together the right team will be essential for your startup to succeed, grow, and thrive. That's self-evident. It's also true that your first few hires will establish your company culture and you don't want to mess that up. Finally, of course, employees are likely to be the most expensive part of your operation—by far—and so that makes it even more crucial that you hire right.

▶ *For your Launch Path Canvas:*

List two or three traits and attributes that you think will be important in team members for your new venture. Don't worry about needing to get this 100% right at this early stage, the purpose here is just to get yourself thinking about the topic. Put these traits in the "Team" box, near the middle of the canvas.

"The world is filled with great opportunities brilliantly disguised as insoluble problems.

JOHN W. GARDNER

CHAPTER 11

HAVE IMPACT

Using The Launch Path framework for launching nonprofit organizations and Social Ventures

One morning about 15 years ago, I had a conversation that forever changed the way I think of impact organizations. I met with Jim Koch in his cramped office on the campus of Santa Clara University, a Jesuit school located at the heart of Silicon Valley and the oldest university in California.[1]

He told me about his vision for being able to improve on the traditional model of nonprofit organizations, using Silicon Valley thinking to create a new kind of startup ("social ventures," he called them) that could harness the power of markets while delivering social impact at scale.

Jim is one of those guys who has the kind of gravitas that makes an entire room go quiet when he speaks. After getting his MBA and Ph.D. from UCLA, he went into corporate management, then moved to the academic world where, as a professor and Dean of the Business School, he helped build Santa Clara University's MBA program into the nationally-ranked business school that it is today. As if that wasn't impressive enough, he also spent time as Acting Dean of Santa Clara's renowned School of Engineering. To have run the School of Business

---

1: The claim to "oldest university in California" is a somewhat fuzzy one, as UC Berkeley has its origins about the same time. Santa Clara University, which began as Santa Clara College in 1851, today officially uses the description "California's oldest continuously-operating institution of higher learning." Stanford didn't come along until 1891.

and the School of Engineering at a prestigious private university in Silicon Valley is a pretty rare feat.

As we sat in his office that morning, Jim talked about how the traditional charity model needed to be updated. Nonprofit organizations tend to live on a hamster wheel of pursuing donations to meet the most urgent problems (or just the ones that donors care about right now). Conventional nonprofit organizations are incentivized to produce fast relief because actual systemic change takes much longer and is much more difficult.

When there is famine somewhere in the world, for example, charities raise money to send in truckloads of food. Once people are fed, the charities and donors move on to the next humanitarian crisis without having ever addressed the underlying reasons why the famine had occurred in the first place. "If what we care about is sustainability," Jim told me, "then we need a new kind of organization. We need to bring entrepreneurial thinking to the impact world by creating social ventures."

Although I had never heard the term "social entrepreneur" before I met with Jim Koch that morning, it turns out that a McKinsey consultant named Bill Drayton had been using it for several years as a way of describing individuals who were creating innovative ways to address society's most pressing social problems (Drayton went on to found Ashoka, an organization dedicated to supporting social entrepreneurs). Unlike traditional nonprofit charities, social entrepreneurs might have a for-profit aspect to their operations, using earned income to create sustainability and drive scale. Riffing on the old proverb that "If you give a man a fish he'll eat for a day, but if you teach him to fish he'll eat for a lifetime," Drayton wrote, "Social entrepreneurs are not content just to give a fish or teach how to fish. They will not rest until they have revolutionized the fishing industry."

I finished my meeting with Jim Koch that morning and drove back to my office, thinking about all of this. I had been President of two nonprofit organizations (one was a 501(c)(3) foundation supporting my kids' school, and the other was an educational nonprofit based on the Stanford campus), and I had already been musing about the notion that there had to be a better way to deliver impact. The vision that Jim articulated resonated with me.

Two years earlier, Muhammad Yunus had been awarded the Nobel Peace Prize for what the Nobel Committee called "efforts through microcredit to create economic and social development from below." It started when he lent $27 to a group of poor families so that they could start a business making and selling handicrafts. He was astonished when they paid it all back, plus interest, and went on to build meaningful livelihoods for themselves.

He then founded Grameen Bank and pioneered the field now known as microfinance, giving loans to people in Bangladesh too poor to qualify for traditional bank loans, mostly used to start simple income-generating businesses. Not only did his bank lift tens of thousands of people out of poverty, it did so profitably. Read that last sentence again because it sums up the radical concept that **an organization can both do good and do well** at the same time.

Jim Koch was exactly the right guy to take these lofty thoughts and put them into structured practice, right at the intersection of his experience of running a leading School of Business and a School of Engineering at a Jesuit university dedicated to bettering humanity. So synthesizing the concepts developed by Bill Drayton, Mohammad Yunus, and others, Jim Koch co-founded at Santa Clara University what is today called Miller Center for Social Entrepreneurship.[2] The Center runs the

---

2: I've condensed the history of Miller Center for Social Entrepreneurship a bit. You can read the full history on their website at millersocent.org

world's leading startup accelerator program for social ventures, and I've served as a volunteer Executive Mentor with the program for more than fifteen years. We've had more than 1,300 social entrepreneurs go through our startup accelerator program, and our graduates have gone on to raise nearly a billion dollars in capital and deliver social and economic impact all over the world. Working with Miller Center has been one of the great honors of my life.

What do these social ventures typically look like? Here are four that I've worked with at Miller Center, just to give you a flavor:

- **Nnaemeka Ikegwuonu** wanted to help smallholder farmers in his native country of Nigeria. So he established a community radio station called the Smallholders Foundation that would deliver relevant content to them (weather, market information, tutorials on improving agricultural yields) in order to help improve their livelihoods. Earned income comes from selling air time to NGO's and others who want to reach the same populations.
- **Diana Sierra** is a successful industrial designer who grew up in Colombia (the country), got a Master's degree from Columbia (the University), and went on to design innovative new products for a variety of global brands. A trip to Africa a few years ago exposed her to a problem that exists all over the world: girls without access to menstrual products often miss a week of school every month, putting them at an academic disadvantage from the moment they hit puberty. Diana put her product design skills to work developing product that could solve the problem, moved to Mozambique, and founded BeGirl, a social venture that has now reached a half-million young women in Africa (see case study in Chapter 9).
- **Manoj Sinha** grew up in India, went to IIT, then came to the US to get his Master's in engineering from the University

of Massachusetts Amherst. Wanting to make a difference for people at home, plus help to save the planet, he launched Husk Power Systems to build and deploy micro-grid electricity systems in rural India. It turns out that rural areas all over the world depend on kerosene lanterns and diesel generators for light and electricity, causing all sorts of environmental damage. Husk's microgrids can save small communities 30% on their electricity costs with 100% renewable power plants. Husk Power now serves over 50,000 rural households and has expanded from India into Africa. On his LinkedIn profile, Manoj describes himself as "Driven by personal values, integrity and relentless pursuit for excellence." That's pretty much all you need to know right there.

- **Charlot Magayi** grew up in Kenya, where many families cooked over charcoal—the only affordable way to fire a stove and cook a meal. As a young mother, she experienced her own child getting respiratory tract infections and burns, very common in families cooking on charcoal. So she finally saved enough money to start Mukuru Clean Stoves, repurposing locally sourced waste metal to manufacture improved, efficient, and reliable cookstoves sold and distributed by local women. They've now sold over 250,000 of their stoves, impacting more than 1.2 million lives across the country while dramatically reducing carbon emissions. Charlot's organization has a sustainable earned income model (selling stoves profitably), plus social impact (getting families off of hazardous charcoal), plus economic development (distribution is all done by self-employed women), plus climate impact (500,000 tons of CO_2 reduced).

While these are four very different ventures addressing very different problems, they are all using entrepreneurial thinking to create social impact in a way that harnesses market forces to give sustainability to their operations. That's a powerful thing.

There's another key aspect to most social ventures: they typically treat base-of-the-pyramid populations as partners rather than just charity cases. Historically, nonprofit charities have arrived, handed out food to poor people, and then left. Social entrepreneurs are more likely to be from a local community or work in long-term proximity with the communities they serve while helping individuals establish businesses, improve crop yields, and reduce dependency.

This is what makes successful social enterprises different from other impact-focused organizations: They have an **earned-income model** that creates **systemic change** by treating underserved communities as **customers and partners.**

Using The Launch Path for Social Ventures

So, with regard to **The Launch Path,** how is building and launching a successful social venture different from a traditional startup? I honestly think it's probably 85% the same. It begins by identifying a problem worth solving; you'll still need to get to Product-Market Fit, you still need to understand how your venture fits within the landscape of competitors and alternatives, and you still need an economic model. But here are a few key differences between launching Social Ventures and a traditional startup:

- **A theory of change plus a business model.**
  Ordinary startups need to have a business model—a rationale by which the organization creates, delivers, and captures value in the form of earned income. Social ventures—if they intend to be sustainable on earned income—need to have the same. But as organizations dedicated to impact, they also need to have an impact model—a theory of change by which they are creating, delivering, and measuring a desired social/environmental improvement.

- **Contributed income vs earned income.**
  Charities and non-profit organizations exist on contributed income (donations and grants), whereas for-profit companies operate on earned income (profit from operations). Many social ventures are launched and operated on a combination of the two—a typical model might be to use contributed income to launch the venture and then become sustainable by having earned income associated with ongoing operations. So when developing the economic model we discussed in Chapter 5, you'll want to distinguish between earned income and contributed income.

- **Measuring Impact.**
  We have well-established ways of measuring the financial performance of an organization: revenue growth, net profit, debt-to-equity ratio, etc. With a social venture, you'll also need to have quantitative and qualitative ways of measuring your impact. Social ventures are sometimes called "double bottom line" organizations because they are operated partly for an economic bottom line (profits that provide economic sustainability) and partly for a social bottom line (lives impacted or carbon emissions reduced, for example).

- **Defining Personas.**
  In Chapter 7, we talked about developing personas for your startup as a way of making sure you understand that the benefits your product delivers to one sort of customer may be a little different than to another. With social ventures, the population that you impact may be different from the customer you are selling to. I like to draw a "how the money flows" diagram with social ventures, showing the different personas involved and how they fit into your overall engine of sustainable impact.

- **Sources and structures of capital.**

  In the old-fashioned bifurcated world of non-profit and for-profit organizations, there were no established sources of capital for mission-driven organizations. Social ventures weren't "non-profit enough" to pitch foundations for grants, and they weren't "for-profit enough" to pitch for venture capital on Sand Hill Road. Fortunately, in the past ten years, this has changed dramatically, and today there are many different sources and structures of capital for social ventures. I'll dive deeper into them in the next section below.

- **Choosing the right entity type.**

  A traditional nonprofit in the US is incorporated as a 501(c)3, a special tax-exempt organization that is required to operate within a constrained set of parameters. Social ventures will often be better off incorporating either a traditional corporation or a B-Corp, a special entity that is recognized by many states. Choosing one of these structures will give you more flexibility with regard to financing the venture. See "A Legal Primer for Entrepreneurs" in the reference section of this book.

- **The "Exit".**

  Many tech entrepreneurs dream of building a startup that will be bought by Google for $500 million or maybe having a billion-dollar IPO. With social ventures, those outcomes are much less likely. So this makes the investor pitch (and capital structure) for social ventures a bit different. You are pitching the impact, of course, but if you are looking for equity capital or debt capital, you'll need to have a proposition by which the capital makes a round trip (i.e., is paid back to the investor with an upside) even if there is no acquisition or IPO in the future.

With those broad exceptions, launching a successful social venture or nonprofit organization requires the same essential process as any other startup. The steps on The Launch Path, as outlined in this book, all still apply.

Sources and structures of capital for social ventures

As mentioned above, social ventures are less likely to be a fit for traditional venture capital since it's unlikely the equity in a social venture can be sold in the future at a huge multiple over the purchase price (the basic equation that venture capital relies on). But here are some of the financing types that are successfully used to provide capital to social ventures (make sure you read the Chapter 6 section outlining the differences between grants, debt, and equity).

- **Traditional Grants.**
  Many social enterprises are able to raise seed capital from foundations structured as a grants. A social enterprise developing some new agricultural technology they plan to sell in emerging markets, for example, might be able to get a grant from the Gates Foundation to develop the technology, with the idea that the enterprise will be self-funded on earned income once the product is launched.

- **Impact Loans.**
  These are loans specifically designed for social ventures and other impact-based organisations. These are sometimes called "soft loans" because the terms may be somewhat more friendly than a commercial bank might offer—perhaps the interest rate is below market rate, or maybe the repayment terms are flexible. The lender (might be a government agency, a foundation, or a private organization) gets the benefit of helping to achieve

social impact while still having the capital make a "round trip" back to the lender, and the social venture gets the benefit of capital with more favorable terms than they would get from a traditional bank.

- **Program Related Investments (PRI).**
  Because of the odd nature of US tax law, foundations will often only issue grants to 501(c)3 nonprofit organizations, and if they make investments into for-profit entities, they may be subject to a special excise tax under Section 4944 (just hang in there with me on this). So a way to invest in a social enterprise is often via a Program Related Investment, which allows them to help fund a social enterprise that aligns with the foundation's mission while still hoping for a financial return on their investment.

- **Demand Dividend.**
  This is a structure that blends aspects of debt and equity. Like debt, it goes on the books as a loan. But like equity, it gives the lender a claim to future profits, with an agreement that profits will be paid out as dividends "on-demand" in order to pay back the loan.

- **Revenue Share Notes.**
  This is a very common and simple arrangement by which the investor gives money to the social enterprise in return for a share of revenue capped at a certain amount. For example, I could give $100K to a social venture with the agreement that they will pay me 2% of all future revenue until I receive $150K back.

- **Social Impact Bonds (SIB).**
  Despite the name, they aren't really a bond in the traditional sense. It's more of a pay-for-performance agreement. Let's say

your startup has an innovative way to address homelessness in a particular city, and you'll need a million dollars to run the program. You draw up a Social Impact Bond in which perhaps a private investor puts up the million dollars, and the city agrees to pay down the bond by $250,000 for each x% reduction in homelessness achieved, capped at a million dollars. If all goes well, the city is happy that the homelessness rate was reduced, the investor is pleased to have made a difference and also got their capital returned, and your social venture ended up with a million dollars.

These are just some of the many sources and structures of capital for social ventures in the current landscape. As with any sort of financing, the key is to find a structure where the interests of the investor are aligned with the interests of the organization. With social ventures getting this alignment can be a little more challenging because the impact component adds another layer and also because the capital isn't likely to return to the investor in the same way that venture capital comes back (acquisition or IPO). But the good news is that today there are sources and structures available that make sense to align investors and social entrepreneurs.

Summary

The world faces many challenges today. We have a climate crisis that threatens the planet, and we can't feed all eight billion people we have now (let alone the ten billion we'll have by 2050), plus, we want economic equality for women and social justice for all. These are big hairy problems.

Traditional charity still has a role to play, as do governments, but social entrepreneurs can bring unique agility, fresh thinking, and innovation to bear on these problems. The World Economic Forum says we have now entered the 4th Industrial Revolution and that "the speed, breadth, and depth of this revolution is forcing us to rethink how countries develop and how organizations create value."

They go on to say that while technology is driving this new industrial revolution, "The real opportunity is to look beyond technology, and find ways to give the greatest number of people the ability to positively impact their families, organizations, and communities."

As someone who has spent his life in Silicon Valley, I believe in the power of entrepreneurship to change the world. Social Entrepreneurs all over the globe today are working at the intersection of innovative thinking, a passion for improving the world, and expertise in harnessing the power of markets. I believe they can deliver change that is powerful and sustainable.

Case Study:
MAUQA

A couple of years ago, I met Suniya Sadullah Khan through my work with Miller Center for Social Entrepreneurship. She and her co-founder, Muhammad Mustafa, had an idea for a social venture that would help poor, illiterate people in Pakistan get jobs as domestic workers (house cleaners, cooks, babysitters, etc.).

Their thesis was that the gig economy had created opportunities for lots of people around the world, but most gig jobs are app-based or online-based, and it's hard to use those tools if you can't read. They believed they could change this by creating an online marketplace that included an app with a user interface designed for illiterate workers. Suniya and her co-founder began planning their venture, naming it Mauqa Online (mauqa is the Urdu word for "opportunity").

Many founders would assume that the correct first step in developing the startup would be to build a minimum viable product (MVP) of the app itself. In fact, that's the direction Suniya and her co-founder were headed in as they searched for a technical person who could help build an MVP.

But then they attended a workshop on lean startup methodology, and Suniya remembers, "That's when it clicked—if we stopped thinking that our MVP had to be 'tech,' we could start experimenting straight away to see what works and what doesn't."

The concept of "on-demand services" barely existed in Pakistan—Uber and its competitors had only launched a couple of years earlier, as had food delivery startups—so Pakistanis were slowly getting used to the whole idea. The only way this venture would work would be if there were enough clients interested in using it to find on-demand domestic helpers.

Suniya and her co-founder believed that there would be, but one of the key tenets of lean startup methodology is to **test your hypotheses**. Suniya "decided to first test if our hypothesis of clients wanting 'on-demand domestic help' was true. So, we started a Facebook page and just posted in different groups with no advertising spend at all. A day later, we had a customer message saying she wanted someone to come and iron clothes for three hours. We didn't have anyone, so my co-founder went and did the job!"

As they ran their new "marketplace" as a Facebook page, they continued to gain key insights. They realized their pricing was too low, so they adjusted it. They found out that some of the helpers didn't have the soft skills clients expected in domestic workers, so they started offering soft-skills training for helpers who signed up.

They soon added a basic website linked to a Google form. The flow of new customers started to increase, and they began to experience some scaling pains. For example, in order to make sure helpers arrived at a client's house on time, Suniya would often ferry them around herself—an approach that was clearly not scalable. So they entered into a partnership with Careem (recently acquired by Uber for 3.1 billion dollars) to handle transportation logistics.

Their next bottleneck turned into an inability to recruit employees fast enough, so they increased their salary offerings above the market rates and offered to pay employees every two weeks (a duration mostly unheard of in Pakistan).

In the aggregate, these learnings not only proved Suniya's hypotheses but also provided invaluable learnings about how they needed to modify their business model—learnings they **would never have gotten if they had started by building an MVP of the app itself.**

"If we had started by building an MVP of the app," Suniya says, "I honestly think our startup would have flopped. By instead launching it with manual processes, and doing everything by hand, we started generating some revenue in our second month and were constantly learning every day about operations, supply, demand, and customer service points that we needed to address. We documented all of this and used the learning when we finally built our customer app, our back-end engine, and now for the helper app."

Here's the thing: In the case of Mauqa, the question wasn't: "Could we build an app?" Of course, they could build the app, so creating an MVP of the app wouldn't have proved anything. Instead, the question was:

"Is there marketplace potential in connecting poor, illiterate people in Pakistan with clients wanting on-demand domestic work? If so, what would the issues be in delivering a marketplace of that kind?" Choosing to create a non-digital MVP and doing everything by hand gave them the validated learning they needed to make their venture a success.

In 2019, Suniya landed a big funding round, and Mauqa started scaling up, adding two more big cities and improving the livelihoods of thousands of people across Pakistan—all because they figured out what kind of MVP they needed for the learnings required to build and scale a successful venture.

Note: Mauqa Online closed its doors in 2021 after scaling rapidly in three Pakistani cities and preparing to expand to the capital, Karachi. Suniya's co-founder Muhammed Mustafa said, "We raised funds to operate in Karachi, but due to the tightening of the regulatory environment by the Financial Action Task Force (FATF), our funds were stuck." Despite this ultimate fate, I've still included the case study because it illustrates nicely the concept of building a successful MVP for a social venture.

KEY TAKEAWAYS:

There are several great lessons in the Mauqa story:

◊ Most founders of an app-based startup think an MVP would be an early version of the app or maybe a clickable digital prototype. But smart founders know that it's important to be clear on what you actually want to test and learn from. For Suniya and her co-founder, they realized the correct MVP needed to be a manual, non-digital version of the service that would test the idea and provide them with key learnings and insights <u>before</u> building the actual app.

◊ For different startups, the risk is in different places. For Mauqa, the risk was whether the "gig economy" was a concept that would be embraced in Pakistan and whether the logistics could be worked out. Great entrepreneurs are always thinking to themselves, "What is the smallest possible experiment I could do right now that would provide the greatest possible learning?".

◊ Founders need to do everything themselves for as long as possible. Suniya went into the neighborhoods where workers were and signed them up personally, calling them when jobs were available. Muhammed went and did an ironing job himself when they couldn't find a worker. Founders who are on the front lines will learn insights much more quickly than founders who delegate those tasks too soon.

The Launch Path Canvas

Lorem ipsum

Name of Startup Venture: Fitaco, Inc

Prepared by: Bret Waters

Date: November 8, 2023

Iteration: 8

Problem ?	Solution	Why it matters ☆	Alternatives	Customer
One clear sentence that articulates the problem your startup solves. Consumers in the US spend $331 billion/year on fast food, and most of it is really unhealthy. The paradox is that consumers today want to eat healthy, but also have a busy life that often drives them to resort to the convenience of fast food.	How does your venture solve the problem you have articulated? Keep this short and concise! Fast food doesn't need to be unhealthy. Our startup is developing a new brand of health-conscious fast food (healthy tacos!), delivered directly to your home or office.	Why is this a problem worth solving? The National Institutes for Health say that today a fast food diet may kill more people prematurely every year than cigarette smoking.	When a customer looks at alternative ways to solve the problem we solve, what will they see? This is a list of competitors and alternatives. Link to a graphic representation of the landscape. There are many, many food delivery services, from Uber Eats to Doordash to Grubhub. See visualization at this link.	It's all about understanding customers. Write a one-sentence description of key customer personas and the problem we solve for each. Circle the one that is most influential. **Adventurous Alex:** A thrill-seeking foodie always on the hunt for unique and spicy taco creations to satisfy their daring palate. **Health-Conscious Haley:** A fitness enthusiast looking for wholesome and fresh ingredient options that align with their nutritious lifestyle at the taqueria.

Path to PMF	Top 3 Benefits	Distribution	Positioning	(continued)
What is our path to Product-Market Fit? Customer Development, MVPs, etc. 1. Farmers' markets where we can get input on our menu items. 2. One truck in the Palo Alto area for a pilot project. 3. Scale slowly to additional markets, based on our learnings.	What are the top 3 benefits that your product or services provides to customers? 1. Convenience. Use our mobile app to place a custom order and it's delivered directly to you. 2. Healthy food, designed by a nutritionist. 3. Tacos. Everybody loves tacos.	What are our distribution channels? Direct to consumer, via resellers, or? We intend to sell direct-to-consumer, via our mobile app and website, with delivery via our own vans. In the future, we may be open to distribution partnerships.	Within this landscape of competitors and alternatives, how is your venture positioned? Our positioning can basically be summed-up in two words: healthy, and delicious. There are many food delivery apps that can deliver something that is delicious but not very healthy. Or you could eat a kale salad. We serve delicious tacos designed by a nutritionist. That's our unique positioning.	**Busy Ben:** An on-the-go professional seeking quick, flavorful, and portable taco choices to enjoy during a busy workday. **Vegetarian Victoria:** A plant-based eater in search of flavorful and creative vegetarian and vegan taco selections that cater to their dietary preferences. **Traditional Tony:** A lover of classic flavors, Tony enjoys indulging in authentic and time-honored taco recipes that remind him of his cultural heritage.

Economics	Team	Defensibility		(continued)
What are the Unit Economics for this venture, what do we expect the CAC<LTV to look like, and what are out capital needs? (Link to full spreadsheet). One unit = one taco. Sell price $5, on which our gross profit is 4.74 Early tests indicate CAC of $11, and we expect an initial LTV of three orders per customer ($25.50), which will grow with time. Our initial capital needs are $220K, which will get us through the pilot launch. We will propose to investors structuring this as a SAFE. See full spreadsheet at this link.	What are the characteristics of the right team to make this venture a success? The right team aligns with our target demographic - people who want to eat healthy and also enjoy the convenience of a quick taco meal. The economics of our venture are such that we'll need drivers and cooks who are affordable, so we will work hard to make it an attractive part-time job for students, and a great evening second job for anybody.	What is your secret sauce that is difficult for competitors to copy? The fact that we own the customer and customer data is a big part of our defensibility. A restaurant selling through a 3rd-party like Doordash owns neither the customer nor the data.		**Family-Oriented Felix:** A parent looking for a family-friendly meal delivery with a variety of options to cater to the taste preferences of both kids and adults. **Budget-Conscious Bella:** A student or frugal diner in pursuit of affordable yet flavorful taco choices that won't break the bank at the taqueria.

STEP 11, FOR YOUR STARTUP

Whether you are explicitly a social venture, or you just simply want to operate your for-profit company in a way that is a responsible member of the community, having clear values matters. It's important for any company to have a positive impact on the community you operate within, and a key component to team culture is being clear on why your startup matters.

▶ *For your Launch Path Canvas:*

Write a paragraph or two about why your venture matters. Share it with your team for input and buy-in. Now distill it down to one crisp sentence and put that sentence in the "Why it matters" box on the **Launch Path Canvas.**

"It takes 20 years to build a reputation and five minutes to ruin it. If you think about that, you'll do things differently.

WARREN BUFFETT

CHAPTER 12
OPERATE WITH INTEGRITY

Great leaders build high-performing organizations based on honesty, transparency, and integrity

My first full-time job, at the age of 21, was with a company named Pacific Lithograph in San Francisco. I was hired as a salesman, and on my very first day, the President of the company, a tall, crusty old guy named Doug Ballinger, called me into his office. I was nervous and wondering why I'd been called into the Big Guy's office already. He said to me, "Listen up, kid. I want you to know that the one thing that will get you fired here is if I ever catch you doing anything dishonest. Dishonest with a customer, or a vendor, or a colleague, or whatever" (he had a few F-bombs tossed in there, just for flavor). "Some people are going to say we're good printers, and some people are going to say we're bad printers, but I don't want anyone to ever say we're dishonest businesspeople. Because here's the most important thing you need to know about business, kid: a reputation for bad quality you can work hard to overcome. But a reputation for dishonesty, you'll never overcome."

Big Doug is long gone, but his words have served me well in the decades since. So I'd like to conclude this book with a few words about honesty and integrity in the startup world.

Silicon Valley has seen its share of startup founder fraud, some of it very well-publicized. The story of Elizabeth Holmes and Theranos has been covered widely in the media and turned into a book and a movie. Once hailed as "the next Steve Jobs," she's now a convicted felon and perhaps the most famous example of an entrepreneur who crossed the line between over-promising and outright fraud.

Over the years, there have been other examples of startup fraud, and some of them are a bit comedic to look back on. In the 1980's, managers at disk drive manufacturer MiniScribe boosted their numbers by packing 26,000 red bricks into disk drive boxes, shipping them to Singapore, and booking them as "sales." A decade later, Pixelon raised $30 million in venture capital, spent $12 million of it on a launch party in Las Vegas, and then filed for bankruptcy the following year.

More recently, in 2021, Softbank invested $150 million in a messaging app called "IRL." When they made the investment, the founders' pitch deck claimed the app had 20 million users and was growing fast. Later it turned out that 95% of those users were bots. The numbers in the pitch deck were completely bogus. Softbank has filed suit against the founders, but it's unlikely they'll get much of the money back. Whoops.

The fact is, startup founders often find themselves walking a thin line between bravado and deceit. You're making big promises in pitch meetings with investors, you're projecting confidence in interviews with the press, and with your internal team, you want to be an upbeat, motivating presence, even on bad days. "Fake it 'till you make it" is the well-worn mantra.

In any business, there's always the temptation to fudge the numbers a little. Accounting rules allow for a bit of leeway here and there, and CEO's are constantly working with the accounting team to make things look as good as possible. Deals that close on the threshold between two quarters will get booked in whichever quarter needs them most. Uncollectible receivables can be kept on the books until after the first of the year in order to improve this year's numbers. Deals signed on May 1 can be backdated to April 30th. "It all comes out in the wash," the saying goes. But it can be a slippery slope from harmless fudging to outright fraud.

The Theranos case, to me, has always been an example of what I call "the promise overhang." Every entrepreneur makes promises about their product that slightly overhang what the product can actually do. That's common for exuberant optimists like startup founders. But when that overhang extends too far, everything collapses.

I don't know Elizabeth Holmes, but I suspect that she started out as an earnest entrepreneur who over-promised a little. But then the promise overhang grew, and after a while, her overpromising turned into lies, as she kept hoping that the product would eventually catch up to her promises. And then the lies became a habit. And once lies become a habit, soon you're committing outright fraud without even being fully conscious of it.

I believe that honesty, transparency, and integrity are moral imperatives for each of us as individuals. But with a business, those principles become an economic imperative as well. A commitment to ethical behavior builds trust and fosters long-term relationships, two things that are absolutely essential to the growth and success of any organization.

In operating with integrity, every day, you'll also be establishing the right tribal culture for your team. A team built around values of honesty, transparency, and long-term decision-making will consistently outperform a team run by a CEO who is in the habit of telling lies for short-term gain. "A fish rots from the head down," as the saying has it. Don't be a rotting fishhead.

Nothing is more important to startup success than the team. A team that senses dishonesty, false promises, or unfairness leads to a toxic environment and high turnover rates, which can dramatically hinder a company's growth and damage its reputation in the industry Conversely, a team that knows that its leaders say what they mean, mean what they say, and can stand behind their product with a clean conscience? That's golden.

For many startups today, ethics and values also can come into play during product development. Technology products can cause privacy risk for users, medical products obviously have risk/benefit issues to consider, and the new generation of artificial intelligence products opens up all sorts of new ethical issues to consider.

There are regulations around many of these things, of course, but as the founding CEO, are you going to establish a company culture of making sure your products are always compliant with regulations, or will you create a culture of finding ways to skirt or avoid regulations wherever possible?

That's your decision to make.

My personal leaning has always been toward clean compliance on everything. I want all the company's energy to go into building great products and happy customers, not dealing with tax audits, regulators, and lawsuits.

I called this chapter "Operate with Integrity," but maybe it really should be **operate with intention**. As you found and operate your company, be intentional about every decision, making sure that all your decisions align with your founding values.

My friend José Flahaux co-wrote a book recently called *Ethics in the Age of Disruptive Technologies*.[1] The book discusses the fact that business ethics have a whole new layer to them now, as technology products often come with ethical dilemmas that didn't exist a generation ago.

1: Ethics in the Age of Disruptive Technologies: An Operational Roadmap.
   ISBN 979-8851448072

ChatGPT builds knowledge by stealing other people's ideas. Social media enables creepy actions by bad actors. Facial recognition can be used in fighting crime but can also be racist. The book suggests that CEO's should establish their anchoring principals for the company and that those principals become the center around which all other values orbit. As José's book says, "Principles without operationalization are just nice words: the proof of ethical intentions is in the actions and outcomes themselves." Operate with intention.

For you, as a startup founder, decide what your anchoring principles will be. Share them with your co-founders and make sure there is consensus and intention. Publish them for all team members, and ask them to hold you accountable—if you ever make decisions that are not aligned with the company's anchoring principles, you want your team members to bring it to your attention.

An early Google employee suggested their anchoring principle should be "Don't be evil," and the Google team embraced it wholeheartedly. When Google had its IPO in 2004, the prospectus contained a letter from Larry and Sergey, the founders, which said, "Don't be evil. We believe strongly that in the long term, we will be better served—as shareholders and in all other ways—by a company that does good things for the world even if we forgo some short-term gains". Over time, the motto was changed to "Do the right thing," but the final sentence of the preface to the employee manual still says "And remember... don't be evil..."

Yes, we can argue today about whether Google has always made good ethical decisions, but you can't argue with the success of the company or the strength of its company culture.

Running a business is hard, and every day can be filled with difficult decisions. Being clear about your moral compass can make those decisions a little bit easier, and will help to create a team culture that builds toward long-term success.

Big Doug was right—run your business with honesty, integrity, and transparency.

If you do that, good things will happen.

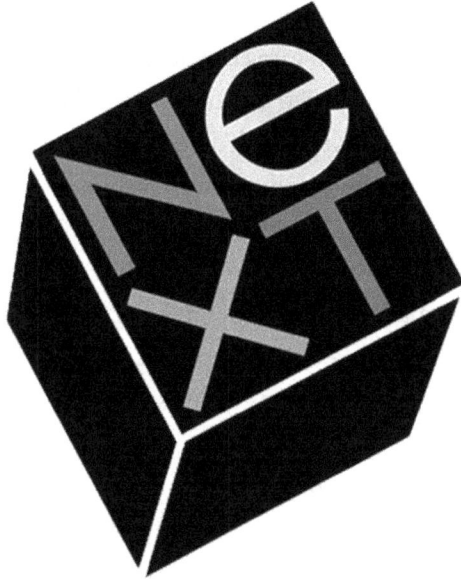

Case Study:
NEXT COMPUTER

In September of 1985 Steve Jobs was fired from Apple, the company he had founded. He was so pissed off that he sold all of his Apple stock except one single share that he kept as a souvenir.

Enraged by what had happened, he went out and founded a new company, NeXT, to build the perfect next-generation computer. He wanted to show the world that he was right and the Apple board was wrong. A few Apple employees followed him, and for the next three years, he disappeared from sight as he and his small team worked days and nights to develop what they believed would be the greatest computer system ever.

I was running a company in Palo Alto at the time, just a few blocks from his house, and we'd run into each other occasionally at the Whole Foods that had recently opened at Emerson and Homer, where he'd go for his fresh vegan juice blends. We'd nod to each other in recognition, but he wasn't really in the mood for conversation. He was focused.

Apple sued NeXT, saying they were building something based on confidential information. Jobs responded, "It is hard to think that a $2 billion company with 4,300-plus people couldn't compete with six people in blue jeans." The suit was dismissed.

Steve Jobs had met previously with Paul Berg, a Nobel prize-winning professor of chemistry at Stanford University, who expressed frustration with the time and expense of researching recombinant DNA in traditional laboratories, and was convinced that a more powerful computer would make a huge difference. Intrigued, Jobs met with universities around the world to better understand what a high-end computer workstation for university researchers might be like. He began hearing some patterns and decided that universities and other research labs could be the beachhead market for his new computer, and from there, they could move into consumer markets.

When the NeXT computer was finally unveiled to the world, it was a genuinely beautiful work of art. It had a die-cast magnesium cube-shaped black case with a lightning-fast 25 MHz CPU inside, a magneto-optical drive—and built-in ethernet!

But most impressive of all was the new operating system, NeXTSTEP. Object-oriented and multi-tasking, it was based on Unix and had power and flexibility that went far beyond any other desktop operating system on the market.

At the launch event held at Davies Symphony Hall in San Francisco, Jobs delivered a brilliant presentation, as always. He talked about how he took everything he had learned developing the original Mac, and invested that knowledge in making something even better. "Macintosh was a revolution in making it easier for the end user," he said, "But the software developer paid the price. If you look at the time it takes to make an application... the user interface takes 90% of the time"

To solve this problem, NeXT had developed their own set of object libraries for developers to use. So instead of having to write the code to draw an interface button on the screen, for example, one line of code would call something from the library that would do that for you. Seems obvious now, but at the time, it was revolutionary.

Jobs said this object library for NeXT software developers would be called ApplicationKit, or AppKit. Included was a visual tool called "Interface Builder," that gave developers the ability to build and connect the objects in their programs graphically.

It's hard to overstate what a big deal this was at the time. By the late 1980's, software development had become incredibly complicated, with far more technology layers than conventional software development methods had ever anticipated. This notion of an object-oriented programming environment changed the whole paradigm.

The NeXT development environment meant that developers could eliminate 80% of the code that all applications share in common, allowing them to focus on the 20% of the code that made their app unique and provided additional value to users. The result, Jobs insisted, would be that a small team of two to ten developers could write an app as fully featured as a hundred-person team working for a large corporate software company like Microsoft. The rapt audience stared in disbelief as Jobs showed how the AppKit could be used to create a new application from scratch.

It was an amazing computer with a revolutionary development environment. The NeXT computer got some solid traction with universities, financial institutions, and government agencies, but its $6,500 price tag was too high to make much of a dent in the consumer market.

Its impact on the industry was huge, however. Tim Berners-Lee used a NeXT Computer to invent the World Wide Web, and on a NeXT machine in Switzerland, he ran the very first web server in the world. John Carmack wrote Doom on a NeXT Computer, creating an entire computer game franchise that lives on today. Adobe, then an unknown little company, developed the PostScript-based graphics engine for the machine. NeXT's WebObjects was the first web application development framework, creating the entire notion of web applications (instead of just static HTML pages).

In November of that year, Steve Jobs hosted an event for reporters and called up onto the screen an application called CyberSlice to order pizza. Long before mobile phones, this app used GIS data to find a pizza shop near you and transmit your order to them. Jobs predicted that the internet would someday be the primary way that people ordered pizza. The reporters laughed and weren't really convinced, but everybody enjoyed the pizza when it arrived.

Ultimately, the NeXT machines were just too expensive to break into the consumer markets so Jobs made the decision to abandon the hardware business and make NeXT a software company with an OS that would run on other hardware. The company was rebranded as "NeXT Software".

Then one day Gil Amelio, the new CEO of Apple, called him up. Partly because of NeXT, a whole new generation of computing was happening across the industry, with the internet at the center of everything, and Apple was way behind the curve. Apple needed to do something, and Gil Amelio proposed that Apple acquire NeXT as a way for Cupertino to leapfrog themselves back to the front of the pack.

A $400 million deal was stuck, and Apple bought NeXT in order to replace the aging MacOS. Steve Jobs would come along as a "special consultant." The NeXT operating system would be rebranded Mac OS X and propel Apple into the next century.

Today, all these years later, the AppKit is still the primary application framework on OS X, and iOS's UIKit is heavily modeled on it. Interface Builder as part of Apple's Xcode Integrated Development Environment (IDE). The iPhone runs iOS, built on the XNU kernel from NeXTSTEP. Same with Apple's tvOS and watchOS.

But the biggest plot twist was yet to come, of course. Seven months after Apple bought NeXT, the new "special consultant," Steve Jobs, conducted a boardroom coup over the July 4th weekend, ousting Gil Amelio from his job as CEO of Apple and reinstating himself as the King of the World.

KEY TAKEAWAYS:

◊   In Chapter 1, we discussed how most great startups begin with a founder who falls in love with a problem worth solving. Max Lechin took it a step further, saying it was "love plus rage" that made him found Affirm. The recently-fired Steve Jobs definitely harnessed love plus rage in founding a new startup that would revolutionize the computer business.

◊   Most great startups begin with a founder who notices a problem worth solving (Chapter 1). Jobs identified that universities and research labs had a problem, and by going out and meeting with many of them (Chapter 2) he was able to fully understand their problem and create ideas on how it could be solved. Universities then provided a beachhead market (as discussed in Chapter 7).

◊   Great entrepreneurs marry the problem, not the solution. When the economics of building hardware didn't work out, Jobs pivoted to making NeXT a software company, solving the same problem.

◊   The presentations that Steve Jobs delivered are legendary. He convinced an entire industry that they were doing software development wrong, and he had a better solution. In Chapter 8, we discussed the fact that great entrepreneurs have the ability to tell a crisp, clear, and compelling story about what they're doing and why it matters.

◊   More than anything else, of course, team matters (Chapter 10). Steve Jobs wasn't an engineer—he never even finished college. But he was able to recruit some of the world's leading engineers, and inspire them to create something beyond what even they thought they could create. It turned out that, indeed, "six people in blue jeans" were able to do what no billion-dollar company had been able to do. When Apple acquired NeXT, they were buying the software, but the real value was in the team they were acquiring. It was that team that would transform Apple from the struggling company they were in 1996, with an operating system that was lagging behind, into the $3 trillion market cap company they are today.

FINAL THOUGHTS

I wrote this book because I believe passionately in the democratization of entrepreneurship. I believe that entrepreneurs everywhere can play an important role in solving many of the world's big challenges and in helping to create opportunity for all.

There is no guaranteed recipe for startup success. But I hope the Launch Path framework that I describe in this book helps you to think through the factors that tend to drive startup success and failure – so that you can create a venture that succeeds beautifully.

The companies I founded were small successes; all three were acquired at fewer than 100 employees. But my ragtag team at Metagraphics developed the first web-based document generation engine, my team at Artmachine developed the first pure-SaaS platform for digital media management, and the brilliant engineering team at Tivix developed ground-breaking software for organizations all over the world. Assembling those teams is my life's greatest professional accomplishment, and watching individuals who I hired go on to great career success has been a profound source of personal satisfaction.

Startup success is all about assembling great teams, and leadership is all about making others better. If you remember those two things, you will succeed and thrive.

Here's to great entrepreneurs everywhere.

Bret Waters
March, 2024

REFERENCE SECTION

A LEGAL PRIMER FOR ENTREPRENEURS

As you launch your startup venture, there are a variety of legal issues that you'll need to think about, from forming a corporate entity to protecting your company's intellectual property (IP). My experience is that you want to get as much of this as possible done correctly right at the beginning, so that as the venture launches you can be focusing all your energy on building a great business, not wasting time with legal and compliance issues.

The big question: DIY or hire a lawyer?

Having a good corporate law firm is a great thing to have. As a startup CEO, it is incredibly beneficial to have an attorney you can call up anytime and run things by. Plus, a good corporate lawyer is usually very well-connected and can be a great source of referrals to other professionals, partners, investors, and perhaps even customers.

But a good lawyer ain't cheap, and many entrepreneurs start with the do-it-yourself (DIY) approach, with the intention to hire a law firm down the road after they have money. The good news is that there are many DIY legal tools and platforms available to startup founders today (see list at thelaunchpath.com).

Finding a good lawyer:

Referrals are almost always the best way to do this. Ask around, email your friends, ask your CPA, etc. You want someone who has experience working with startups (yes, a family law attorney could figure out how to form a corporation, but in the long run you will really benefit from an attorney with deep startup and corporate experience).

In Silicon Valley, most law firms will give you a reduced flat-rate on corporate formation, because they want the long-term business with your venture (and they'll probably want stock warrants in return). The Palo Alto law firm Wilson Sonsini handled the original corporate formation of Google on a special deal, and went on to make tens of millions on the IPO. Now every law firm is hoping they'll be next.

Choosing and forming a legal entity

One of your first legal decisions will be the sort of legal entity to form. Here are the options in the US (other jurisdictions have similar legal entity types, although their names may be different).

- **Sole Proprietorship**: This is the default under the law. If you do nothing, your business will be a sole proprietorship. Under this structure there is no legal separation between you and the company, which means that if the company gets sued or has debt, you are personally liable. For tax purposes there also is no separation between you and the business, so the business profits (or losses) are just simply part of your personal taxes. Also there is no equity structure (you can't sell 23% of yourself to somebody), and no concept of survivability for the business (when you die the business ceases to exist, in the eyes of the law).
- **Partnership**: Exactly the same as above, but more than one person involved with the business.
- **Limited Liability Corporation (LLC)**: Separate legal entity, so you are not personally responsible for the business debts, but there is full tax flow through (the company's profits or losses go on your personal tax return). Equity structure allows for multiple "members," but there is no concept of shares of stock

(it makes it difficult, for example, for someoneto own 3% of the business (and no way to issue stock options or have classes of stock).

- **C-Corp:** This is the standard "big daddy" corporate structure. Full liability shield (the business is a separate entity so you are not personally responsible for business liability). Separate taxation—the company files its own tax return. Maximum equity flexibility—issue as many shares of stock as you want, sell the stock to anyone (subject to a bunch of SEC laws), have different classes of stock, etc.

- **S-Corp: Like a C-Corp except with tax flow-through.** There are also some limitations on the number and types of shareholders, and you cannot have different classes of stock.

- **501(c)3**: The standard model for nonprofits (charity) organizations. The profits are exempt from taxation, and individual contributors can get a tax deduction for their donations (subject to certain limitations). Note that as an officer of the nonprofit you can still pay yourself a full market rate salary (subject to standard income tax).

- **Benefit Corporation** (B-Corp): Recognized by 33 states, a Benefit Corporation's directors and officers operate the business with the same authority as in a traditional corporation but are required to consider the impact of their decisions not only on shareholders but also on society and the environment. In a traditional corporation, shareholders judge the company's financial performance; with a benefit corporation, shareholders judge performance based on the company's social, environmental, and financial performance.

What is the deal with Delaware?

In the US, corporations are formed at the state level, not the federal level, and a strange twist is that most major companies are incorporated in the tiny state of Delaware.[1] The reason is primarily that if your company ends up in court it will be more efficient to litigate in Delaware because the judges are experienced with business matters and there's a whole court system called Delaware Court of Chancery, considered to be the best court for resolving business disputes.

Legal Entities for Businesses in the US.

	Survivorship.	Liability Shield.	Tax Flow-Through	Shares of stock.	Classes of stock.	Notes
Sole Proprietorship	No.	No.	Yes.	No.	No.	Default. If you do nothing, this is what you are.
Partnership	No.	No.	Yes.	No.	No.	Same as sole proprietorship, but with multiple owners.
LLC	Yes.	Yes.	Yes.	No.	No.	Owners are called "members"; no shares of stock.
S-Corp	Yes.	Yes.	Yes.	Yes, limited to 100 Shareholders	No.	You create a C-corp and then make an "election" to be treated as an S-corp.
C-Corp	Yes.	Yes.	No.	Yes, unlimited.	Yes.	The "big daddy" option. Well-understood and preferred by VC investors.
501(c)3	Yes.	Yes.	Exempt.	No.	No.	Also called a "non-profit" organization. Except from taxes.
B-Corp	Yes.	Yes.	No.	Yes, unlimited.	Yes.	Not recognized in all states.

Venture capitalists prefer it, so if you intend to eventually raise venture funding then you might as well incorporate in Delaware as a "C-corp" because that's the preference for most investors, but it will increase your cost and administration slightly, because you'll need to be registered both in Delaware and in your home state.

Summary:

If you plan to eventually raise venture capital, you'll need to be a C-Corp in Delaware. If you don't, then an LLC or an S-Corp may be easier and have some personal tax advantages. But do your own research and hire a good lawyer if you can.

1: There are some other states, such as Wyoming and Nevada, that are trying to compete with Delaware as being the preferred place to incorporate.

When should you form a legal entity for your startup?

Many startups begin as an informal, part-time side project, so when do you know it's time to spend the money to form a legal entity? The short answer is **that you should form a legal entity when you get to the point the business takes on liability.** Examples might include signing a lease, signing a loan, or hiring employees. And these days even launching a website can potentially create liability. Along the journey from startup idea to a launched business, you will cross a threshold where you're starting to take on personal liability. Form a legal entity before you cross that threshold to protect yourself by separating the business's liabilities from your personal assets.

Protecting yourself from personal liability

One of the main purposes of creating a legal entity for your venture is so that, in the eyes of the law, you and the company are two separate things. Your personal assets and liabilities are separate from the company's, and visa versa. So don't mess this up! Make sure that all leases and purchases and loans are in the name of the company, not yours. Keep completely separate bank accounts and never mix personal funds with business funds. Make sure the company files its tax returns and other regulatory requirements. If your business gets sued at some point, the other side's lawyers will try to "pierce the corporate veil" and come after your personal assets. One of the ways they will do that is by trying to claim that you weren't really properly operating as a corporation and so you don't deserve liability separation between your personal matters and your business matters. Don't let this happen. Be smarter than that.

Protect your company's intellectual property

As soon as you create your legal entity, the next thing you should do is to transfer the domain name, the logo, software, sketches, and everything else to the company. Typically this is done by typing up a "Bill of Sale," listing everything, and selling it to the company for some nominal amount. There are a bunch of reasons this is important— one of them is that in case of a future co-founder break-up you don't want to find out that the domain name doesn't actually belong to the company. Also, for any future investor conversations that are going to want to see documentation that everything belongs to the company they are investing in.

Next up is Confidential Information and Invention Assignment Agreement (CIIAA). All employees should sign one (including the founders!) with the company. Among other things, it states that anything "invented" by the employees while on the job belongs to the company, not the individual. Again, investors are going to require that these agreements be in place, and so you should too!

Trademarks, Patents, and Copyrights

Protecting your company's intellectual property is important, and there are three broad ways in which you can do this:

- **Trademarks** are a way of protecting a recognizable sign, design, or expression that identifies products or services from a particular source and distinguishes them from others. These are relatively easy and inexpensive to file for. You can find out more on the website for the US Patent and Trademark Office (uspto. gov) and there are many online companies offering services for obtaining Trademarks.
- **Copyright** protects original works of authorship such as writings, illustrations, blog posts, etc. Once you publish something that you have created, you are automatically the copyright holder (often people will put "Copyright 2023 John Smith" at the bottom, just to make it clear. You can also register your copyright,

just to make sure (especially if you plan to license rights), and you can read more about this at the US government website copyright.gov.

- **Patents** are slightly trickier. A US patent gives you, as the creator of an invention, the right to exclude others from making, using, selling, or importing, an invention like yours. You can use Google Patents to search to see if anyone already holds a patent on something similar, and you can find more information at uspto.gov. There are many online legal self-help services available for patents, and a good IP attorney can add a lot of value to this process. Remember that just having a patent doesn't necessarily do you much good—you'll need very expensive litigation to protect it if you feel another company infringes upon it.

Privacy Regulations

If your startup has a website, it will need to be compliant with various online privacy laws. No matter where your startup is located, you'll probably have website users in California and in Europe, so you'll want to read up on the California Online Privacy Protection Act (COPPA) and the General Data Protection Regulation (GDPR in the EU) since those are the two operative sets of privacy regulations. If you are capturing certain kinds of personal information (health information, for example) there are specific regulations surrounding that stuff, and if you expect to have users under 13 then there's a new set of requirements. The point is this: if you are collecting any information on your users at all, you'll need to do your research on the applicable data protection regulations. Compliance around online privacy is extremely important these days.

Taking Money from Investors

Types of investment structures are covered in Chapter 6, but the main thing here is to document everything clearly! There have been many disputes between startups and investors because a check was written without clear documentation on the terms of the investment. Avoid this! With an equity investment you will pretty much always need a law firm because you are selling stock, which gets into highly-regulated territory, and this is one of reasons that SAFEs have become a popular way of accepting early-stage investment without triggering the need for the complex legal paperwork of an equity financing. See Chapter 6 for more details on SAFEs and other investment structures and strategies.

Employing People

In the US, most labor law is state-specific, and obviously around the world research on which employment regulations apply to your startup. But here are the three things you need to be especially aware of as a startup founder:

- At the beginning, startups tend to like to hire people as freelancers, to avoid the cost and hassle of running payroll and paying payroll taxes. This typically runs afoul of labor law eventually, so proceed with caution. In California, for example, the number one thing that startups get fined for is paying people as freelancers when legally they should have been paying them as payroll employees. This can be painful and expensive.
- Once you form a corporation, as the founder you are now an employee of the company, subject to all labor laws. Strangely, this means that if you are not paying yourself then you are in violation of minimum wage laws. Yes, I know that's ridiculous but it's also true. So check the laws that your startup is subject to—you may need to pay yourself minimum wage in order to stay out of trouble.

- Every employee—even you and your co-founders—need to sign an employment letter with the company, clearly stating employment terms including confidentiality terms and IP rights (explicitly stating, for example, that any software code written belongs to the company and not the individual). In the "resources" section below you will find document generators that can produce a Confidential Information Invention Assignment Arbitration agreement (CIIAA) that every employee (even you and your cofounders!) should sign.

There are many other employee issues, of course, that a good employment law attorney can review with you. The laws tend to be very employee-friendly, and penalties can be severe, so you want to make sure you are completely compliant in every way.

Summary

Your startup will operate within a legal system that will protect you (and sometimes frustrate you). As a startup founder, you want to spend all of your time and energy on building a great company and taking care of customers, not dealing with frustrating legal hassles. So take the time to understand the legal side, and keep things as clean and tidy as possible. A good startup lawyer is a great asset to have, but there are also lots of great self-serve legal platforms available today.

GLOSSARY OF STARTUP FINANCING TERMS

Angel Investor
A high-net-worth individual who invests capital in startups, typically in exchange for equity ownership, convertible debt, or SAFE's. Unlike a venture capital investor they are investing their own personal money.

Bootstrapping
Starting a business without outside capital, and growing it organically.

Burn Rate
The rate at which a company is using-up its current cash on hand, with expenses currently outpacing revenue.

Cap Table (Capitalization Table)
A list of all the equity holders in a company, and how much equity (shares of stock) they currently own. A Cap Table typically also shows how many shares are authorized but not yet issued, as well as outstanding stock instruments (stock options and warrants) that may be exersized in the future.

Convertible Note
A very common investment structure for seed-stage financings, a convertible note starts as debt and then converts to equity upon some future trigger. A common scenario is a 24-month promissory note, with interest accruing but no payments required, with conversion to equity upon the company's next equity financing. At that trigger the note then automatically converts to equity at face value plus all accrued interest, at the same valuation as the new equity investors have agreed to in the round. It is common for convertible notes to contain a "sweetner",

where the early investors get to convert their notes to equity at an X% discount from the new equity investors.

Debt Financing

With a debt financing, the company has an obligation to re-pay the capital, principal plus interest, over some amount of time. The debt holder has no claim of equity ownership of the company and no claim to any future profits of the company (beyond repayment of principal plus interest). In the case of liquidation of the company, debt is always senior to equity.

Due Diligence

The process of investors researching and analyzing a startup's financial, legal, and operational aspects before finalizing an investment.

EBITDA

A silly acronym for earnings before interest, taxes, depreciation, and amortization. It's an artificial concept developed by investment bankers in the 1980's when leveraged buyouts were all the rage. The only time you should think about EBITDA is if someone wants to buy your startup then EBITDA will make it look more profitable than it really is. Other than that, forget about it. As Warren Buffett says "References to EBITDA make us shudder. It is not a meaningful measure of performance".

Equity Financing

Any financing where the investor is buying part of the company in return for the capital invested. An equity investor has a claim to a percentage of all future profits of the company, and to a share of any future sale (or liquidation of the company). Unlike debt there is no operating repayment obligation. The percentage ownership share of an equity investor is always *New Capital / (Pre-money Valuation + New Capital)*. So, for example, if we agree that Pre-money Valuation of the company is \$2M, and the investor is putting in \$1M, then the investor now owns 33.3% of the company ($1/(2+1)$). Simple math—the hard part with an early-stage company is agreeing on what the pre-money valuation should be.

Exit
A liquidity event where investors can cash out their investment, typically through a merger, acquisition, or initial public offering (IPO).

IPO (Initial Public Offering)
The process of a private company selling stock to the public, by listing its shares on a stock exchange.

Liquidity Event
An event where investors can convert their equity into cash, typically through an IPO or acquisition.

Preferred Stock
In an equity financing is done (see above), the investor may get stock that has certain preferential rights. The typical example is venture capital financing where the investor receives Preferred Stock, while employees hold Common Stock, and the Preferred Stock is senior to Common Stock in the case of liquidation of the company (ie, the investors get their money first before any distribution to employees and other common stock holders)

Pre-money Valuation
The valuation of a startup before a new round of investment.

Post-money Valuation
The valuation of a startup after a new round of investment (Post-money valuation always equals Pre-money valuation plus the amount of new money).

Revenue Sharing Note

Structured as debt, with the repayment defined as a percentage of the company's revenue instead of a fixed payment. So, for example, it might be a $100,000 loan, with the payment defined as 2% of the company's monthly revenue, capped at 1.5x the loan amount. This can be especially well-suited to seasonal businesses, which generate more cash in some parts of the year than others,

Runway

The amount of time a startup's available capital will last based on its current burn rate (revenue minus monthly expenses).

SAFE Financing

Developed by Y-combinator as an alternative to Convertible Notes, SAFE is an acronym for Simple Agreement for Future Equity. The principle difference from a convertible note is that a SAFE financing is not a loan, it is more like a warrant (gives the investor the rights to purchase shares in the future) but without pre-determined pricing on those shares. It is designed to be a lightweight instrument that can be issued without undue legal expenses and complications, while deferring the question of valuation.

Series A, B, C, etc.

Stages of financing rounds as a startup grows. The name comes from the fact that lawyers once printed out a series of stock certificates for investors in each round of financing. Since lawyers have no imagination, they called the first series of stock certificates "Series A", then "Series B", etc. They are arbitrary names without any particular meaning. In practice, the first equity financing is typically called a Series A (previous rounds are typically called "Seed, or Pre-Seed" and likely to be convertible notes or SAFE's.

Term Sheet

A non-binding document outlining the terms and conditions of an investment (or M&A transaction), serving as a basis for negotiation. See the next section, Anatomy of a Term Sheet.

Valuation

The estimated worth of a startup, which is required in order to determine the percentage of ownership that equity investors receive for their investment.

Valuation Cap

With Convertible Notes and SAFEs, the entrepreneur and investor are agreeing that the investment will convert to equity at an undetermined valuation in the future. In the case of a future crazy-high valuation, the investor may end up feeling this is unfair. Let's say I put $1M into a very early stage company and then two years later a VC firm says they'll do an equity round at $100M valuation. This means that my money will convert to 1% of the company and I'm going to scream bloody murder—I put a million dollars in when it was a high-risk, early-stage deal, I should be getting more than 1%!! Putting a Valuation Cap into the Convertible Note or SAFE solves this problem. If we agree on a Valuation Cap of $10M, then I know I'll own at least 10% of the company, even if there is some crazy-high valuation at the time that my money converts to equity.

Venture Capital (VC)

Investment funds formed to invest in early-stage, high-potential startups in exchange for equity (see the longer section in this book about how the venture capital business works). It is a high-risk, high-reward asset class.

Venture Capital vs Private Equity

VC and PE are both types of funds created to buy stock in private companies and then sell that stock in the future, hopefully at a much higher price. Venture Capital (VC) focuses on buying equity in early stage companies and then waiting for a future liquidity event (M&A or IPO). Private Equity (PE) is more focused on "fixer-uppers"—buying an established company, spending a few years fixing it up, and then reselling it at a higher price.

Warrants

Warrants are an instrument that gives the right (but not the obligation) to buy stock at a certain price within a certain time window. The price at which the stock can be bought is called the exercise price or strike price.

ANATOMY OF A VC TERM SHEET

FITACO, INC.
TERMS FOR PRIVATE PLACEMENT OF Series A PREFERRED STOCK

The following is a summary of the principal terms with respect to the proposed Series A Preferred Stock financing of Fitaco, Inc. , a Delaware corporation (the "*Company*"). Except for the section entitled "Binding Terms," this summary of terms does not constitute a legally binding obligation. The parties intend to enter into a legally binding obligation only pursuant to definitive agreements to be negotiated and executed by the parties.

Offering Terms

Securities to Issue: Shares of a new series of preferred stock of the Company (the "*Series A*").

Aggregate Proceeds: $1,000,000 in aggregate new capital.

Purchasers: Accredited investors approved by the Company (the "*Purchasers*").

Price Per Share: Price per share (the "*Original Issue Price*"), based on a pre-money valuation of $2,000,000, including an available option pool of 20% of the post-money fully diluted capital of the Company.

Liquidation Preference: One times the Original Issue Price plus declared but unpaid dividends on each share of Series A, balance of proceeds paid to Common Stock. A merger, reorganization or similar transaction will be treated as a liquidation.

Conversion: Each share of Series A is convertible into one share of Common Stock (subject to proportional adjustments for stock splits, stock dividends and the like) at any time at the option of the holder. Conversion ratio will be subject to adjustment on a broad-based, weighted average basis in the event of subsequent issuances at a price less than the Original Issue Price (as adjusted) subject to customary

---

You'll find the full example term sheet on **thelaunchpath.com**

A term sheet is simply a non-binding document outlining the terms of a proposed investment. If accepted, it becomes a guide for the lawyers who will draw up the actual legal documents required to complete the financing. As with anything, all of these terms are negotiable. Let's dive in and understand what the terms mean.

This example is for a venture capital Series A (first equity financing) for our amazing new venture, Fitaco. Remember that venture capital investors are buying stock in your company (it's not a loan), with the expectation that they will sell the stock at a large profit in the future, either when the company is acquired (by another company), or has an Initial Public Offering (an IPO, when the stock is sold to the public). They also want some protection in case things don't work out and the company has to be wound-down and the remaining assets sold-off. Here are the items on a typical venture capital term sheet, followed by an explanation of each in italics:

- **Securities to issue**: Shares of a new series of preferred stock of the Company (the "Series A"). *This means that in return for their investment, the investors will be issued stock.*
- **Aggregate Proceeds:** $1,000,000 in aggregae new capital. *There may be several investors in this round, for a total of a million dollars.*
- **Price per Share:** Based on a pre-money valuation of $2,000,000, including an available option pool of 20% of the post-money fully diluted capital of the Company. *This means that the pre-money valuation will be $2M, and that the company is carving-out an option pool in order to recruit and retain great talent by being able to offer stock options to employees (see Glossary for definitions of pre-money and post-money valuations).*
- **Liquidation Preference:** One times the Original Issue Price plus declared but unpaid dividends on each share of Series A preferred stock. A merger, reorganization or similar transaction will be treated as a liquidation. *This says that in the case of a future liqidation of the company, the investors will get their original investment back before anything is distributed to the founders, employees, and other common shareholders. This one says "One times the original" investoment, but a more agressive term sheet might say "two times", meaning that the investors will put $1M into the company, and if liquidated they will get the first $2M before anyone else gets anything. Pay attention to this one!*
- **Conversion:** Each share of Series A is convertible into one share of Common Stock at any time at the option of the holder. *Investors want to hold preferred stock until the IPO, when they*

want to convert to common stock and sell. This gives them the right to do so, on a 1:1 basis.

- **Voting Rights.** Votes together with the Common Stock on all matters on an as converted basis. \Approval of a majority of the Preferred Stock required to liquidate or dissolve, including any change of control. *This says that the preferred shareholders (investors) get to vote on everything as if they had converted to common stock (ie, their vote counts as much per share as founders and employees), but that selling or liquidating the company requires a majority vote of the investors (ie, you can't sell the company without their approval).*

- **Voting for directors**: The holders of Series A Preferred will be entitled to elect two directors. The holders of common stock will be entitled to elect three directors. Any additional directors will be elected by the holders of preferred stock and common stock voting together. *This defines the initial Board of Directors as having two seats chosen by the investors and three seats chosen by the founders. This should map closely to the percentage of stock owned. In this example, the investors will hold 41% of the company and have 40% of the board seats.*

- **Financial Information**: Purchasers who have invested at least $100,000 ("Major Purchasers") will receive standard information and inspection rights. *This means that anyone who invested more than $100K can call you anytime and ask for current financial information, etc. But your cousin Sam who put $2K in can't do that.*

- **Proprietary information agreements**: The Company will have all employees and consultants enter into proprietary information and inventions agreements. *Very standard. They want to make sure that all the IP created belongs to the company, not the founders and employees.*

- **Future Rights:** Major Purchasers will have the right to participate on a pro rata basis in subsequent issuances of equity securities. *This means that on your next round (Series B) of financing, these investors will have the right to also invest in that round if they want.*

- **Key Holder Matters:** Each Key Holder will have four years vesting beginning December 2, 2023. Full acceleration upon "Double Trigger." Each Key Holder shall have assigned all relevant IP to the Company before closing. *You are your co-founders are "Key holders". If you wrote the software code (IP) personally you will need to assign it to the company (so that it's clear that it's owned by the company and investors, not you). Also, your founders' stock will need to put on a vesting schedule, so that you don't leave the company in less than four years. If the company is sold and you are fired ("double trigger"), then the vesting is accelerated and you get all your stock back. Founders scream ("I already own my founders' stock, you can't put it on a vesting schedule!", and venture capitalists just smile and explain they need protection to make sure you don't leave).*

- **Expenses:** Company to reimburse counsel to Purchasers for a flat fee of $25,000. *That's right! You get to pay your lawyer and the investors' lawyer for handling both sides of the financing transaction! This may seem bizarre, but it is considered standard because VC's want the transaction expenses to be paid out of the fund.*

- **Diversity Rider:** In order to advance diversity efforts in the venture capital industry, the Company and the lead investor, Delicious Ventures, LLC, will make commercial best efforts to offer and make every attempt to include as a co-investor in the financing at least one Black or other underrepresented group including, but not limited to LatinX, women, LGBTQ+ check writer (DCWs), and to allocate a minimum of 10% or $100,000 of the total round for such co-investor. *A rider that can be added into a term sheet, in an attempt in get more diversity within investment syndicates.*

- **Binding Terms:** For a period of 30 days, the Company will not solicit offers from other parties for any financing. Without the consent of Purchasers, the Company will not disclose these terms to anyone other than officers, directors, key service providers, and other potential Purchasers in this financing. *Once the term sheet is signed, the parties agree to work to close the deal within 30 days. During that time, you will not go out and try to find an investor who will beat these terms, nor will you tell anyone else the details of these terms.*

These are the typical items you will find on a standard term sheet for a Series A venture capital financing, but they will vary depending on the investor, the company, and advice of counsel. I'm providing this simply with the hope that it will be helpful to you to be familiar with some of these terms as you pursue your own startup venture. But I ain't no lawyer, and I don't intend any of this to be legal advice.

www.ingramcontent.com/pod-product-compliance
Lightning Source LLC
Chambersburg PA
CBHW070348200326
41518CB00012B/2174